Menacing Virgins

Menacing Virgins

Representing Virginity
in the Middle Ages
and Renaissance

Edited by
Kathleen Coyne Kelly
and Marina Leslie

DELAWARE

Newark: University of Delaware Press
London: Associated University Presses

Associated University Presses
440 Forsgate Drive
Cranbury, NJ 08512

Associated University Presses
16 Barter Street
London WC1A 2AH, England

Associated University Presses
P.O. Box 338, Port Credit
Mississauga, Ontario
Canada L5G 4L8

The paper used in this publication meets the requirements
of the American National Standard for Permanence of Paper
for Printed Library Materials Z39.48-1984.

Library of Congress Cataloging-in-Publication Data

Menacing virgins : representing virginity in the Middle Ages and Renaissance /
    edited by Kathleen Coyne Kelly and Marina Leslie
        p.   cm.
    Includes index.
    ISBN 0-87413-649-0 (alk. paper)
    1. Literature, Medieval—History and criticism.   2. European
literature—Renaissance, 1400–1600—History and criticism.
3. Virginity in literature.   I. Kelly, Kathleen Coyne.   II. Leslie,
Marina.
PN682.V56M46   1999
809′.93353—dc21   98-19983
                                                                                      CIP

PRINTED IN THE UNITED STATES OF AMERICA

Contents

Foreword

MARGARET W. FERGUSON

Wᴀɪᴛɪɴɢ for the gynecologist, thinking about this collection of incisive essays on medieval and Renaissance representations of virginity, and leafing through one of the magazines provided for women who wait in doctors' offices, I was stunned to see in large, bold type the word "Virgin" above a picture of a naked baby; the caption recommended a certain brand of diapers with the arresting claim that "virgin" means "never before used." The highly fanciful etymology (according to the *OED,* at least, the English word "virgin" and its Romance language cognates derive from the accusative form of the Latin *virgo,* meaning "maiden") seemed worthy of Isidore of Seville, although he might have been surprised to find the phrase "never before used" suggestively explaining the "virgin" virtues both of a buxom baby (gender not revealed in the photo) and a brand of disposable plastic diaper. What struck me as most bizarre about the advertisement—and also most germane to the many paradoxical aspects of what counts as "virginity" as analyzed in the book you are reading—was the implicit economic and cultural message to acquire and *USE* the virgin item. The excessiveness, the transgresssive weirdness, of the advertisement's implied logic of virginity, a logic that caught the baby body as well as the diaper in its loop, only served to dramatize a psycho-economic feature typical of many of the notions of virginity we have inherited from the past: the virgin item's cultural value lies partly in the fact that it has *not yet* been used: the specter of an imminent or eventual use, consumption, or violation is indeed central to many cultural conceptions of virginity from the Middle Ages to the present.

Western notions of virginity—and of its allied but by no means always synonymous concept, chastity[1]—have historically been knotted with a number of paradoxes. One of the most enduring of these, as the editors of this volume observe in their introduction, arises from the fact that virginity is identified "both with wholeness and with absence or lack"; the virgin is "intact" but also she (or he) who has *not* (or not yet) been defiled by or initiated into sexual congress

7

with another human being, usually construed as a member of the opposite sex.[2] Some paradoxes pertaining to virginity have loosened over time, while others have emerged or tightened with socio-economic, institutional, and ideological changes such as those associated with the Protestant Reformation or the so-called "rise of capitalism." Continuities of long duration can nonetheless be discerned; female "virginity," for instance, was seen as a temporal "stage" of a more encompassing category of "chastity" by patristic writers who distinguished between "virgins," "wives," and "widows" (see editors' introduction, note 2), as well as by Protestant writers who viewed "chaste marriage" as the end or *telos* of maidenly virginity. Some medieval patristic writers, however, like some sixteenth- and seventeenth-century Protestant ones, brooded on the actual or potential contrasts, even conflicts, between "virginity" and "chastity." "Virginity" could signify bodily "intactness," whereas "chastity" could signify a higher quality of spiritual integrity; and patristic writers were divided, as Jane Tibbetts Schulenberg has demonstrated, on the question of whether a nun who lost her ("literal") virginity through rape could still possess chastity in its spiritual sense. This debate turned on the question of whether a rape could occur without the woman in some sense "willing" it—a question that is alive and well today, and that underlies the debate between the Elder and Younger Brother in Milton's *Comus.*

A potential opposition between "virginity" and "chastity" also appears in texts overtly or covertly concerned with Queen Elizabeth of England; if a "maiden"—like Queen Elizabeth or Hermia in Shakespeare's *A Midsummer Night's Dream,* with its central if enigmatic figure of a "fairy queen" who resists husbandly control—should refuse to become or stay a wife, the society may be threatened by "disorder." In Hermia's case, a maidenly willfulness threatens both the father's and the king's authority; in refusing to be like the wax tablet upon which the father "imprints" his wishes, Hermia risks becoming an overly militant or "menacing" virgin, like the classical Amazons or like the "barren" nun evoked by Shakespeare's Theseus in his (failed) effort to make Hermia obey her father's command to marry Demetrius. The specter of an active virginity, which entails a repudiation of a husband's or father's "ownership" of a woman's sexuality, haunted English Protestant discourses on the household and its theoretically analogous sphere, the state; the idea of the "active virgin," whether represented by Lysistrata or implied by the complaints about marriage articulated from a female perspective in the Middle English poem *Hali Meiðhad* or in the anonymous seventeenth-century poem "Advice to Virgins" (both texts discussed in the editors' introduction), involves a potential threat to the household regime. No wonder, as Richard Halpern has remarked, that the "active virgin" is often depicted as *wandering* rather than remaining quietly in the enclosure of the patriarchal *domus*.[3] "In excess," Halpern states, "both virginity and sexuality overturn domestic rule," and when this happens, or is imagined as happening, virginity becomes a menace to the ideal of "married chastity."

The ambiguity upon which the title of this book plays highlights the historical lability of concepts of virginity/chastity: the qualities connoted by those terms can be seen as infinitely valuable and hence in need of vigilant protection; but the signified qualities can also be construed as threatening to various vested interests, as the Catholic institution of the convent was sometimes seen as threatening to the secular system of aristocratic inheritance, and as the virgin saints depicted in Christine de Pizan's *Book of the City of Ladies* (1405) were seen as threats by various figures of patriarchal authority protectively coded as "pagan" but with attributes strikingly similar to those possessed by male authorities—sacred and secular both—during Christine's own era.

As the editors of this book remark in their introduction, the historical lability of the concepts of virginity and chastity requires us to analyze the process of their cultural construction; if "virginity" in particular seems ostensibly to be a biological concept, the bizarre history of virginity "tests" provides support for Kirsten Hastrup's argument that "biological categories are always transformed into meaningful categories which are defined by their relationship *to*, and interaction *with*, other categories of society."[4]

Certain metaphors for female virginity seem especially tightly correlated with socioeconomic changes of great import: the metaphor of the "virgin land," for instance, authorizes and rationalizes a drive for colonial possession in the early modern era, and during that same period (which Marx saw not as the "Renaissance" but as a period of uneven "transition" from feudal to capitalist social formations), a positive trope of virginity as a "treasure" sometimes and significantly shifted, in certain Protestant discourses, into a negative image of "hoarding." The shift occurred under the pressure of the Protestant denigration of monasticism and a correlative (and highly overdetermined) revaluation of the institution of marriage as a higher (and more profitable) state than it was held to be in the patristic tradition descending from St. Paul's dictum, "Better to marry than to burn."

Paradoxes pertaining to the nature of *female* virginity in particular tend to cluster around issues or images of temporal duration, epistemological and ontological status, and cultural value. In her essay entitled "*Il Trionfo della Pudicizia*: Menacing Virgins in Italian Renaissance Domestic Painting," for instance, Cristelle Baskins cites a fourteenth-century treatise on "buoni costumi" (good clothing) that compares a woman's reputation for chastity both to a beautiful flower and to a husband's crown. The two analogies dramatize the problem of defining the "essence" of a phenomenon that seems in many representations of it to depend as much on others' views of its existence (a "reputation" for chastity) as on a woman's possession of something allegedly tangible, like a maidenhead, or of something precious but intangible like "spotless" behavior. The analogies in the clothing treatise also dramatize the problem of wifely chastity's temporal duration: if such chastity is like a beautiful flower, it will "naturally" and inevitably decay, and will therefore become a logically inappropriate vehicle for the concepts of economic and social value embedded in the alternate image of the husband's "crown."

When the "husband" of the virgin is Christ—as it is in the patristic tradition based on St. Paul's praise of the superiority of virginity to (carnal) marriage for both men and women and in the ascetic institution of Catholic monasticism—-the conceptual paradoxes underlying the ideal of virginity dramatize the recurring impulse toward "sexual puritanism," as John Bugge calls it, in the history of Christianity.[5] A striking paradox that pertains, again, particularly to ideas of *female* virginity arises from the fact that while the term "virgin" itself calls insistant attention to the woman as a sexed being, the religious ideal of virginity insists on a "desexing" of women; as Marina Leslie notes in her essay in this volume on Margaret Cavendish's *Assaulted and Perfected Chastity*, Church Fathers bestowed their highest praise on those models of female virginity who had "successfully repudiated their own sexuality"; the most admirable (female) virgins "transcend" their sex but are not described as sexless; rather, they are described as "virile," or "male."[6]

As I have been hinting—and as the essays gathered in this volume amply attest—concepts of male virginity, although no less important than those of female virginity for the Catholic Church and for certain Protestants too, have tended to raise epistemological, ontological, and economic questions that are different from—though also significantly related to—those that have attended Western discussions of female virginity. One can make no definitive distinction between gender-inflected concepts of virginity at any given historical moment, or, indeed, in certain texts (a male author may consciously or unconsciously identify with a virginal female character, for instance); but one can nonetheless be alert to the persistent *asymmetries* arising along lines of gender both in representations of and in ideological prescriptions for virginity and chastity. As Kathleen Coyne Kelly argues in her fascinating study of "Menaced Masculinity and Imperiled Virginity in Malory's *Morte Darthur*" (also in this volume), there are no tests for male virginity in those medieval medical treatises and literary texts that repeatedly discuss and dramatize tests for female virginity. And because, in a medieval gynecological treatise such as *The Secrets of Women,* the assertion that female virginity can be tested goes hand in hand with an acknowledgment that virginity can be counterfeited, female virginity becomes a magnet for epistemological questions—and for an obsessive focus on the visible/invisible hymen—in a way that male virginity does not. Nonetheless—and this is a point that invites further examination than can occur in this volume—the *kind* of epistemological and moral questions raised by the long-standing cultural concern with "testing" for (female) virginity arguably exerted great influence on the questions both male and female Protestants asked about whether they were "elect" or not. The search for "signs" of election, always demanding attention but never leading (in this life) to certainty, clearly underlies Milton's creation of and identification with a virginal "Lady" subjected to a symbolically excessive spiritual/physical test by Comus. Asymmetries of gender do not of course disappear when a male writer figures himself as female, but their social and ideological implications become very hard to tease out; the same poet who was nicknamed "the Lady of Christ's" by his Cambridge classmates also defended himself against obscure charges of sexual promiscuity (as Lauren Shohet points out in her essay in this volume) by arguing that sexual sinning is worse when performed by men than by women because men are "innately" superior to women. Acknowledging that his view is unusual, Milton spells out his argument in the early prose tract known as the *Apology for Smectymnuus:*

> But having had the doctrine of holy scripture unfolding those chaste and high mysteries with timeliest care infused, that "the body is for the Lord, and the Lord for the body" [cf. 1 Cor. 6:13], thus also I argued to myself: that if unchastity in a woman, whom St. Paul terms the glory of man, be such a scandal and dishonor, then certainly in a man, who is both the image and glory of God, it must, though commonly not so thought, be much more deflowering and dishonorable; in that he sins both against his own body, which is the perfecter sex, and his own glory, which is in the woman, and, that which is worst, against the image and glory of God, which is in himself. . . .[7]

Milton's strong sense of the man as the "perfecter" sex has as one of its less critically discussed logical conclusions a deep investment in what we would now call homoerotic as well as homosocial relationships.[8] Exploring the relation between medieval and Renaissance theories and practices of male friendship on the one hand, and discourses of virginity on the other, is another path of critical inquiry opened, although not fully pursued, in this volume. It is a significant path, it seems to me, for an increased historical understanding of virginity. Both female and male virgin bodies are clearly implicated, for instance, in certain proto-capitalist invectives against hoarding, although ironic, even cynical effects sometimes emerge from the transfer of classically-inspired (male) libertine arguments against female virginity (e.g., "gather ye rosebuds while ye may") to new contexts such as the first seventeen of Shakespeare's sonnets. These, famously, enjoin the beloved young man to reproduce himself (for his family's sake) rather than hoarding his sexual treasure; but in the context of this sonnet sequence, as we see retroactively, the alternative to sexual hoarding is not the specter of Catholic virginity/celibacy but rather that of the male-male friendship praised in such texts as *The Two Gentlemen of Verona* and in Montaigne's essay "De l'Amitié." The ideal of male friendship was colored by Renaissance writers' awareness that pre-Christian authorities (Plato, for instance, and Theocritus) had fully sanctioned physical love between men. Milton's Latin elegy for his friend Charles Diodati, like Shakespeare's sonnets, suggests a deep concern with that classical tradition and, more generally, with the vexed relation between classical and Christian notions of licit sexuality. Because he was a "stainless" youth who "did not taste the delight of the marriage bed," Milton's Damon receives "the rewards of virginity"; but the rewards for refraining from sexual congress (of any sort) seem, as so often in Milton, to be conceived as a license to blend classical and Christian notions of pleasure and thus to enjoy fully that which has heretofore been prohibited. Miltonic concepts of virginity, temperance, and asceticism come to signify temporal—and temporary—modes of self-discipline *willed* by the subject and rewarded by a barely representable sensual bliss. At the end of the poem about Damon, the young man is imagined participating in "festal orgies . . . under the heavenly Thyrsus," the wand of Bacchus that joyously encouraged sexual pleasure across or beyond the usual bounds of gender difference. Damon anticipates Milton's angels, who can "either sex assume" but who are all portrayed as male; they too enjoy an eternal bliss of sexual pleasure, at least according to Raphael, who blushes when Adam asks about how spirits "mix," with "virtual or immediate touch" (*PL* 8, 617–18).

It seems somehow appropriate that a serious and provocative book about medieval and early modern representations of virginity should be composed by many hands, and should suggest the need for even more work on the topics so richly explored by the essays gathered here. The book menaces any idea the reader might entertain that she or he possesses an "intact" understanding of what virginity "is" or "means"—or has been and meant in an inevitably partial selection of past times and places. It seems equally appropriate to the subject at hand and to the spirit (and body) of this book that its preface close with an acknowledgment of its own fragmentary and problematic status as an introduction, of some sort, to the essays—and editors' introduction—you are about to read. Prefaces, as Jacques Derrida writes (with specific reference to the philosophical preface to a book by a "single" author—so my use of Derrida necessarily involves slippages and displacements), tend to "announce in the future tense ('this is what you are going to read') the conceptual content or significance . . . of what will *already* have been *written*. And thus sufficiently *read* to be gathered up in its semantic tenor and proposed in advance."[9] I realize, however, that I have not begun fully to read the essays printed after (though written before) this preface; hence I offer these reflections to you, and to the book's editors and contributors as well, with a sharp but not wholly paralyzing awareness that neither the preface nor the volume is intact. Preface-writing is indeed, as Derrida observes, a "ludicrous" operation, "not only because writing as such does not consist in any of these tenses (present, past, or future insofar as they are all modified presents); not only because such an operation would confine itself to the discursive effects of an intention-to-mean, but because, in pointing out a single thematic nucleus or a single guiding thesis, it would cancel out the textual displacement that is at work 'here.' (Here? Where?)."

I end by ventriloquizing Derrida's text—which is translated and hence already in some sense violated, according to a historically powerful metaphor that equates "original" texts with intact female bodies[10]—because he has done so much to teach us, by negative and positive example (both types evident in the elaborate meditation on "hymen" in "The Double Session"), that we cannot take tropes of virginity for granted. Whether they occur in texts written by men, women, or those "undecidable" hypothesized subjects denoted by "anonymous," such tropes adumbrate sexual-political visions that often enable, or justify, significant social practices. From diaper advertisements through school counselling programs to songs by popular stars, tropes of virginity are very much still with us, and very much in need of the analytic and historicizing estrangement they receive in this book.

Introduction: The Epistemology of Virginity

Kathleen Coyne Kelly and Marina Leslie

[C]arnal integrity is in no way approved of, unless spiritual purity is associated with it as companion.

—Aldhelm, *De virginitate*

[I]f a woman is covered with a piece of cloth and fumigated with the best coal, if she is a virgin she does not perceive its odor through her mouth and nose; if she smells it, she is not a virgin.

—Nicholus of Florence, *De passionibus mulierum*

> This idoll which you terme *Virginitie*,
> Is neither essence subject to the eie,
> No, nor to any one exterior sence,
> Nor hath it any place of residence,
> Nor is't of earth or mold celestiall,
> Or capable of any forme at all.
> Of that which hath no being, doe not boast,
> Things that are not at all, are never lost.
>
> —Christopher Marlowe, *Hero and Leander*

[V]irginity is one of the secrets that men find most exciting.

—Simone de Beauvoir, *The Second Sex*

In discussing what she calls "the myth of Virginity," Simone de Beauvoir says that the virgin, "[n]ow feared by the male, now desired or even demanded . . . would seem to represent the most consummate form of the feminine mystery. She is therefore its most disturbing and at the same time its most fascinating aspect."[1] This collection of essays offers an exploration of the poetics and politics of this enduring cultural myth, and of virginity's inherent paradox, identified as it is with both wholeness and with absence or lack. The presence—or absence—of virginity is central to the construction of female identity, both as subject and object, in the Western European Middle Ages, and its legacy persists into the Renaissance and beyond.

15

Although the following essays will describe a range of virginal attributes found in representations of both female and male sexuality, they also demonstrate the degree to which depictions of virginity in the Middle Ages and Renaissance are gendered—or coded—as female, even when male virginity is ostensibly the subject. At the same time, the feminization of virginity in Western European culture did not prevent the female virgin from accruing a variety of stereotypically masculine qualities; early patristic writings on the resolute female virgin frequently represent her as a *virilis femina,* and this image can be found throughout the Middle Ages and Renaissance. The very instability of the designation *virgin* goes well beyond the social interrogation or technical verification of the virginal body to touch upon the grounds for the cultural construction of sex and gender.

The virgin, as our title suggests, can be seen alternately or even simultaneously as menaced and menacing. Each essay in this volume focuses on some aspect of the peculiar cultural ambivalence toward virginity in medieval and early modern Europe. A common thread, then, ties these essays together, while the book as a whole demonstrates both the tremendous variety of literary virgins as well as the poetic potency of the topos of virginity across a range of disciplinary and discursive practices.[2] The essays forge connections between narrative and law, art, music, and history, situating virginity at the interstices of a number of social and cultural practices governing the construction of the body, the regulation of property and propriety, and the institutionalization of *pietas* and *eros* in church and at court.

The Latin *castitas* and *virginitas* and their vernacular cognates carried a number of possible meanings in the Middle Ages and the Renaissance. Of course, the writings of the Church Fathers provide the spiritual and theological underpinnings for any and all definitions of chastity that obtained in Christian Europe. Paul established what would become the normative view on virginity with his insistence on the necessity of both bodily and spiritual integrity ("the unmarried woman or girl is anxious about the affairs of the Lord, how to be holy in body and spirit" [RSV, 1 Cor. 7.34]). Yet the writings of Ambrose, Jerome, Augustine, and others do not furnish us with an ideologically uniform, internally consistent body of thought on the subject of virginity/chastity.[3] Depending on the context, an author who used the terms *castitas* and *virginitas* might be referring either to one's never having experienced coitus (i.e., a "virgin" in a purely physical sense); *or* to an individual's commitment to the religious celibate life (regardless of whether that individual was single, married, or widowed); *or* to sexual faithfulness in a monogamous marriage.[4] Sometimes the word *virginity* is used to denote physical intactness, and the word *chastity* to refer to the more encompassing idea of spiritual integrity.[5] Kirsten Hastrup usefully situates the shifting definitions of virginity in the process of their cultural construction when she notes that "biological categories are always transformed into meaningful categories which are defined by their relationship *to*, and interaction *with*, other categories of society."[6]

The subject and function of virginity have been well documented within the context of medieval Church doctrine, especially with respect to the cult of Mary, the virgin *par excellence* in the writings of the Church Fathers and later medieval commentaries.[7] Perhaps as a consequence of the often monologic picture that emerges from religious writings, current studies on the ontology of the body in medieval texts have tended to give short shrift to the literary virgin except as religious icon, and to overlook her more ambiguous figuration in other genres. For example, the *Roman de la Rose* and the Wife of Bath's Prologue vividly demonstrate an ambivalence toward the social and secular value of virginity, an ambivalence that simultaneously reproduces and subverts the dominant ideology. In the vernacular romance, the encomiastic treatment of virginity that we find in medieval religious and didactic treatises gives way to a preoccupation with the maintenance and proof of female virginity. Here, the fear that a consecrated virgin may compromise her chastity, and therefore lose her place among the heavenly elect, is transmuted into the fear that the virgin—that is, the unmarried daughter or sister—may lose her value.

As the virgin moves out of the compass of the church (where she is a noncirculating commodity, a treasure saved up) and into the realm of the secular (where she is an object of exchange, a marker in a game of privilege and empire), she is less likely to be seen as a hieratic symbol of spiritual rewards, becoming instead an instrument for the transference and securing of social and political legacies. Such a shift—indeed a reversal—in emphasis may well reflect how the very commodification of chastity and its identification with the feminine contributes to the symbolic destabilization of the Christian ideal of virginity in the Middle Ages. The essays in the medieval cluster suggest the considerable ambivalence in representations of virginity, and demonstrate that the Church did not and could not confer upon virginity an unambiguous or uncontested value.

In the Renaissance, virginity continued to be equated with sacred as well as secular capital, suggesting that there was, by no means, a complete rupture with the anxieties or the representational strategies of the Middle Ages. Scholars interested in the poetics of virginity in the English Renaissance have tended to concentrate on Elizabeth I and the impact that her virginal politics had on the literature and culture of her era. Indeed, Elizabeth as the cynosure of the age has created a focus but also a blind spot in the study of the poetics of virginity in the Renaissance.[8]

The shift under James I toward a more patrician model of rule celebrated the king as *parens patriae,* and his masculine fertility was seen to contrast with and to correct the barren virgo/virago iconography of Elizabeth's reign.[9] James's transformation of Elizabeth's sexual politics was made clear from the very beginning of his reign when—as Thomas Dekker reports—he entered the city of London in 1603 as a bridegroom prepared to meet his bride.[10] Nonetheless, it would be a serious distortion to assume that the sexual poetics of rule governed the lived experience of those who were ruled. Elizabeth may have represented chaste female government, yet the ascendance of an absolutist state system did much to reinforce patriarchy in sixteenth-century England. Moreover, virginity did not go out of style in Stuart England; rather, it was increasingly invoked as a social value regulating female sexuality and governing the advantageous disposition of daughters.[11] Chastity continued to hold great symbolic power in the political and religious idioms of both sides of the conflict of the Civil War, as the essays here on Milton (by Lauren Shohet) and Cavendish (by Marina Leslie) amply demonstrate. The essays in the Renaissance cluster deliberately look past Elizabeth and include examples outside the confines of England in order to broaden our understanding of models of chastity in the Renaissance.

In the social and secular sphere, a girl's virginity in both the Middle Ages and in the Renaissance was, as we have noted, an important counter in the homosocial relations between men, securing as it did both patrilineage and property. Yet even in the context of regulated marriage, virginity's social value was complex, and, at times, self-contradictory. John Rogers has argued suggestively that the "central paradox" of virginity lies in the fact that "the very state that qualifies a woman for her subjection to the patriarchal law of marriage, is the same condition, if maintained, that best permits her to evade its hold."[12]

The possibility of choosing virginity to evade the "hold" of marriage was long celebrated as one of celibacy's chief attractions. An early medieval poem, the "Love Ron," attributed to the clerk Thomas of Hale, tells us that a "Mayde cristes" (maid of Christ; i.e., a nun) has asked for a "luue-ron" (love poem) that will help her to contemplate her heavenly bridegroom. Both this world and the men in it are changeable, inconstant, false, and the source of all grief, says the poet. "Hwer is paris & heleyne," he asks. Along with other famous earthly lovers, "Heo beoþ i-gylden vt of þe reyne / so þe schef is of þe cleo" ("they have glided away out of the rain, as sheaves slide off the sloped roof").[13] Virginity, on the other hand, entitles one to eternal happiness; it is the most precious of all gems.[14]

The author of the early Middle English text known as *Hali Meiðhad* (c. 1225) selects another poignant image to convey what women can expect once they marry. Married women of whatever station— including queens, countesses, and ladies, must "lickið honi of þornes. Ha buggeð al þet swete wið twa dale of bittre" ("lick honey off thorns. They pay for all that sweetness with twice as much bitterness").[15] But those who consecrate themselves to a life of virginity will never know such grief:

> Lutel wat meiden of al þis ilke weane, of wifes wa wið hire were, ne of hare werc se wleateful þe ha wurcheð imeane, ne of þet sar ne of þet sut i þe burdðerne of bearn ant his iborenesse.[16]

> Little does a virgin know of all this misery, of the unhappiness of a wife with her husband, or of the disgusting act they do together, or of the pain and misery of pregnancy and childbearing.

This and other arguments *contra* marriage, aimed expressly at women (morning sickness, breast-feeding, the worries and cares of family, including sick children and jealous, lazy, and abusive husbands), have their classical antecedents, and they were easily pressed into service in praise of virginity during the formative years of the Church. *Hali Meiðhad* is one in a long succession of texts that took seriously the Pauline privileging of virginity over marriage, and attempted to carry it to its logical conclusion.[17]

Although arguments *against* virginity are the stock in trade of Renaissance lyrics by men, the sentiments of *Hali Meiðhad* do survive the English Reformation in women's verse. Sometime before 1648— that is, before her own marriage—Katherine Philips railed against the pangs of childbirth, and against crying children and "blustering husbands" in her poem, "A marry^d state affords but little ease."[18] In a similar poem titled "Advice to Virgins" (written "By a Lady," according to the manuscript), the fear of lost beauty—and the resultant loss of husbandly interest—is added to the list of married woes. In contemplating the pains and humiliations of marriage, the author of "Advice to Virgins" opines:

> A Womans humour hardly can Submit
> To be a Slave to One she do's Out Wit.[19]

Whereas the medieval texts offer Christ as the ideal, perfect lover, "Advice to Virgins" seems less intent on demonstrating its Christian piety than in rejecting male idolatry. "Saint like" suitors seem "Gods 'till Marry'd but prov'd Divels then" (35–36). The final lines of the poem once again play on religious sensibilities:

> And therefore Madam, be advis'd by me,
> Turn, Turn Apostate to Loves Deity.
> Suppress wild Nature, if she dares Rebel
> There's no Such Thing, as Leading Apes in Hell.

> (59–62)

Hali Meiðhad and "Advice to Virgins" are separated by more than the piety of the former and the urbanity of the latter, for, while the arguments against marriage continue into the seventeenth century, the alternatives to marriage are much less clear. The Henrican Reformation, with its dissolution of the monasteries, severely hindered English women committed to the cloistered life and who were unwilling or unable to travel to Catholic strongholds on the Continent, and virginity's institutional prestige was much eroded by the European Reformation generally. Protestant attacks on the Catholic Church often expressed a disdain for, if not outright hostility toward, celibacy (i.e., institutionally-sanctioned virginity). As A. D. Harvey puts it, "the conventional Protestant view was to regard any attempt to exalt virginity as reeking of Popish superstition."[20] The fear of women sequestered together and running their own affairs contributed to the arguments for disbanding what had become centers of female autonomy and learning.[21] In Protestant Europe, the nunnery became synonymous with the brothel, making Hamlet's well-known advice to Ophelia a brutal pun.

In the Renaissance, then, the burgeoning literature devoted to female chastity (and increasingly directed to a growing female readership) is thus reconfigured to suppress the monastery and the convent, and to foreground the home and the court instead. The numerous tracts on virginity written by the Church Fathers and then expanded upon and concretized in medieval devotional literature are still read, but they are supplemented—and finally replaced—by the marriage manual and conduct book.[22] Yet in the Renaissance, as in the Middle Ages, a woman's chastity remains her greatest prize, her ultimate value—indeed, her only value. In *Instruction of a Chris-*

ten Woman, the subject of Nancy Weitz Miller's essay in this collection, Juan Luis Vives declares:

> No man will look for any other thing of a woman, but her honesty [chastity] the which thing only, if it be lacked, is like as in a man, if he lack all that he should have. For in a woman the honesty is instead of all.[23]

Although an enormous body of literature written during the early modern period urged women to give up their prized virginity, these writings were not at all ideologically inconsistent with the aforementioned paeans to virginity. John Donne, in one of the "paradoxes" attributed to him, states: "surely nothing is more unprofitable in the Commonwealth of *Nature,* then they that dy old maids, because they refuse to be used to that end for which they were only made. . . . *Virginity* ever kept is ever lost."[24] Parolles in *All's Well that Ends Well* is even more vituperative; for him, virginity is

> against the rule of nature. To speak on the part of virginity is to accuse your mothers, which is most infallible disobedience. . . . Virginity breeds mites, much like a cheese . . . is peevish, proud, idle, made of self-love, the most inhibited sin in the canon. (1.1.135–45)

These rather extreme statements document the fact that, after the English Reformation, virginity was generally viewed as a temporary stage through which a young girl passed on the way to chaste marriage. Virginity was a valuable commodity, but it had a very limited shelf-life.

To chart the history of virginity as a steady, evolutionary progression from a religious ideal in the Middle Ages toward a more secularized ideal in the Renaissance would obscure the extreme instability of the concept of chastity in both periods. What this collection demonstrates again and again is that medieval and early modern attitudes toward virginity are not generalizable and evolutionary, but specific, changeable, and often conflicted. Yet it is clear that virginity's signifying force is in no way annulled by the contradictions that the following essays document. For even if the secret of virginity eludes representation and is constrained by a rhetoric of silence, the figure of the virgin is everywhere on display in the Middle Ages and Renaissance, an object of anxious fascination, and the focus of an enduring cultural obsession. The aim of *Menacing Virgins* is to begin to delineate the nexus of religious, political, economic, and aesthetic values that, in the medieval and early modern periods, contribute to the Western European myth of virginity, and to examine how those complex cultural forces animate, empower, discipline, disclose, mystify, and menace the virginal body.

Our first essay in the medieval cluster is "'Blæju Þöll—Young Fir of the Bed-Clothes': Skaldic Seduction." William Sayers examines early medieval Icelandic poems that were addressed to young, unmarried women. Such poems constituted a form of "seduction," and were therefore legally actionable. Sayers sounds a theme that runs through a number of other essays in this volume: that virginity is not necessarily a physical state, but a condition largely dependent upon social conventions and mores. As Sayers puts it, "the menace to and from maidenhood in medieval Iceland was greater in the public domain of gender (social virginity) than in the private world of physiology and sexuality." The male gaze, here formalized into verse that was widely circulated, was menacing precisely because it was so public, capable of pre-empting the authority of a father (or other male guardian) to give the virgin's body in marriage.

Maud Burnett McInerney, in "Rhetoric, Power, and Integrity in the Passion of the Virgin Martyr," forges a connection between the medieval representation of the menaced but verbally accomplished virgin martyr and earlier, classical images of feminine power and eloquence. Exploring the parallels between the Middle English *Seinte Margarete*, for example, and representations of Ovid's Medea, McInerney offers a profound reconsideration of the presumed equation of female virginity and silence. Her focus on the voluble virgin martyr conjures what McInerney describes as "an ancient tradition of magical eloquence usually associated in the pagan world with feminine practitioners of the occult arts." This essay traces the "aggressive verbal power" of the martyred virgin through Prudentius' *Peristephanon*, the *Legenda Aurea*, and Chaucer's Second Nun's Tale, to suggest the persistence and the prevalence of her paradoxical construction as a figure in which "physical passivity is linked to an aggressive eloquence, and a sexualized martyrdom to imperishable integrity."

In "King by Day, Queen by Night: The Virgin Camille in the *Roman d'Eneas*," Wendy Chapman Peek demonstrates how the "radical virginity" of the Amazon queen Camille challenges the ideology of romance, in which marriage and dynastic consolidation are central and prevailing concerns. Peek draws on the work of Julia Kristeva to explain the poet's fascination with the recalcitrant virgin. Employing Kristeva's theory of the abject, which, in Kristeva's words, "disturbs identity, system, order," Peek argues that "Camille is the terrifying presence which discloses the ideological limits of the dominant culture."

Kathryn Lynch considers the menacing virgin from a very different perspective in "Diana's 'Bowe Ybroke': Impotence, Desire, and Virginity in Chaucer's *Parliament of Fowls.*" The formel eagle may well be only a bird, but she is a reluctant virgin bride as well. It is her virginity that is the subtext to much of the debate among the birds, Lynch argues. "The eagle's repressed sexuality thus invokes the famous 'taboo of virginity,' which reflects a deep male fear of untouched female sexuality." Chaucer has constructed, however facetiously, a tale of the virgin who "simultaneously repels and attracts." Avian virginity becomes an occasion for the narrator to explore his own anxiety about creativity and the subject of poetry, and the formel eagle's hesitancy comes to symbolize the poet's own vacillation about his role.

In "Menaced Masculinity and Imperiled Virginity in Malory's *Morte Darthur,*" Kathleen Kelly explores the concept of male virginity in the medieval romance; more specifically, she demonstrates the difficulty of recuperating the male body in Malory's text. When the male body is threatened with penetration and fragmentation—which is the very moment when we would expect to view it most fully and explicitly—either the fetishized female body is substituted for it, or the male body itself is feminized. Either way, masculinity, along with the code of knighthood that constitutes it, remains protected from critique.

In the first essay in the Renaissance cluster, "*Il Trionfo della Pudicizia:* Menacing Virgins in Italian Renaissance Domestic Painting," Cristelle L. Baskins directly connects textual representations of virginity to material culture and the visual arts in her readings of fifteenth- and sixteenth-century Italian wedding furniture. Baskins considers the iconography of Italian Renaissance domestic paintings and their figurative display of the commodity of virginity. "How," she asks, "did Renaissance brides imbued with 'chaste thinking' make that shift from maiden to matron, how did they learn to pay the marriage debt?" As a way of answering this important question, the essay discusses the representation of the battle between Cupid and Chastity, a frequent subject in domestic painting, drawn from Petrarch's *Trionfi.* Exploring the ambiguities and ambivalences in Gherardo del Fora's depiction of this scene, Baskins considers the very mixed message about female chastity, violence, chastisement, and constraint that such an image would have presented to a fifteenth-century Florentine bride.

In "Metaphor and the Mystification of Chastity in Vives's *Instruction of a Christen Woman,*" Nancy Weitz Miller argues that Vives's text exemplifies the paradoxical thinking that informs Renaissance ideas about virginity. In the marriage game, virginity is supposed to attract attention and to provide protection from unwanted attention. Such a paradox gives rise to competing metaphors that construct virginity: virginity as protection, as "armor," and virginity as valued, as "treasured"—and hence worth "stealing." In addition, the notion that virginity both attracts and repels leaves the issue of responsibility for male desire unresolved, while locating the sin of failed virginity in the woman.

Lauren Shohet revisits Milton's *Comus* in "Figuring Chastity: Milton's Ludlow Masque," showing how Milton puts the masque—associated in his day with sexual license and wantonness, and, by extension, anarchy—to a new use by making chastity itself the subject. Miltonic chastity, she argues, is comprised of "personal chastity as necessary precondition for composing poetry; chastity as ethical process, chastity as mode of figuration; and chastity as epistemological and interpretive principle." Moreover, Shohet recuperates the function of the figurative in the *Mask* within its own epistemological context; the figurative, rather than being in opposition to the real (as contemporary critics structure it) is actually a link, a bridge, between the real and the ideal.

In "Lost Honor and Torn Veils: A Virgin's Rape in Music," Lydia Hamessley examines the "Accenti queruli" of Giovanni Felice Sances in order to explore the disjunction between the narrative of rape and the exquisite music in which this narrative is set. The narrator is a man who tells the maiden Lidia that so long as she keeps silent about his "seduction," she may keep her reputation as a virgin. As Hamessley shows, the listener is easily lulled into accepting this story and passing over the disturbing fact that this was no seduction, but a rape.

In "Evading Rape and Embracing Empire in Margaret Cavendish's *Assaulted and Pursued Chastity*," Marina Leslie explores the masculine heroics of this odd romance's virginal heroine. Leslie looks at how a female author employs and revises the figure of the virago and her ambiguous—often misogynist—legacy by "negotiating between the Scylla of the absolutist virago and the Charybdis of the monstrous usurping androgyne." Situating Cavendish in her Civil War context, Leslie argues that the author produced "a gendered allegory featuring the martial maid as both the emblem of disordered times and the tonic to cure them."

*   *   *

This collection grew out of a panel organized by Kathleen Kelly and Marina Leslie for the 1993 Southeast Medieval Association meeting. The editors thank Michael Kuczynski for his invitation to present work at this conference. We particularly want to thank Wendy Peek, one of the original panelists and a contributor to this collection, for suggesting the felicitous and ferocious title that we took for both the panel and the collection—"Menacing Virgins." We'd like to thank those enthusiastic conference-goers who originally inspired us to develop a collection, and all those who took part in the subsequent electronic discussion on virginity and on rape on MEDTEXT-L, CHAU-CERNET, and MEDFEM-L (Michael Calabrese, Shirley Carnahan, Susannah Chewning, Jeffrey Cohen, Sian Echard, Jody Hoppe, Wendy Pfeffer, Daniel F. Pigg, Christine Rose, Elizabeth Rowe, Paul Spillenger, Jocelyn Wogan-Browne). Our deepest gratitude goes to Margaret W. Ferguson for her interest and for her willingness to contribute a preface. Finally, we would like to thank our editor Jay Halio for his support of the project. We are pleased that, collectively, the essays in *Menacing Virgins* constitute a conversation across the rhetorical and real boundaries constructed by discipline and period; certainly the conversation that we have had as editors has tended to dissolve these boundaries in sometimes unexpected and always rewarding ways. We hope that we have succeeded in moving beyond a "thematics" of virginity to use virginity as an instrument for interrogating the assumptions and presumptions of periodization and the "integritas" of isolated disciplinary practice.

Menacing Virgins

Part I
Virginity in the Middle Ages

"Blæju þöll—Young Fir of the Bed-Clothes": Skaldic Seduction

William Sayers

In the mid-thirteenth-century Icelandic *Eyrbyggja saga*, Vermundr returns from Norway and a favorable reception at court with the gift of a pair of Swedish berserks, professional men-at-arms who were subject to a fighting frenzy in battle that made them impervious to fear and, it was thought, to fire and iron as well. As is frequently the case of Norwegian gifts in the ideologically complex family sagas, the berserk brothers, Halli and Leiknir, are a questionable addition to the Icelandic community of the Snæfellsnes region. When Vermundr refuses to arrange a suitable marriage for Halli, the troublesome brothers are passed along as a malicious gift to his brother Styrr, whose ethical position in the saga is more compatible with their negative potential. Taken into the rural household, Halli and Leiknir work on Styrr's farm, but soon their temporarily sublimated aggression leads them to aspire to better their economic condition. Halli, with Leiknir's support, pays court to Styrr's unmarried daughter, Ásdís.

Two poems, in the formal style and rigorous *dróttkvætt* meter of the medieval Norse skalds, are included as part of the berserks' suit of Ásdís. The supposed circumstance of the poems is the haughty but silent Ásdís's stroll past the work site where the berserks are engaged in tasks imposed by Styrr. This intellectually demanding verse was most often employed in the praise of a ruler or in the poet's promotion of his own image as a brave, resourceful and faithful warrior. Yet it is here turned to the flattery of a farm girl, as I will discuss in more detail below. Here and following, I furnish the original poem and a literal translation designed to capture the complicated punning and metaphorical aspects of these verses. First Halli speaks, and then Leiknir:

Hvert hafið, Gerðr, of görva,   þvít í vetr, en vitra
gangfögr liðar hanga,   vangs, sákat þik ganga,
ljúg vætr at mér, leygjar,   hirðidís, frá húsi,
línbundin, för þína;   húns, skrautligar búna.[1]

31

Where will you make your outing, fair-walking, linen-wrapped (= with headdress) Gerðr (goddess) of the joint-hung's (forearm's) fire (gold rings) (= woman) — tell me no lie — since I have not seen you this winter, wise coffer-guardian of the peg's field (= gaming board) (= woman), go more richly dressed from home?

Sólgrund Siggjar linda undir,	hoddgrund, hvat býr
sjaldan hefr of faldit	Hlín, oflæti þínu,
jafnhátt; öglis stéttar	hýrmælt, hóti fleira
elds nú's skart á þellu;	hvítings, an vér lítum?[2]

Sun-field of the islands' belts (sea) (= wearer of gold, woman), seldom have you worn so high a headdress; now the pine of the hawk's seat's (hand's) fire (gold) (= woman) wears finery; treasure-field (= woman), what more than what we see is hidden under your pride, fair-spoken Hlín (goddess) of the white [drinking-horn] (= woman)?

Some fifty stanzas of this erotic verse, in the demanding metrics of *dróttkvætt*, are preserved in the Old Norse-Icelandic poetic corpus. Extant courting poems belong to a contextual, rather than generic, category called *lausavísur*, "loose" or "occasional verse." Their aesthetic merits, topical interest, and later incorporation into the family and Norwegian kings' sagas account for their preservation. Otherwise, social circumstances would have worked against the survival of love songs; such versifying was simply not in the interest of the Norwegian and Icelandic establishments and their ideology. Moreover, post-conversion Church condemnation of love poetry, which presumably threatened the sacrament of marriage, should also have worked against preservation.

Questions that a scholar may legitimately ask of a tradition of courting verse concern the origins, legal and social situation, and phenomenological affinities of erotic poetry, the status of unmarried women, and the image of woman that is projected and promoted in this sub-genre. In the present study, attention will focus on how maidenhood, in the specific cultural definition of early medieval Iceland, can be approached, addressed and appropriated through verbal art; how "woman" challenges but may also authenticate the poet; and how, in her susceptibility to the seductive menace, the virgin can in turn pose a threat to familial plans and social order, as in the case of the berserk brothers Halli and Leiknir. Before doing so, it is necessary to describe some of the cultural functions and features of both poetry and "woman" in early medieval Iceland.

Although the biographical "skalds' sagas" incorporate a substantial amount of erotic verse along with the usual poems of praise, censure, and self-advancement, their focus is on contention between men, to which courting scenes generally provide a prelude. Such contention reaches its acute phase after the woman's marriage to a rival. On the other hand, amorous relationships, except in the case of *Kormáks saga*, are given relatively little analysis. The skalds' "biographies," that is, the prose narratives as distinct from the verse, may influence our efforts to determine the status of courting poets and courted women in the first centuries of Icelandic history. As no other verse is known from Halli and Leiknir, there is a good possibility that the verses quoted above are the work of the saga author or some other intermediary in the storytelling tradition, not of the two berserks. Therefore, attention will rest on the poetic artifacts themselves, an approach that foregrounds individual poems and lesser-known poets.

Since poetry's origins are constantly being recalled in the self-reflective verse of the Norse skalds, we would do well to consider whether *ars* and *amor* were significantly linked in the beginning of things. Snorri Sturluson's paired works, Gylfaginning (*The Deception of Gylfi*) and Skáldskaparmál (*Poetic Diction*), treat the origins of poetic art from a variety of perspectives, but female beings are not involved in the evolutionary history of poetry, except in the seduction of Gunnlöð, a giant's daughter, by Óðinn (under the name of *Bölverkr* "Ill-Doer"), a seduction designed to acquire the mead of poetic inspiration: "Bolverk went to where Gunnlod was and lay with her for three nights and then she let him drink three draughts of the mead."[3] This incident can be interpreted as a commentary on that necessary component in art that derives from the Other (giants as representatives of alterity), from the feminine, and from the natural cycles of death and regeneration.[4] Given Óðinn's clear motives, and without interrogating those of Gunnlöð, male access to females for sexual and other exchange—seduction, if we count this as a simple deception—is an important part of the male-driven elaboration of poetry, one narratively dominant over, but not obviating, woman's role as custodian of the mead. As we shall see, the subsequent interdependence of human poet and "patroness" (willing or unwilling object and recipient of poetry) will replicate this original relationship in similar, if not identical, complexity.

However, the tacit approval accorded the god's action by the myth did not unequivocally extend to Icelandic society's view of seducers and their verses.[5] The legal situation is remarkable on two counts: erotic poetry is proscribed, in the sense that it is legally actionable, and this proscription figures in a context in the law code *Grágás*, in which defamation and magical practices are similarly condemned.[6]

Erotic verse, verbal abuse, and magic (with pre-Christian antecedents) share a similar severity in sentences: outlawry. But it is apparent, even from the brief foray into the origin myth above, that there
was a deeper rationale for the grouping. Factors here include the
metamorphosis of speech into poetry, the transformational effect of
verbal art (amorous, slanderous) on its subject and public, and the
alteration of reality effected by sorcery (not least, love magic). Another common denominator of the three crimes is human sexuality:
man's praise of women, his mockery of "effeminate" men (to draw
on the vocabulary of the value system under consideration), and
early Scandinavian magic called *seiðr*, which is thought to have had
a significant association with female sexuality and generative power.[7]
Sorcery, the defamation of men, and the seduction of women are
located on the social margin; a further affinity among magic, public
calumny, and erotic verse can be found in their immediate social
effects. A poet's suit or seduction, like coarser slurs, impinged on
the honor of senior males in a family, and therefore might be turned
to political purposes quite distinct from winning a girl's heart and
body. Despite the ban, the family sagas show that courting and defamatory verses were practiced and feared, and that their creators
were prosecuted, legally and extra-legally, when the plaintiffs had
sufficient political power to execute their vengeance.

The position of early medieval Norse women before the law has
attracted considerable recent critical attention, not least because of
their relative empowerment compared with the women of southern
Europe.[8] Some of the apparent theoretical independence of women
in the pre-Christian period, such as the ability to initiate divorce,
may have been curtailed with the introduction of Christian canon
law, which sought to render marriage indissoluble and, it is claimed
by some, to protect these same women from arbitrary divorce by
their spouses. Yet women lacked the authority to exercise in the
wider political sphere the power that was resident in land or a chief-
tainship that they might own. Not only was their legal agency constrained, their recourse to law and appearance in its courts were
similarly limited. In the matter of erotic verse, a woman over twenty
might initiate a case against the author of poems about her, but its
prosecution would rest in her kinsmen's hands.

The thirteenth- and fourteenth-century family sagas, celebrating
a Golden Age through the deployment of a selective realism, are
concerned with marriage chiefly as it relates to legitimate descent,
inheritance, land-holding, interfamilial rivalry, political alliances, and
action—in short, the viricentric, extra-domestic world of competition
in an island nation that experienced shrinking natural resources

within a century of its founding. As a consequence, impulsive marriages in the family sagas often end poorly, whether the impulse was
that of the partners or their parents; marriages arranged by senior
males may end poorly too, if a headstrong woman is not consulted.
The ideal saga balance seems to include initial negotiation among
males, referral to the woman, and her acquiescing deferral of the
decision back to her family head. There is little place here for the
suitor's verse.

Since Norse myths dealing with cosmogony and sociogony show
the male principle at work, one might provisionally conclude that
the life of the spirit is masculine, as is art, law, and social organization, with mere materiality relegated to the feminine and subject to
natural law. Where would physical virginity and the sociocultural
construct that could provisionally be called "inviolate feminine gender" fit into this scheme of things? And I stress that it is indeed a
scheme. In the pre-conversion world that Christian Icelandic saga
authors of the thirteenth century chose to recreate, physical virginity,
along with sexual inexperience or experience, seems not to have
been matters of major concern.[9] For example, the tutelary divinity of
virgins, Fulla, is a shadowy figure in myth, central to no preserved
tale.[10] In our sources, no transcendent quality is ascribed to physical
purity, nor is its loss lamented except in texts of a homiletic Christian
nature.[11] Adolescent sexuality seems taken for granted, although
there is little explicit commentary on it, save when a fornication suit
is a card played in a larger political struggle. The non-sequestration
of unmarried women, norms of hospitality and the communication
needs that were served by visits between the remote farmsteads
made it difficult to deny male visitors some minimum access to
young women in the semi-public hall. As I shall show, the menace
to and from maidenhood in medieval Iceland was greater in the
public domain of gender ("social virginity") than in the private world
of physiology and sexuality.

*　*　*

Skaldic verse is showcase art, the virtuoso deployment of an eru-
dite vocabulary, mythological motifs, and metrical complexity. Only
the most gifted poets succeed in rising above conventions of style
to achieve individualized content and distinct contours of personality
(as a later critical perspective might describe it). This basis in stereo-
type—which we should not color too negatively—also affects the
image of women singled out by the poets for address and description. In fact, they are for the most part only variations on the theme
of Woman, although possibly personalized through topical refer-

ences that are lost to a later audience. The resulting tension between the general and the specific can be illustrated by a return to Halli and Leiknir's rather similar stanzas, and by the identification of a favorite device in erotic verse, the encryption of the name of the woman addressed among the poetic images. This is designed as an intellectual puzzle, one with fairly simple conventions, but calling for a good knowledge of mythological lore and other poetic vocabulary. Jenny Jochens suggests that concealing the name may have been done to preclude prosecution, but the convention also seems one that poets were ready to exploit. The individual name, Ásdís in this case, is then the most specific and topical piece of information in the verses, although its presence is entirely due to and realized through convention.[12]

Let us consider more specifically how women are conceived in these verses. The attributes of Ásdís in the two examples relate exclusively to conventional gender functions: she is the wearer of fine clothes and jewelry, the custodian of the gaming board and its pieces, and of the drinking horn. The first two contribute to her beauty but also underline her socioeconomic status. The latter two refer to responsibilities of women in the hall of Icelandic residences: to carry out duties imposed by the norms of hospitality, serving ale and assisting in entertainment. The individual women the poets address with a multitude of terms are all reflexes of a single perfect female, the iconic totality of social womanhood, the embodiment of conventional virtues in an attractive appearance. But in none of this are there references to woman as mother. Pregnancy, child-bearing, and the offstage nurturing role of woman are disregarded in favor of her service in the male world of the public room. The male gaze is without analysis. The young woman is objectified to the point where personality is suppressed. Skaldic poetry offers less a range of character types than a repertory of social functions. Even the qualities of mind and character to which allusion is made are those of social relationship, such as cordial speech. Other frequent objects of reference are to women's beauty as brightness, e.g., "loga . . . ór eisu" [flame from glowing embers];[13] the production, use, and care of textiles (tablecloths, bedclothes, cloaks, head-dresses); and the possession and wearing of other objects of worth.

Þórarinn *svarti* Þórólfsson of Mávahlíð offers a typical example in verses intended to restore his reputation as a virile man of action: "*nú kná alnar leiptra jörð at fregna til orða" [now can the earth of the flashes (gold) of ells (of cloth) (= woman) question (my) words].[14] Ormr Barreyjarskáld ("the skald of Barra," in the Hebrides), with no concern for incongruity, calls the woman "*Draupnis drógar dís" [the guardian spirit of Draupnir's sweat (gold)].[15] For Óláfr Haraldsson the woman is "*grjótölnis landrifs lind, merkð golli" [linden of land-reef's (sea's) stone-snakes (gold) (= woman), marked with gold] and "*valklifs bands björk" [birch of the band of the whale-cliff (sea) (= gold)].[16] Gunnlaugr complains of Helga: "*fold flóðhyrs nemr flaum af skaldi" [the flood-fire's (gold's) land (= woman) deprives the poet of joy].[17]

Skaldic verse, when flattering, is essentially ennobling, because it raises its objects, at the cost of individuality, to archetypal, even semi-divine, status. Women are directly equated with a range of female supernatural beings, usually in a kenning construction, such as "Gerðr [a valkyrie] of the arms' fire" (gold bracelets). The economy of the kenning system keeps immanent a whole mythological corpus, so that Woman moves in a charged mythic landscape. The transformational effect of erotic verse that elevates the young woman to the sphere of the divine recalls poetry's association with magic, and historically may even have affected her reputation and sense of self-worth.

Although the kenning is generally thought of as periphrasis or circumlocution—ways round to meaning—when the technique is so common it not so much leads by an artistic route to hidden meaning as it leads away from familiar identity (such as the landowner's daughter) toward the universal. The technique is one of displacement. Even the scrambled syntax of this non-narrative verse contributes to a sense of alocality, until the elements are sorted, ordered, and the poem solved. Also contributing to the emotional distance between poem and public, between poet and apostrophized woman, is the frequent use of the third person for both man and woman. In the reference to idealized attributes and functions, reliance on nominal forms (names, nouns, adjectives) creates a static picture. The capacity for movement is an inherent agency, unspent power. In the relative absence of kinetic verbs, action is deferred in favor of potential action. The act implicit in the relationship between the parts of kennings must be supplied by the listener, e.g., "the goddess of the drinking-horn" = she who proffers it to men.

Women are viewed in isolation, relating only to abstract concepts of perfect womanhood on the one hand, and to the poet, he too an archetype, on the other. The women of skaldic poetry do not form a community, nor are they seen as members of families, save in the poems of frustration and contention, allied with defamatory verse, that show them married to the poets' rivals. Yet this deference and conferral of worth in the hermetic, almost claustral, world of the inward-turning poem creates a very specific potency for the woman apostrophized, one better known in western European literature from the works of the troubadours, Dante, or Petrarch. Given the limited range of activity, real and potential, accorded to women in the poetry, a few simple, everyday acts can be raised to mysterious, monumental status, like beauty itself: in King Óláfr's verse, the woman walks past, greets the poet or is silent, or rides away on horseback, taking his peace of mind with her.[18] Although for the poet speech is among the most important of acts, woman, despite the epithet "fair-spoken," has no voice in these monologic poems and seems unable to construct a meaning for her experience.[19]

Greatly magnified in a theme otherwise developed by poets at Norwegian courts in longer poetic works and in prose tales, woman can be equated with the land itself, awaiting its ruler to whom she also confers legitimacy:

Ár stóð eik en dýra,	nú hefr (bekkjar) tré bliknat
jarladóms, með blómi	brátt (Mardallar gráti
harðla grœn, sem hirðar,	lind hefr) laufi (bundit
hvert misseri, vissu;	línu-jörð) i Görðum.[20]

Formerly there stood a fine oak very green with blossoms in every season, as the keepers of the earldom knew; now the tree's leaves have quickly faded in Russia; the linden of the benches has bound the linen-land (= head) with the tears of Mardoll (= Freyja) (gold).

The poet is subject to the contingency that in the early Norse world view was associated with chaotic forces external to man's law and social organization, of which the land and the natural world, with its giants, trolls, and dwarves, along with woman in her regenerative capacity and driven by her sexual imperative, are major parts. The poet can impose order and his person only through the creation of a rigorously formal verse so that woman, like land and nature, comes provisionally under the control of male art. But the imposition of organizing male intelligence is not possible without the catalyst of the poetic mead, which has partaken of many forms and conditions, including female custodianship.

This poetry on the social margin paradoxically praises only attributes at the social center, the norm. Although the dissemination of such verse may have been illegal and thus be seen to subvert social order, the verse itself is engaged in a construction of female gender completely aligned with the ideology of this same society. As consciously as any modern art form, it illustrates Foucault's contention that discourses systematically form the objects of which they speak. The erotic poet enshrines concepts of female gender in such a way that its representatives can be individualized exclusively through the superiority of his art, that is, only the esthetically successful one-of-a-kind poem can make a woman both universal and individual.[21]

* * *

Despite his engagement in the elaboration of female gender, the poet is preoccupied with the advancement of his own image. The skald is acutely concerned with male gender, how he appears in the eyes of both women and men. In this self-reflective verse, for which poetic composition, its effects and rewards are a preoccupation, there is a formal symbiotic relationship between poet and woman that antedates the personal context or rises above individual acquiesence and gratification. Just as woman in these verses is seen in essentially male-serving social functions, she is the prerequisite for the poet's activity in the artistic sphere. There is then a double spectral relationship: the poet gives the woman back an enhanced, mythologized image of herself, while the simple existence of the woman as target for the verse gives the poet the opportunity for stylized self-realization, like iron filings patterning themselves around a magnet.

In the elaboration of his poetic persona, the skald's select situations of seafaring and battle, hypermasculine as they are, are often contrasted with the distant, calm life of the woman addressed—or, if she is married, with the sloth of an uxorious, stay-at-home husband. This conscious staging of self via such oppositions seems touched by self-pity, but the poet's own judgment would more likely be heroic stoicism. Skaldic verse is a highly contrastive medium with a variety of *chiaroscuro* effects, aided by the conventional contrast or at least a shift in subject matter between the two *helmings*.

The concern with evaluation competes with action, which often remains potential or is summarized in abstract terms before its inception or after its close, as in, for example, references to combat. Þórleifr *jarlsskáld* Rauðfeldarson simply calls a woman "svarri" [haughty one] as he angrily plans revenge for a wrecked ship.[22] Björn Ásbrandsson, the "Hero of the Breiðvíkings" (*breiðvíkingakappi*), speculates that Hlín of the sea flames (gold) in her white clothing would be anxious for the seafarer's (the poet's) safety, if she knew that he lay alone and chilled among rocks instead of in her bed.[23] Egill Skallagrímsson's grandfather's comrade-in-arms, Ölvir *hnúfa*, imagines that the woman has closed her eyes in sleep while he is caught among the skerries.[24] Stefnir Þórgilsson addresses a Danish woman, Gerðr of the woollens, whose father he has angered, but he would rather stand bowed and rain-swept by the post than lie warm in her arms.[25] Similarly, Þórketill *klyppr* Þórðarson says in sorrow over a battle loss: "*hygg eigi byggva beð né svá dýnu hjá Þér, bjór-ranns Nanna" [I do not intend to occupy your bed nor the down bolster by you, Nanna of the beer].[26] From an even more threatening situation on land, Hrafn Önundarson, Gunnlaugr's rival, says that the woman will hear of his courage in judicial combat at the assembly, even if he receives his death blow.[27]

Or the poet's thoughts may return from the nautical setting more actively to love. Hallfreðr exclaims:

Fúss emk enn, þótt ósa   þvít álgrundar endis
aflvöll drepi stalli,   áttgóðrar mér tróðu
mjök skýtr Mörnar vakri,   betr unnum nú nytja
minnask við Kolfinnu,   nær an heitin væri.[28]

I am still eager to kiss (punning on the word for "remember") Kolfinna, although the power-laden estuary (sea) strikes our mast step; strongly is thrust Mörn's (elf's) nimble one (the ship); as I now would love to enjoy the well-born fagot of Endil's (sea-king's) eel-foundations (sea stones, gold) (= woman) almost better than if she were pledged [to me].

From this, it is a short step to equate the woman with a ship:

Þykki mér, es ek þekki   en þás sér á Sögu
þunnísunga Gunni,   saums í kvinna flaumi,
sem fleybrautir fljóti   sem skrautbúin skríði
fley meðal tveggja eyja,   skeið með gyldum reiða.[29]

It seems to me when I espy light-coiffed Gunnr (valkyrie) as if a quick ship floated on the swift way (sea) between two islands; but when needle's Saga (goddess) is seen in the flow (crowd) of women it is as if a finely outfitted war-ship glided by with gilded rigging.

The circuit of imagery can be closed in another way, with the poem likened to a ship[30] or when lovemaking itself is equated with seafaring in *double entendre*. The Norwegian chieftain Hárekr Ey-vindarson admonishes the widows of Lund and maids of Denmark not to smile if in his late years he no longer has the courage to steer his ship out onto the open sea.[31] But if seafaring is a metaphor for lovemaking, what appears to be far is actually close, just as, in other ways, skaldic verse seeks to put the intimate at a distance. In a juxtaposition of death in naval combat with the erotic, Hallfreðr is prepared to make the final sacrifice for the ultimate reward:

Lítt hirði ek, lautar   ef ek næða Sif slœðu
lundr hefr hætt til sprunda   sofa karms meðal arma,
viggs, þótt verðak höggvinn,   mákat ek láss við ljósa
varra, í höndum svarra,   lind ofrœkðar bindask.[32]

Little do I care that I may be struck down in the arms of the proud one;
the wake's hollows' (sea's) steed's (ship's) tree (warrior) (= poet) ran
the risk for the woman; if I were granted to sleep between the arms of
Sif of the garments chest; I cannot keep from my compelling love for the
linden tree of the bright keys (= woman).

Skaldic verse as a whole is not prudish, as the more offensive,
slanderous verses illustrate in their salacious references, but the
finely dressed women of skaldic verse generally stay clothed. The
social identity conferred by fine dress is maintained intact even when
preserving bodily integrity is not an issue. The tone is often more
austere than sensual.[33] Only in moves toward the coarser end of the
stylistic range is there reference to active sexuality, and this is often
directed past the young woman to insult her guardians. Kormákr
notes Steingerðr's fine eyes and beautiful feet;[34] Hallfreðr finds female beauty enhanced by a summer in the mountains: "*sævar báls
hirði-Naumur koma allar sléttfjallaðar heim frá seljum" [The care-
giantesses (or Naum as proper name) of sea-fire (gold) (= women)
all come home smooth-skinned (-haired?) from the shielings].[35] Although the sexual tenor is generally kept cool, an expression like
"blæju þöll" [young fir-tree of the bed clothes] surely carried an
undercurrent of sexuality.[36] Another typical situation in erotic verse
could be put under the sign of the assignation—future, thwarted, or
now irrevocably past. But here, too, the ambivalent skald seems to
anticipate the troubadour love-lyric in preferring his lady's absence
to her presence. One of the earliest skalds, Auðun *illskœlda* ("wicked
skald"), regrets a woman's failure to appear as promised and hangs
his verse on the verb *smjúga* "to creep through an opening."[37] Björn
hítdælakappi recalls how the astute woman sent the servant to muck
out the barn so that he could slip into the house.[38] Björn Ásbrandsson
looks back elegiacally on an autumn day spent with "armlinns þella"
[arm-linen's pine], a day they might have wished the longest between
the yellow woods and the blue sky ("í miðli guls viðar ok blás").[39]
Archly, Eindriði Einarson affirms that on the island all the girl's body
was far from him but her lips ("*mér kom allt meyjar hold fjarri i
eyju nema varrar");[40] those who claim more happened will suffer for
it. But the stylistically transparent poem (note the simplex *mey* "girl")
does not ring true, so that frankness must be read as fraud, the same
tension as in the verbal construction "kom . . . fjarri" [came . . . far].

Hallfreðr notes: "snót . . . vér munum hvern dag dýra" [wise one, we remember other, nicer days].[41] Gunnlaugr, too, has only memories. He recognizes that he can never win "hörvi drifna hafnar jörð" [(the giantess) Earth (as wearer) of the cloak of refined flax], but when they were younger he first lay on the one and then on the other of the arms of "lautsíkjar lyngs landi" [the land of the field-salmon's (snake's) heather (gold)].[42]

Snapshots of the actual moment of seduction are few, despite the voyeuristic nature of the genre. One example from the corpus of Björn *hítdælakappi*, the interpretation of which is made more difficult by wordplay, may be contrasting the poet's present situation with that of Oddný Eykyndill ("Island-Candle") at home in her husband's arms, but the place assigned to this stanza in the sequence of poems in the saga suggests the earliest phase of the poet's relationship with the girl and it may be he who is both seducer and seaman.

Hristi handa fastar   meðan vel stinna vinnum
hefr drengr gamans fengit;   veldr nökkvat því klökkva,
hrynja hart á dýnu   skíð verðk skriðar beiða,
hlöð Eykyndils vöðva,   skorða ör á borði.[43]

The warrior has made Hrist (valkyrie) of the forearms' fire (gold) (= woman) experience [the body's] pleasure; Island-Candle's muscles' piling (or lacework) falls hard and fast on the feather-bed, while we make the stiff oar flexible at the gunwale (bed-side?); he (she?) is rather equal to the task (the cause of it?); I have to propel the ski of the [beaching] prop (ship) forward.

Yet allusions to physical union are never put in a marriage context; no future social life together is projected.

*　*　*

Woman is situated on a mythological plane in skaldic verse and is constantly apostrophized. To what kind of enhanced power is the appeal being made? In a stanza at some distance from the truly erotic, Þjóðólfr Arnórsson makes three references (one a direct address) to a watching woman:

Rétt kann rœði slíta   ært mun, snót, áðr sortuð
ræsis herr ór verri;   sæföng i tvau ganga,
ekkja stendr ok undrask   þöll leggr, við frið, fyllar
ára burð sem furðu;   fúr, kleyf, á þat leyfi.[44]

The ruler's host knows how to tear the straight oars from the sea; the widow stands in wonder at the bearing of the oars as before a marvel;

the rowing will be in peace, wise one, before, blackened, the sea-gear (oar) breaks in two; the young fire-fir (wearer of gold) gives her approval.

Roberta Frank has identified a significant component in many skaldic poems (and not just erotic verse) in her article title, "Why skalds address women." The seemingly arbitrary introduction of the woman, through what is often a one-word interpellation, creates a novel tension. How does this woman relate to the situation of the poet? As witness to male deeds seems the immediate and perhaps superficial answer, and it returns us to the matter of specularity raised above. "Þrúðr kann mart en þrúða" [glorious Þrúðr (valkyrie) understands much].[45] Yet the woman interposed in the verses is more than spectatrix; she is also authenticator and judge, even if we must assume her to have been physically distant from the scene described. As a consequence, the structure of the male/female relationship in erotic skaldic verse is more complex than may seem the case at first glance. Just as the king's deeds are mute and ephemeral without the poet, so the poet's actions and his verse require a female audience in the case of courting verse, but more problematically so, he requires her in other circumstances. The poet's fields of action are battle, the sea, the hall, but also poetry itself, and on all of these he requires female confirmation, even vindication, as if it were the minimal desired return on the poem. The usually authoritative voice of the poet is then qualified by an apparent lack of self-sufficiency. It is as if Óðinn returned to Gunnlöð for a testimonial. The role accorded women by skaldic verses, enthroning them in conventional gender norms, is not within the social agency perhaps unhistorically ascribed to them in the family sagas but rather in a court of appeal where male gender is tried.

Against the coercive contractualism and seductive power of the *ad mulierem* poem, part of the latent female power over male actors is found in the suspension of judgment. The virgin's menace is one of silence. Yet it would be hazardous to speculate that physical integrity made her a more perfect, "uncorrupted" arbiter, one seeing and judging her "first man." But the poet has finessed the threat of silence through another convention of the genre. Since these are not dialogue or debate poems, woman is given no opportunity to reply. Negative assessment is precluded, as silence is returned to male control, assisted by the closed temporal horizon of the poems, the absence of social action projected beyond the end of the verse. However, female subjectivity cannot be entirely precluded. To adapt a statement by Jeffrey Jerome Cohen on an essay by Sarah Stanbury:

> [I]nsisting on a space for female subjectivity even within texts bounded by an ostensibly masculine visual frame . . . argues for a new trigonome-

try of vision that allows "shifting incarnations" and women who "dare to stare back.'"[46]

Thus a further tension is added to erotic verse through the heteronomous construction of gender, woman and man posing and poised before each other in expectation of cue, response, and judgment.

* * *

The tendency within the courting poems toward the static and depersonalized, the creation of seemingly undifferentiated female identity, should not be thought to outweigh the very personal circumstances of the poems' creation and distribution, and the consequences of the poems for social dynamics. If woman exercised power over the poet through reticence, on a less theoretical level erotic skaldic verse posed substantial threats of its own. From the interior workings of the poetry, its syntactic interfolding, onomastic puzzles, and the mutually dependent stances of poet on parade and feminine observer, it is to the external social context that we now must turn to explore how the poems worked in the community of hearers, and what potential dangers they created by their very composition and in their consequences when circulated. Taking the poems at face value, the majority stay well within the bounds of good taste and could scarcely be construed as insulting or personally demeaning to the women addressed, although wordplay and innuendo are never to be counted out. But since the ostensible range of outcomes within the poem stops short of a marriage union, the verse may be qualified as essentially seductive in aim, designed to gain the girl's attention and win her favor, whether or not this found expression in sexual union. If physical virginity were in jeopardy, reputation, less firmly or necessarily based in actual event, was at even greater risk.

Medieval Icelandic society, we now realize, was considerably more competitive than the earlier view of the family sagas as accurate depictions of the wholesome life of free farmers in a proto-democracy would have us believe. As in most societies, contract marriage and its merging of economic resources was an important maneuver in assuring family success and viable socioeconomic units centered on the farmsteads. But in the straitened circumstances of the resource-scarce island, honor, too, becomes a commodity, affecting the individual's status and effectiveness in the community. Thus, a young man's unwanted attentions, which as physical presence were difficult to deflect because of the norms of hospitality and, in the form of circulating verses, were even more difficult to suppress, could affect not only the marriageability of dependent women but even more importantly the honor of their male family heads. This is the fundamental reason that erotic poetry was grouped with defamatory speech. Male honor was threatened by the challenge to male authority that took the form of unauthorized address to and comment on young dependent women, whose economical assets at marriage and procreative futures were intended to remain firmly in family hands.

What were the social expectations medieval Icelandic society had of women? In the male-authored conception of the family sagas, women's inclination to and capacity for social good seem limited, even though women may fill in for men as proxies when male leadership is inadequate, as in the scenes of incitement to vengeance. More generally, in the fictional saga world, society's ambivalent expectations of women seem to have been, at best, that they conform to male direction (thus providing neutral support for the status quo); at worst, that they promote intra- and inter-familial conflict from the narrow stage of the household through envy, jealousy, social pretensions, and the frustration and anger of dysfunctional marriages. In the male view, woman contributed to the contingent in human affairs: "*Rýgr vas alin fira börnum at rógi" [woman was born to [cause] strife (calumny, slander) for the children of men].[47] Like the poetic mead, honor seems only provisionally and contingently resident in the female vessel. Honor's custodians, the senior males, may reluctantly have placed or recognized it there, but it is open to appropriation by the intruder. But in this, female disempowerment is far from complete. Just as the woman could say "No" to the poet and also refuse him the recognition that the conventions of skaldic verse seem to call for, she could say "Yes" and thus preclude the future her family might have planned. Woman's feared susceptibility to flattering art and her possible escape from social control could have far-reaching social effects. Physical violation was then only the most tangible and immediate consequence of successful courting poetry.

Courting verse and seduction come down, in *realpolitisch* analysis, to matters between men. By idealizing women in social terms and never explicitly stating their socially disruptive potential, erotic verse does not deconstruct the dominant ideology of early Iceland but does put individual exponents and players to the test in the maintenance of personal and family honor within the constraints of that ideology. The isolated Icelandic farmsteads and fields were more intense social crucibles than many have recognized.

We now examine how erotic verse may have circulated in this social context, and how, at its most ambitious, it might have had a regulatory or destructive effect on social life. Time seems arrested within these declamatory and static poems, as if momentary homeostasis were needed for each listener to reach understanding. Skaldic poetry is elitist in posing intellectual challenges of decipherment: recognizing mythological names and motifs and specialized vocabulary, reordering poetic syntax, identifying different kinds of wordplay, and appreciating the varieties of metrical patterning. If we conclude that skaldic verse, because of its complexity, was not transparent on first hearing, the listener who attempted interpretation must have had the verse repeated or memorized it for further review, and this, like the ensuing effort at comprehension, represents an intellectual co-opting and the creation of a miniature "community of intention" or "understanding." As the poet orders experience through his composition, so the public replicates originary acts in the imposition of order on verbal chaos and through the process of understanding. Such verse is demanding, manipulative, seeking to initiate a contractual relationship; when successful, the listener develops a stake in the poem. From this perspective, the seduction of the young woman, aided by the description of her beauty and accomplishments, is a publicly staged and involuntarily abetted event. In one sense, it is the mind, not the body, that is the vulnerable point of the poet's attack, and the poem, as a cultural weapon gendered male, is the true violator.

Old Norse literature is relatively close-mouthed on the matter of the public performance of sagas and on other storytelling, although there are numerous scenes of the presentation and recitation of skaldic verse, some fairly realistic in the sense that a prior period of composition is envisaged, while others promote the fiction of extemporaneity. But there is less information on how erotic or defamatory poetry may have circulated in the community. The family sagas have the stock figures of itinerant women and day laborers carrying information between households,[48] but there must have been many other means and occasions for a clever poem to be disseminated. The very preservation of the verses until an age that had the means to commit them from memory to vellum does suggest their currency outside the immediate circle of the principals. As noted, the tendency toward depersonalization of the characters— woman, poet, rival—might be thought to work against survival. The dense interdependence of metrical and stylistic features would contribute to accuracy of record, but only if other factors assured the continued life of the poem: overall aesthetic quality, the interest of topical reference, the place of such poetry in a community ethos, and what we might describe as a greater tolerance for erotic verse than that evidenced by the law code. The legal position of some kinds of verse on the social periphery cannot be read as a true statement on either its incidence or its consequences. Finally, over time there must have been a willingness among later Icelanders viewing the national past—authors and publics—to preserve some of these initially problematic artistic creations. Just as surely as the law codes, poetry can be a means chosen by the society to describe itself or its past. As with the treatment of feud in the family sagas, this seems a strategy of promoting containment, rather than denial or erasure.

*   *   *

In a society that prized personal honor, virginity is valorized as an integrity of gender that is very different from the Christian conceptions of physical purity and its loss through sin. The physical divestment might be compared to the usurpation of grazing land, a frequent saga motif and factor in feud. In Icelandic terms, the virgin in control, acting against the wishes of a father, can "feminize" the entire family, that is, make it appear effete, effeminate. Here, the Icelandic farm girls join the adulterous queens of continental romance. Within the medieval value system, their sin is only a "natural" one, while it speaks more pointedly to the insufficiency, physical and political, of the monarch.

As well as the qualitative evaluation of poets, unmarried or widowed women exercised select forms of quantitative control in Icelandic society—control over space in land ownership and transfer, and over time in the choice of sexual partner—that determined which family lines would continue into the future. And while fertility was, in this era, not an option that could be chosen or rejected, the ability or disability—the body's refusal—to bear children was yet another means of female control over families. As we have seen, this generative power also extended to the poems themselves, when the woman's beauty, status and accomplishments stimulated the poet to compose. And, like a father withholding legitimacy from a newborn, woman is accorded judgment over the poeticized account of the poet's life. This is part of the larger circuit of exchange and interaction in which the virgin generates poetry, while poetry may negate that virginity, physically or in reputation. Both poet and virgin, when they meet in the lists of art, stand to win and lose.

In natural terms, medieval gender theorists might have claimed that the female body was incomplete without the fecundating male.

In cultural terms, we have seen that the male gender of the poet and the male-directed agenda of the family are similarly incomplete without female participation. With respect to our exclusively male-authored sources, we can only pose the summary question about the extent to which women in their socialization may have "bought into" the ideology outlined in this study. In the individual case, the woman seduced by proscribed skaldic verse does not truly threaten the community ethos. The menace she might be thought to pose is first active at the level of the family. Since honor is a constant-sum game, her actions contribute to the inevitable social dynamic, redistributing the commodity of honor and its potential for translation into economic and political power. In this, poetry's social agency recalls its mythic origins in the successive violent appropriations of the mead of poetry. Poetry did not reach man for a designated purpose. Skaldic poetry need not be called feminized because of the poet's ploy of deference to woman's judgment or because of its socially disruptive effects. It is rather, and not surprisingly, another facet of early medieval maleness, a further means of diminishing a rival's honor to enhance one's own, like the frequent charge of passivity in a homosexual act. The poet seeks control over language, over woman, over men, over his own image, and the poem of seduction targeted male gender no less than female virginity.

Erotic poetry carried a physical risk for the poet as well as the addressee, and this is perhaps the most concrete menace of the virgin: stimulating courting verse, she lays the poet open to the retribution of her kinsmen. To return to Halli and Leiknir, before they had made their extemporized verses to the parading Ásdís, they had already proved burdensome to Styrr who had consulted his chieftain Snorri Þorgrímsson on a possible solution. The evening after Ásdís walked by the berserks' construction site, Styrr lured the tired workers into a steam-fed bathhouse. He raised the temperature to intolerable limits, and when the berserks, now powerless after the labor and debilitating heat, rushed out, he struck them down. Styrr's ironic verse epitaph over the warrior-poets reads like a warning to all those who threaten male order through women.[49] And as if to mark, too, the distance of courting verse from ordered society, it is the establishment figure and dealmaker Snorri who now weds the daughter of Styrr: "ok var þat mál manna, at hvárrtveggi þótti vaxa af þessum tengðum" [people said that both became more powerful through this alliance].[50] Snorri is no courting poet and Ásdís' views on the arrangement are not given.

The self-centered skalds would doubtless have wanted the last word. In a fragment thought to be from a poem to a woman, Ormr Steinþórsson says:

Þvit hols hrynbáls   Billings á burar full
hramma, þats berk framm,   bjarkar hefk lagit mark.[51]

For I have put the mark of the birch of the hollow's paw's (hand's) clanging fire (gold ring) in Billingr's son's (dwarf's) drink that I am performing.[52]

This resolves as "for I have put woman's mark on the poem that I present," and woman's mark on the poetry of early northern Europe is a distinctive and intriguing one. The subjacent sensuality of this poetry must be sought through an effort of intellect, and this process reflects early medieval Iceland's tension between, and complementarity of, virgins and seducers, mutually elaborated representations of female and male gender.

Rhetoric, Power, and Integrity in the Passion of the Virgin Martyr

MAUD BURNETT MCINERNEY

Tales of the deaths of virgins such as Margaret, Eulalia, Agnes, and Cecelia are told across Europe, from late antiquity until the high Middle Ages. These stories, sometimes but by no means always written for a female audience, form a very particular sub-genre within the broader category of martyrological narratives. All are characterized by a special emphasis on dramatic confrontations between protagonist and antagonist, between virgin martyr and the pagan tyrant, cast in the form of interrogations that alternate dialogue with torture. All express a double pair of features that distinguish the stories of virgin martyrs from those of their male counterparts: physical passivity is linked to an aggressive eloquence and an eroticized martydom to imperishable sexual integrity. What I propose to explore in this essay is the link between the apparent inviolability of the virgin martyr and the rhetorical power that derives from it, provokes assault upon it, and finally preserves it. The texts to which I will appeal are separated by years, miles, and attitudes; *Seinte Margarete* was written in the English Midlands in the thirteenth century for a female (and possibly virgin) audience,[1] and Prudentius's *Peristephanon*, composed in late fourth-century Spain to celebrate a newly Christian Roman Empire, while Chaucer's Second Nun's Tale may be intended for the sophisticated and worldly audience of the *Canterbury Tales*.[2] In all of these texts, the passion of the virgin martyr is transformative; in them, not only does weakness become strength, but feminine speech, defined as deceptive or vapid or both since the days of Eve, becomes truthful, eloquent, possessed of the power both to inspire and to threaten.

The female martyr has often been perceived as being more moving than the male martyr because of her greater weakness. Her passion, being more pathetic, is supposed to have greater audience appeal.[3] In *Seinte Margarete*, Margaret is certainly physically docile enough in her confrontations with Olibrius and the torturers; she is described

50

as "meokest alre milde" (46:12), and in fact prays for the opportunity to suffer for the sake of God. Passivity, of course, is the very root of martyrdom; the Greek, *pascho,* means "I suffer" or "I endure," and in its Latin form becomes the name of the genre: *Passio.* The particular kind of suffering Margaret will endure, however, is characteristic of the passion of the female martyr in that it links sexuality, virginity, faith, and eloquence in an indissoluble knot.

Olibrius, the Roman prefect described as "þe ueondes an foster" (46:19, "the devil's own child"), desires Margaret as soon as he sees her keeping her sheep. He decides that he will make her his wife if she's freeborn, his mistress if she's not, and is doubly disappointed to discover that she is a Christian since this means that she is both vowed to virginity and a criminal under Roman law. His attempts to convert her by getting her to worship his idols, however, are indistinguishable from his assault on her chastity. When she tells him that she believes in the Christian god, he immediately retires to ponder how he can corrupt her virginity, "hwucche wise he walde merren hire meiðhad" (50:1). Margaret too equates her faith with her virginity. She describes herself as "iseiled wið his in-seil" (52:5, "sealed with Christ's seal"), in language that recalls Ambrose's famous homily on virginity. When Olibrius's men first arrest her, she prays to Christ, linking the welfare of body and soul: "ant biwite þu mi bodi, þet is al bitaht to þe, from flesliche fulþen; þet neauer mi sawle ne isuled beo in sunne þurh þet licomes lust þet lutle hwile likeð" (46:34–48:1, "Preserve my body, which is entirely promised to you, from fleshly filth, so that my soul may never be sullied with sin through bodily lust which lasts but a little while"). She perceives Olibrius's interest, in other words, not as a double assault on her virginity and her faith, but as a single assault on her virginity *as* faith.[4]

The text also makes it quite clear that the contest between Olibrius and Margaret is as much verbal as it is physical; through torture, he attempts to control her body, in order, it becomes increasingly evident, to silence her words. Margaret's elaborate denunciations of Olibrius, couched in imagery from the Psalms, contrast with his more and more frantic demands for silence, and alternate with an escalating series of tortures in which the emphasis is always on the beauty of her naked body. Stop, Olibrius says after his first conversation with her, these words are worthless: "Let, ne beoð þes wordes noht wurð" (50:23). Next, he has her stripped naked and beaten until her "leofliche lich" ("her beautiful body") streams with blood (52:8–9). Later, he begs her again to stop saying such foolish things, "unwitti wordes" (52:24). Margaret doesn't stop, of course, but calls Olibrius a heathen dog and a raging lion, thus in effect reducing his arguments to the wordless and meaningless noise of beasts. This has the effect of rendering him almost insane with fury. Unable to silence the living virgin, he is finally reduced to the ultimate sadistic fantasy:

> Ah buh nu ant bei to me ear þen þu deie o dreori deð ant derf; for ʒef þu ne dest no, þu schalt swelten þurh sweord, ant al beo limmel toloken; ant þenne Ich wulle tellen, hwen þu al totoren art, in euchanes sihðe þe sit nu ant sið þe, alle þine seonewen. (54:36–56:3)

> Submit now and pay homage to me before you die a wretched and painful death; for if you do not you will be put to the sword and torn limb from limb; and then, when you are torn to pieces, in front of all those who sit here and see you now, I will count all your sinews.

Olibrius no longer desires Margaret as his wife or mistress; now he longs for her total and abject humiliation. His words remind us that martyrdom was very much a spectator sport; he imagines his victory over Margaret as total, because it will be public; the consistent irony of the genre is, of course, that this humiliation will always rebound on the torturer, as those who witness the sufferings of the saint will be converted, effectively removed from his jurisdiction and placed under that of God. Olibrius's use of the verb *tellen,* which means to enumerate, or to speak, is particularly noteworthy. He imagines her body as a sort of obscene rosary: he will tell Margaret's sinews just as a Christian might tell her beads. Significantly, Olibrius wants Margaret reduced to her most basic physical components, which will no longer be able to talk back to him, but over which he will at last have verbal power: he, the voice of authority, will be able to *tell* her, the silent flesh.

This emphasis on silencing the martyr raises the question of what, precisely, is so threatening about Margaret's words. I have mentioned above the debt that her prayers owe to patristic language; but they also evoke another tradition of powerful eloquence, demonstrated during Margaret's second confrontation, with the agents of the devil in fiendish rather than human form. Throughout her tortures at the hands of Olibrius, Margaret has prayed that she may be allowed to see the one who is really torturing her: the devil himself. Finally, during a respite in her suffering, when Olibrius has imprisoned her in a dungeon, in order, presumably, to give himself time to come up with new and better tortures and arguments, this wish is granted, and Margaret is visited by a demon. He comes rushing at her out of a corner of her cell in the form of a golden dragon, not human, but fully masculine:

> His lockes ant his longe berd blikeden al of golde, ant his grisliche teð semden of swart irn. His twa ehnen / steareden steappre þen þe steoren ant ten ʒimstanes, brade ase bascins in his ihurnde heaued on eiðer half on his heh hokede nease. Of his speatewile muð sperclede fur ut, ant of his nease-þurles þreste smorðrinde smoke, smeche forcuðest; ant lahte ut his tunge, se long þet he swong hire abuten his swire; ant semde as þah a sharp sweord of his muð scheate, þe glistnede ase gleam deð ant leitede al o leie; ant al warð þet stude ful of strong ant of stearc stench, ant of þes schucke schadewe schimmede ant schan al. (58:11–20)

> His locks and his long beard shone with gold, his grisly teeth were like dark iron. His two eyes shone brighter than stars or jewels, broad as basins in his horned head on either side of his high hooked nose. Fire flashed in his foul mouth, and a smother of smoke streamed from his nostrils, foulest of fogs. And he stuck out his tongue, so long he could swing it around his neck; and it seemed as though a sharp sword sprang from his mouth, which glittered like lightning and flickered like flame. And the place was full of a strong and powerful stench, and shimmered and shone in the demon's reflection.

Margaret has succeeded, in other words, in summoning up the devil, and though she does so by God's grace, this is hardly an unproblematic achievement. The apparent similarity between miracles and magical acts, and between prayer and incantation drove Thomas Aquinas to expend considerable ink on distinguishing between them.[5] Magic, after all, can be understood quite simply as the ability to make the unseen seen, and vice versa.

Margaret reacts to the sudden appearance of the dragon in her cell by falling to her knees and praying:

> Þe sunne reccheð hire rune wiðuten euch reste; þe mone ant te steorren þe walkeð bi þe weolcne ne stutteð ne ne studegið, ah sturieð aa mare, ne nowider of þe wie þet tu hauest iwraht ham ne wrencheð ha neaure. þu steorest þe sea-strem, þet hit flede ne mot fir þen þu merkedest. Þe windes, þe wederes, þe wudes ant te weattres buheð þe and beið. Feondes habbeð fearlac, ant engles, of þin eie. þe wurmes ant te wilde deor þet o þis wald wunieð libbet efter þe hahe þet tu ham hauest iloket, luuewende Lauerd. (58:32–60:7)

> The sun runs its course without rest; the moon and the stars move through the heavens and never stand or stop, but are always in motion,

and never do they wander from the way you have wrought for them. You steer the streams of the sea, so that it may not overflow the bounds you set for it. Winds, storms, woods and waters bow before you and obey you. Devils and angels fear your wrath. The snakes and the wild beasts of the woods follow the law you have decreed for them, beloved Lord.

The prayer has a powerfully animistic quality, but it is not explicitly Christian; the saint makes no reference to Christ, the Incarnation, or the Passion, and her words would not be out of place in the mouth of one of the practitioners of *magia naturalis* or white magic, who imagined the world as "alive in semiotic correspondences between and among the elemental, astral and divine universes; man and woman were part of the whole signifying cosmos. Theirs was a uniquely privileged position: poised at the center of the universe, they participated in all of its complex workings."[6] Gerhild Scholz Williams is describing Paracelsus and his contemporaries in the preceding sentences, but she goes on to remind us that they were a part of a tradition that includes "the philosophers of antiquity and the theologians of the Middle Ages." Indeed, Margaret's prayer evokes not only the white magic of Paracelsus, but also a very different invocation, that of the enchantress Medea in Book 7 of Ovid's *Metamorphoses:*

> "Nox," ait, "arcanis fidissima, quaeque diurnis
> Aurea cum luna succeditis ignibus astra,
> Tuque triceps Hecate, quae coeptis conscia nostris
> Adiutrixque venis cantusque artisque magorum,
> Quaeque magos, Tellus, pollentibus instruis herbis,
> Auraeque et venti montesque amnesque lacusque
> Dique omnes nemorum dique omnes noctis adeste!
> Quorum ope, cum volui, ripis mirantibus amnes
> In fontes rediere suos . . ."[7]

"Night," she said, "most faithful keeper of secrets, and those stars which, with the golden moon, succeed the flames of day, and you, triformed Hecate, who know of my undertakings, come assist me, and the magical charms and arts with which you, Earth, instructed the Mages with powerful herbs, and the breezes and the winds and the mountains and rivers and lakes and all the gods of the woods and all the gods of night, come! With whose aid, when I wish, I make the streams return through their marvelling banks to their sources . . ."

Medea's prayer to Hecate and the powers of darkness is fairly representative of invocations used by classical witches; there are similar passages in Virgil, Horace, and Lucan, linking the enchantress' power to the movements of heavenly bodies, the forces of winds and water, and calling upon minor divinities of woods and wild places. All the same elements exist in Margaret's prayer; angels and devils take the places of the minor deities, and there is a similar emphasis on controlling the courses of the waters, although of course Margaret places that control in the hands of God, whereas Medea claims it for herself. I am not suggesting that there is a direct influence of the Latin text upon the Middle English one (although, of course, the *Metamorphoses* was well-known in the thirteenth century) nor that Margaret is a witch (although the Romans often accused early Christians of witchcraft). Still, the language of Medea's invocation and Margaret's prayer evokes an ancient tradition of magical eloquence usually associated in the pagan world with feminine practitioners of the occult arts.

There is a further point of explicit resemblance between Margaret and Medea. In giving a summary of her magical experience, a sort of occult *curriculum vitae,* Medea mentions her ability to make snakes explode: "Vipereas rumpo verbis et carmine fauces" (*Meta.* 7, 1. 203, "by words and charm I make the throats of serpents explode"). This is apparently a standard talent among Roman witches, reported also by Virgil (*Bucolics* 8.71) and Pliny the Elder (*Natural History* 28.4.19). The Latin *carmen* can mean both "song" or "poem" but also "magical spell"; when used in the context of witchcraft, it should probably be understood as a magical charm incorporating both verbal and somatic components, words as well as gestures or the manipulation of herbs or minerals.[8] Margaret ends her prayer with the sign of the cross, so that it contains all the elements of a magical *carmen.* The result is that the dragon who attempts to swallow her explodes: "his bodi tobearst" (60:22). Margaret's power over the devil operates as more than simply an inversion of Eve's defeat in the garden of Eden; the saint is often represented in sculpture and painting as standing with one foot on the neck of the beast (variously reptilian or mammalian, scaled or shaggy) she has conquered, a pose that associates her iconographically with Diana-Artemis, whose function as patroness of women in labor Margaret also inherits (78:25–28).[9] All of this serves to remind us that the distinction between Christian saint and pagan witch was anything but absolute.[10]

Margaret's physical passivity under torture is thus only half of the story; it is paired with a kind of aggressive verbal power that is anything but pathetic, and that may have antecedents in the pagan magical tradition.[11] Margaret may invite a certain degree of compassion (although I must admit to a certain degree of sympathy for Olibrius's increasing frustration and futile rage, which seem much more human than the saint's equanimity), but her words, at any rate, are far from passive. In order to determine whether the virgin martyr's aggressive and powerful eloquence is necessarily gendered within the context of the hagiographical tradition, I would like at this point to expand the scope of my inquiry beyond St. Margaret, looking sideways to the *Legenda Aurea,* and back to the origins of the tradition.

The *Legenda Aurea* was one of the most popular and influential hagiographical collections of the Middle Ages; it is also one of the most comprehensive, and thus provides a useful testing ground for determining which features are generically essential to the narrative of the virgin martyr.[12] Including those saints like Cecelia who, although married, refuse to sleep with their husbands, twenty out of twenty-four female martyrs in the *Legenda* are virgins.[13] Virgins are also the most argumentative of all martyrs. Male martyrs in the *Legenda* tend to be laconic during their passion; this is especially true of soldier-saints like Eustace, Maurice, and Sebastian. Of the twenty virgins, on the other hand, a dozen participate in fairly lengthy debates either with a pagan judge or with the devil himself. Christina continues to denounce Julian after her tongue is cut out (*LA* 1.471), Lucy and Cecelia go on arguing after their throats are cut (*LA* 1.57, 2.373). While their arguments in all cases fail to have any effect upon their torturers, except to render them beside themselves with fury, they succeed in converting bystanders by the thousands.[14] Finally, it is instructive to consider the case of Euphemia; she is an apparently uninteresting saint, lacking in any distinguishable character traits, remarkable chiefly for the variety of tortures inflicted upon her. Priscus, the judge, attempts to bring about her death in a variety of ingenious ways: he has her beaten and burned, he tries to hang her and to have her raped to death, he suspends her by her hair, starves her, has her pressed "like an olive" between huge rocks, throws her to wild beasts, and finally (successfully) has her stabbed to death (*LA* 2.211–12). Euphemia has few lines in this catalogue of sadistic horrors; her name, however, bespeaks the essential eloquence of the virgin martyr. *Euphemi,* in Greek, means "I speak well."

Nowhere, however, can the connection between virginity and eloquence be seen more clearly than in the eloquent virgin who forms the link between the enchantress Medea and the virgin martyr Margaret, the Sybil of Cumae. Augustine inscribes the Sybil among the pagan children of God; Jerome too places her among the virtuous pagans in his famous misogamous tract, *Against Jovinian,* and even uses her as an *exemplum* of virginity, which he sees as the source of prophecy. Abelard quotes and seconds Jerome on the relationship between virginity and prophecy, describing virginity not only as a peculiarly feminine quality, but as a specifically physical one, a "prerogative of the flesh."[15] In the Middle Ages the Sybil, as well as being a virgin and a prophetess, was also a poet, the author of the "Sybil's Song," composed perhaps as early as the seventh century, but well-known across Europe in the eleventh. In her Song, which, like Margaret's prayer, echoes Medea's invocation in its appeal to cosmic powers, the Sibyl is represented as a virgin whose body is intact as far as human contact goes, but whose very intactness invites the divine to invade it, to shake it into speech:

> Mundus origo mea est, animam de sidere traxi,
> Intactum corpus concutit omne deus.
> <Narrabo quodcumque deus mihi spirat in ore,>
> Si bene devotum senserit ampla fides.
> Multum mea mecum dixerunt carmina carmen;
> Carmina quae scribo, noverit illa deus . . .
>
> The universe is my origin, my soul I have drawn from a star,
> My virgin body God has set trembling in every limb.
> <I shall tell whatever God puts in my mouth.>
> if my abundant faith has had true insight into hallowed matter.
> Many a song my own singings have uttered within myself;
> the songs which I write, those God knows . . .[16]

The closed body of the virgin, pagan or Christian, could symbolize a hidden knowledge; whatever speech issued forth from it would be worth hearing, as Peter Brown argues in *The Body and Society:*

> Here was a wellshaft of deep certainty for which they themselves [male admirers] thirsted. She was the one human being who could convincingly be spoken of as having remained as she had first been created. Her physical integrity came to carry an exceptionally high charge of meaning. To late antique males, the female body was the most alien body of all. It was as antithetical to them as the desert was to the settled land. When consecrated by its virgin state, it could appear like an untouched desert in itself: it was the furthest reach of human flesh turned into something peculiarly precious by the coming of Christ upon it.[17]

This quality of physical integrity, this figuration of the female body as hollow and therefore capable both of containing the divine and being sealed to exclude all other influences, is the aspect of female virginity in which it was impossible for males, no matter how chaste, to share fully. What, after all, is a male virgin? The Apocryphal *Acts of John* appears to identify purity with celibacy: "Thou who hast kept

me also till this present hour pure for Thyself and untouched by
union with a woman; who, when I wished to marry in my youth,
didst appear to me and say: . . . 'John, if thou wert not mine, I should
have allowed thee to marry.'"[18] Chastity is not, however, identical
with virginity, and its formulation in exclusively heterosexual terms
leaves open the question of homosexual contact. Chastity, for a
man, appears to have to do not with keeping outside influences out,
but with keeping what is inside in, with the retention of seed. This
explains the widespread anxiety about nocturnal emissions that produced a sizeable body of literature during the Middle Ages.[19] If non-
ejaculation is the criterion, the male virgin must have been as rare
as hen's teeth, and it is no surprise that, when applied to men, the
words "virginity" and "chastity" appear to be interchangeable, as they
are not when applied to women. A definition of female virginity is
easier to establish (if not to maintain, as we will see): a virgin is a
woman who has not been penetrated, who is physically intact. Female virginity is an apparently absolute state, and this very abso-
luteness was deeply disturbing to many (male) writers of the early
Church, probably not least because it appeared to posit an access
to the divine that was inaccessible to men.

Because of this patristic anxiety, attitudes towards virginity developed along parallel and even antipathetic lines in late antiquity, representing the virgin body both as the object of praise and the target
of opprobrium, and both of these impulses will be acted out in the
martyrological narrative. This paradox must be understood in the
context of the development of the ideal of sexual renunciation delineated by Brown, according to which virginity changed from an essentially social or even economic quality that enhanced the worth of
pagan girls on the marriage market to a spiritual value that was,
on the contrary, antisocial. The process was gradual; in the earliest
Christian writings, the letters of St. Paul, sexual continence is never
recommended as a virtue in and of itself; Paul's "better to marry
than to burn," so often quoted in isolation in order to demonstrate
the Apostle's contempt for the married state, was actually made in
the context of an attempt to maintain the social systems of late Antiquity in the face of a group of people who had decided to renounce
marriage, sexuality, and society as a whole in order to better await
the coming of Christ. Such a project clearly did not bode well for
the continuance of a newly established cult beyond the first generation.[20] By the end of the second century, however, the ideal of chastity
was not only well established but increasingly popular and influential; texts such as the *Acts of John* became templates for the devout.
Similarly, the *Acts of Paul and Thecla* (the archetypal virgin martyr

and transvestite saint who had, according to legend, traveled with Paul after hearing him speak) could declare "Blessed are they who have kept the flesh pure, for they shall become a temple of God. . . . Blessed are the continent, for to them will God speak."[21]

In the third century, Origen elaborated the theory (one might even say the doctrine) of abstinence. According to Brown,

> Origen tended to present virginity as a state that declared the joining of an "immaculate" spirit with its well-tempered, material frame. As a result of this shift in perspective, virginity could no longer be regarded simply as a perilous state of suspended sensuality, imposed on the frisky young by their elders in the relatively short period between puberty and marriage. Nor was it an anomaly, made plain by the suspension of a natural destiny to marriage, undergone, in the pagan world, by a few prophetesses and priestesses. Virginity stood for the original state in which every body and soul had joined. It was a physical concretization, through the untouched body, of the pre-existing purity of the soul. In the words of an author appreciated by Origen, the continent body was a waxen seal that bore the exact imprint of the untarnished soul. Identified in this intimate manner with the pristine soul, *the intact flesh of a virgin of either sex stood out also as a fragile oasis of human freedom.* Refusal to marry mirrored the right of a human being, the possessor of a preexistent utterly free soul, not to surrender its liberty to the pressures placed upon the person by society.[22]

The italics in the passage are mine, intended to highlight an interesting and problematic feature both of early Christian thought on the nature of virginity and of Brown's book. Both are concerned to make virginity something it had never been in pagan times: a state available to both sexes. Classical authors had few illusions on the subject;[23] even the Hellenistic romance, which placed such emphasis on mutual love and fidelity, admitted a difference of degree between male and female "virginity," a fact that Foucault represents without comment in *The Care of the Self* :

> A virginity exposed, assailed, doubted, slandered, safeguarded—*except for an honourable, minor lapse that Clitophon allowed himself*—and finally justified and certified in a sort of divine ordeal, which makes it possible to proclaim concerning the girl, "she is still the same up to the present day, as when you sent her away from Byzantium; it is to be put down to her credit that she remained a virgin when surrounded by a gang of pirates, and overcame the worst of them." And speaking of himself, Clitophon can also say, in a symmetrical fashion: "You will find that I have imitated your virginity, if there be any virginity in men." [Italics mine][24]

Virginity here is clearly represented as inherent exclusively in the female body, an absolute state that the male body can only approximate.

During the early centuries of Christianity, however, certain writers felt driven to redefine the classical conception of virginity, to reverse what had always been true—only a woman can be a virgin—and make it into a reflection of their own profound distrust of all things female—no woman can be a virgin.[25] In Carthage, perhaps as early as 204, a group of Christian virgins decided that they would no longer veil themselves in church, since they interpreted the veil as a mark of sexual shame, a shame that they were free of because they had dedicated their bodies to Christ (only married women, presumably sexually active, wore a veil). Tertullian's reaction to this claim was the furious tract *De virginibus velandis* in which he argues, as Bloch has noted, "that a virgin seen is no longer a virgin."[26] Tertullian insists that every public exposure of an honorable virgin is (to her) a suffering of rape:

> and yet the suffering of carnal violence is the less [evil] because it comes of natural office. But when the very spirit itself is violated in a virgin by the abstraction of her covering, she has learnt to lose what she ought to keep. O sacrilegious hands which have the hardihood to drag off a dress dedicated to God![27]

The profound irony of this passage (and one wonders to what extent the irony is deliberate) is that Tertullian casts himself in the role of the one whose "sacrilegious hands" expose the virgin to the scandal of public scrutiny. By arguing that "a virgin ceases to be a virgin from the time that it becomes possible for her not to be one,"[28] Tertullian, by the stroke of the pen, deflowers the young girl whose behavior has so provoked him, and does so in a manner that, according to his own admission, is worse than "carnal violence." In order to counter the threat posed to masculine authority and the social hierarchy of the African Church, he denies her virginity, enacting what is in essence a rhetorical rape.

The blessed virgins of the martyrological narrative behave just like those maidens of Carthage who were Tertullian's target: they stand forth, unveiled, before the crowd. That there was an implicit connection between the state of virginity and martyrdom is demonstrated by the development of the genre. The first historical female martyrs, Perpetua and Felicity, were not virgins but married women—mothers, in fact. Perpetua, a contemporary of Tertullian, died in 203 A.D., leaving a supposedly autobiographical account of her imprisonment that stands as the only narrative in a female voice from this early period, and which was presumably expanded by one of her fellow-Christians to include an account of her death. Perpetua's passion belongs as much to the late classical tradition of modest womanhood as to the Christian:

> And so after being stripped and enclosed in nets they were brought into the arena. The people were horrified, beholding in the one a tender girl, in the other a woman fresh from child-birth, with milk dripping from her breasts. So they were recalled and dressed in tunics without girdles. Perpetua was tossed first, and fell on her loins. Sitting down she drew back her torn tunic from her side to cover her thighs, more mindful of her modesty than of her suffering. Then having asked for a pin she further fastened her disordered hair. For it was not seemly that a martyr should suffer with her hair dishevelled, lest she should seem to mourn in the hour of her glory.[29]

Perpetua's behavior would have been no less appropriate in the description of the torture and death of a noble Roman woman in, say, Tacitus's *Annals*. In contrast to the later, legendary accounts of passions, we should notice here that the emphasis in Perpetua's account is on her imprisonment and her visions, rather than on her interrogation by the procurator Hilarion. Perpetua's passion is neither confrontational nor verbal; her eloquence is the passive eloquence of the written page rather than the active debate of the later martyr with her persecutor.

In the centuries following the martyrdom of Perpetua, the exaltation of virginity and concomitant devaluation of marriage ensured that married Perpetua would be eclipsed by the virgin Thecla. Thecla may or may not have existed, but her story, first told as early as the second century, already has many of the elements familiar from later hagiography: betrothed to a suitably wealthy man, she flees marriage in order to share in St. Paul's celibate life, is condemned to be burned alive in the amphitheater (a fate that she escapes through a miraculous cloudburst), narrowly escapes being raped, and disguises herself as a man in order to follow the Apostle and lead a Christian life.[30] The popularity of Thecla forms part of a wave of ascetic enthusiasm and is probably not susceptible to a single, simple explanation; nevertheless, it is plausible that a partial reason for Thecla's popularity may lie in her extremely active and vocal career as a preacher and teacher, a career that is all the more extraordinary given the fact that pagans and Christians were united in perceiving the garrulousness of women as a negative feature, a voice that must be repressed. St. Paul (or one of his early followers—the passage may

be an interpolation) wrote to the Corinthians in 54 A.D. prescribing
the role of women in the Church:

> Let a woman learn in silence with all submissiveness. I permit no woman
> to teach or to have authority over men; she is to keep silent. For Adam
> was formed first, then Eve; and Adam was not deceived, but the woman
> was deceived and became a transgressor. Yet woman will be saved
> through bearing children, if she continues in faith and love and holiness,
> with modesty.[31]

This passage sets up a clear opposition between bringing forth words
and bringing forth children; the woman who speaks, instead of giving
birth "in modesty," a phrase that almost always implies silence in
both classical patristic writers, is a threat to society, and especially
to men. Her words are represented as a potentially contaminating
influence with the power to stain all who hear them, or as inherently
deceptive, undermining even the possiblity of truth.[32] Thecla's evan-
gelism served to undercut the Pauline prohibition on feminine
speech, and, according to Elaine Pagels, "Christian celibates may
have invoked Thecla's example to justify the right of Christian women
to baptize and to preach."[33] Thus, at the very beginning of the Christian tradition, active, potent speech is already linked to virginity,
while the married woman is figured instead as passive, modest,
silent.

Prudentius, in his *Peristephanon*, written in the late fourth century,
relates the martyrdoms of three women, Eulalia, Agnes, and Encratis,
and twelve men or groups of men.[34] The sexual status of the men
is never mentioned; they are described as ex-soldiers, bishops, or
deacons, but whether they are married or not is apparently irrelevant.
The women, in contrast, are identified first and foremost as *virgines;*
just as soldier-martyrs such as Emeterius and Chelidonius renounce
their military glory, so female martyrs must renounce the only valid
social position to which they had access, the role of wife and mother.
Prudentius writes of Eulalia that

> iam dederat prius indicium
> tendere se Patris ad solium
> nec sua membra dicata toro.
>
> (ll. 16–18)[35]

> . . . she had already given sign that she turned herself towards the seat
> of the Father and her limbs were not destined for the marriage bed.

The aggressive rhetorical ability of the virgin martyr is also present
in the *Peristephanon*. Eulalia is described as *vociferans* (l. 66, "shout-

ing"), behavior not generally considered attractive in an adolescent girl. She seeks out martyrdom actively, speaking publicly in the forum and confessing God "pectore et ore" (l. 75, "with heart and mouth"). The governor, like Olibrius, is aroused specifically by her words (l. 96, talibus [verbis]). Eulalia denounces the pagan idols and also explicitly invites the violation of her body in terms that both evoke and repudiate sexual intercourse:

> ". . . ergo age, tortor, adure, seca
> divide membra coacta luto.
> solvere rem fragilem facile est:
> non penetrabitur interior
> exagitante dolore animus."
>
> (II.91–95)

> ". . . Go ahead, tormentor, scorch, chop,
> cut up these limbs formed out of clay.
> It is easy to ruin such a fragile thing.
> You shall not penetrate the soul within
> with any burning pain."

The governor replies by reminding her of the "great joys" she is giving up: a splendid marriage and the affection of her family. Curiously, his words reflect those of St. Paul quoted above: woman is for marriage and for childbirth, not for speaking out in public. This paradoxical similarity between pagan judge and Christian apostle serves as a reminder that the virgin's eloquence poses a threat to patriarchal authority regardless of religious orientation. This is because the category of virgin transforms those qualities that are negative in the category of woman, and that therefore demand repression. In the virgin martyr, feminine weakness becomes strength, feminine loquacity becomes eloquence, and this strength and eloquence have a single object: to put the virgin herself beyond the rules and limitations of a society that casts women as silent, passive childbearers.

St. Ambrose, whose image of the Virgin as a sealed fountain captured and institutionalized the image of virginity as an extraordinary feminine state, also realized the magnitude of its loss: "And indeed, when a girl is deflowered by the customary process of marriage, she loses what is her own, when something else comes to mix with her."[36] The logical conclusion to such a statement is inevitable: if a virgin is verbally threatening, render her no longer a virgin and the threat will disappear. Tertullian deflowered the virgins of Carthage with words; the persecutors in the martyrological narrative will attempt the same thing in more physical ways. Indeed, the threat of

rape is one of the defining characteristics of the story of the virgin
martyr. In Prudentius's story of Agnes, the sexual element is explicit;
the nameless tyrant's threats will recur in many later narratives:

> "Si facile est," ait
> poenam subactis fere doloribus
> et vita vilis spernitur, at pudor
> carus dicatae virginitatis est.
> hanc in lupanar trudere publicum
> certum est. . . .
> omnis iuventus inruet et novum
> ludibriorum namcipium petet."
>
> (14, ll. 21–30)

> He said, "If it is easy for her
> to bear pain and suffering,
> spurn life as valueless, yet still she values
> the modesty of her sworn virginity.
> She shall be thrown into the public whorehouse. . . .
> All the young men will rush in to find
> a new slave for their lusts."

Agnes replies to this threat with confidence: "[Christus] praesto
est pudicis nec patitur sacrae integritatis munera pollui" (ll. 34–35,
"Christ stands by the chaste and will not suffer the gift of holy integrity
to be polluted"). Similarly, when Lucy is threatened with rape in the
Legenda Aurea (1.56), she insists that the body can only be defiled
if the spirit consents. The whole issue of a woman's complicity or
non-complicity in rape is side-stepped however, here as always, for
the rape never occurs. The first man to look lustfully on Agnes dies
(*LA* 1.142); those who attempt to carry off Lucy find her too heavy
to move (*LA* 1.56); a man who attempts to lay his hand on Euphemia
is paralyzed (*LA* 2.210). The paradox for the persecutor is this: the
virgin, who must be raped, in order to silence her, cannot be raped;
she is a maiden who cannot lose her maidenhead. She draws her
inviolability, like her eloquence, from her virginity, for it is this that
makes her the Bride of Christ, and perhaps also the bride of death;
the distinction between the two is never really clear. In either case,
she belongs to the other world; from the moment that she declares
her faith, she is always already dead, and she is deadly. Nowhere is
quality more clearly expressed than in the *Legenda Aurea*'s St. Christina: fifteen hundred bystanders are burned alive by flames intended
for her, her pagan father dies mysteriously after condemning her to
death, and his successor drops dead at the sight of her (1.470–71).

In *Seinte Margarete*, the actual threat of sexual violation is located in the human form of Olibrius. The devil who appears to Margaret after she causes the dragon to explode, however, makes it quite clear that his main mission in life is to destroy virginity wherever it manifests itself:

> ah þe gode Ich ga aa bisiliche abuten, ant ham Ich folhi neodelukest þe cunnið to beon cleane wiðuten monnes man ant fleoð flesches fulðen, ȝef Ich mahte eanies weis makien ham to fallen ant fulen hamseoluen. (66:7–10)

> I am always busily circling around the good, and I follow most closely those who strive to keep themselves clean and untouched by man, fleeing fleshly filth, to see if I may somehow make them fall and foul themselves.

He is equally emphatic that Margaret's eloquence, which I have argued derives from her virginity, is what gives her power over him:

> Marherete, meiden, inoh þu hauest ido me. Ne pine þu me na mere wið þe eadie beoden þet tu biddest se ofte; for ha bindeð me swiðe sare mid alle, ant makieð me se unstrong þet Ich ne fele wið me nanes cunnes strengðe (62:24–27).

> Margaret, virgin, you have done enough to me. Don't torture me any more with those prayers you say so often; all in all, they have bound me so sorely and made me so weak that I feel that I have no more strength.

Seinte Margarete thus brings together the quasi-magical eloquence demonstrated by Medea and the Sybil and the idea of an unassailable virginity. This virginity both gives rise to the virgin's voice and provokes the attacks aimed at silencing it.

Chaucer's Second Nun's Tale demonstrates most strongly of all, albeit in a rather backhanded way, a generic connection between the physical state of virginity and the kind of aggressive eloquence I have been discussing.[37] St. Cecile's prayers for the preservation of her virginity are described as incessant from her earliest childhood: "She nevere cessed, as I writen fynde, / Of her preyere, and God to love and drede, / Bisekynge hym to kepe hir maydenhede." The threat to the martyr's virginity comes in one of its alternative forms here; she is not threatened with rape by a violent aggressor, but is married to an eligible young man named Valerian, who is apparently unaware of her vow of chastity. Even during the marriage ceremony, her prayers continue, in silent counterpoint to the music of the organs:

> And whil the orgnes maden melodie,
> To God allone in herte thus sang she,
> "O Lord, my soule and eek my body gye
> Unwemmed, lest that it confounded be."
>
> (134–37)[38]

Here we have again the association of purity of soul with integrity of body, already familiar from the tale of St. Margaret, along with the image of the virgin's body as a hollow, musical space, as in the Sybil's Song. On Cecile's wedding night, she informs her new husband that she is under the protection of a rather bloodthirsty angel, who will kill him instantly if he lays a finger on her:

> "And if that he may feelen, out of drede,
> That ye me touche, or love in vileynye,
> He right anon wol sle yow with the dede,
> And in youre yowthe thus ye shullen dye . . ."
>
> (155–58)

Cecile, like Margaret and Medea, has power over unseen other-worldly beings. As is the case with Christina, sex with her has death as its price.

Valerian allows himself to be converted, and he and Cecile then go to work on his brother, Tiburce, converting him too with the aid of the invisible yet fragrant crowns the angel gives them. Eventually all three are arrested and brought before the Roman prefect Almachius, and it is in the context of their trials that the difference between the virgin martyr and her male counterparts becomes most clear; Cecile's passion repeats the pattern established by Margaret, of torture alternating with dialogue. Both the explicit and even eroticized descriptions of physical suffering and the debate with the persecutor are absent from the passions of her husband and brother-in-law. When Valerian and Tiburce are brought before Almachius, Chaucer reports no direct speech at all from them. They are completely silent:

> But whan they weren to the place broght,
> To tellen shortly the conclusioun,
> They nolde encense ne sacrifise right noght,
> But on hir knees they setten hem adoun
> With humble herte and sad devocioun,
> And losten bothe hir hevedes in the place.
> Hir soules wenten to the Kyng of Grace.
>
> (394–99)

Their confrontation with the pagan judge, such as it is, is over in a single stanza. When it is Cecile's turn, however, she berates Almachius for fourteen stanzas, most of this in direct speech. This disproportion is particularly interesting in light of the sources Chaucer was working with; Sherry Reames has demonstrated that Chaucer drastically abridged the speeches of Valerian and Tiburce as he found them in the eighth century *Passio* and in the *Legenda Aurea,* making the two men, in Reames's words "almost ciphers in the second half of the narrative."[39] Cecile's verbal ability is correspondingly enhanced—or as Reames sees it, over-enhanced.

Almachius's first words to Cecile are civil, solicitous, courtly even: "'I axe thee," quod he, "though it thee greeve, / Of thy religioun and of thy bileeve'" (425–27). Cecile responds by attacking his argumentative method:

> "Ye han bigonne youre questioun folily,"
> Quod she, "that wolden two answeres conclude
> In o demande; ye axed lewedly."
> Almache answerde unto that similitude,
> "Of whennes comth thyn answeryng so rude?"
>
> (428–32)

Cecile's particular form of verbal superiority is thus identified as rhetorical, even scholastic, rather than tinged with magic like Margaret's. Rhetoric, of course, as it was taught in the great schools, was supposed to be an exclusively masculine province; and, as the Wife of Bath reminds us at such length, it was often intimately connected with antifeminist discourse. Almachius seems somewhat shocked by Cecile's forensic abilities; her "rudeness" is evidently not what he expected from a nobly born Roman maiden. And Cecile continues as she started, assaulting the pagan law he represents as irrational, a "wood sentence," which she will logically demolish:

> "And if thou drede nat a sooth to heere,
> Thanne wol I shewe al openly, by right,
> That thou hast maad a ful gret lesyng heere.
> Thou seyst thy princes han thee yeven myght
> Bothe for to sleen and for to quyken a wight,
> Thou that ne mayst but oonly lyf bireve,
> Thou hast noon oother power ne no leve.
>
> But thou mayst seyn thy princes han thee maked
> Ministre of deeeth, for if thou speke of mo,
> Thou lyest, for thy power is ful naked."
>
> (477–86)

Cecile inverts the usual procedure of the interrogation of the virgin martyr, stripping Almachius' power naked, just as other judges have stripped the virgins themselves naked. The repetition of the pronoun "thou" here, ending with the emphatic "thou lyest" turns Cecile's logic into an *ad hominem* attack, to which Almachius responds by saying that he doesn't care what she says about him, but that he can't bear to hear her speak ill of his gods; personal insults he will suffer "as a philosophre" (l. 490), a phrase that again establishes the whole confrontation as a contest between logicians. Cecile launches a few more insults at him, calling him a "lewed officer and a veyn justise" (ll. 496–97), before turning again to her own kind of logic to demonstrate the powerlessness of these divinities:

> "Ther lakketh no thyng to thyne outter yen
> That thou n'art blynd, for thyng that we seen alle
> That it is stoon—that men may wel espyen—
> That ilke stoon a god thow wolt it calle.
> I rede thee, lat thyn hand upon it falle
> And taste it wel and stoon thou shalt it fynde,
> Syn that thou seest nat with eyen blynde."
>
> (498–504)

Here, she uses the evidence of his own senses against him, to prove him a fool, a "nyce creature." This is too much for Almachius, who has been relatively calm (philosophical, to use his own word) so far. He loses his temper, and commands that Cecile be boiled to death in her own house, in a sort of Roman version of an overheated sauna. Cecile survives this torture, and Almachius sends a messenger to decapitate her. After three strokes, however, Cecile's head has not been completely severed, and due to a peculiarity of Roman law the executioner cannot strike her again. Even in this state, Cecile will not be silenced, and Chaucer's narrative at this point achieves a kind of Grand Guignol quality:

> But half deed, with hir nekke ycorven there,
> He lefte hir lye, and on his wey he went.
> The Cristen folk, which that about her were,
> With sheetes han the blood ful faire yhent.
> Thre dayes lyved she in this torment,
> And nevere cessed hem the feith to teche
> That she hadde fostred. Hem she gan to preche,
>
> And hem she yaf her mobles and hir thyng . . .
>
> (537–40)

The partial beheading and the fact that Cecile goes on preaching after it are both found in Chaucer's sources, according to which she also arranges for her house to become a Christian church. But Chaucer's rendition of this scene approaches the absurd with the markedly casual departure of the executioner, the sheets used to staunch her wounds, the poet's insistence that the saint "nevere cessed" talking, and especially the image of Cecile divvying up her furniture and her possessions. It is hard to take entirely seriously a saint whose distaste for the worldly is so absolute that she rejects marriage, and yet who takes such pains about her household effects, which Chaucer's stanza prioritizes by placing them in the first line, well before the souls that she does not commend to pope Urban until line 545.

It is this curious tone in the Second Nun's Tale, simultaneously strident and ringing slightly false, that has disturbed so many readers. Beichner finds Cecile "in contempt of court," and calls her "contentious and belligerent."[40] She has been accused of doing no more than "insult and goad" her persecutor,[41] even described as "an aggressive logocentrix."[42] But Cecile's behavior makes sense if we see the tale as at least partially parodic, Chaucer's version of what he clearly felt to be the defining characteristic of the virgin martyr: she talks too much, and even if you half kill her, you cannot get her to be quiet. The poet's understanding of his subject, in other words, implies a certain sympathy with the pagan prosecutor, rather than with the virgin martyr, whom he represents as an extreme and not very appealing character.

Perhaps this apparently irreverent attitude can be explained by the relationship between teller, tale, and audience. The author of *Seinte Margarete*, whoever he or she may have been, was probably a religious and certainly intimately involved with a group of women who were living a life intended to mimic, insofar as possible in the Middle Ages, that of the virgin martyrs. The author is writing, as it were, from inside the tradition. Prudentius's relationship to his material is immediate in a different kind of way; writing as he does in a Roman empire that has been Christian for less than a century, the persecutions he describes are still close to him in time, rooted in places he has seen, perhaps even in eyewitness accounts. Christianity as a state religion is still far too new to be taken for granted. By the time Chaucer chose the legend of St. Cecilia upon which to excercise his skills with rhyme royal, the subject had become aestheticized by the intervention of many years and many texts, not least that of Jacques de Voragine, which, as I have argued, highlights the generic similarities of its narratives. The devotional tale may have been, for Chaucer, a more purely literary construct than for his predecessors. Still, whether exploited to the point of parody or elaborated in more personal and psychological terms as in the case of *Seinte Margarete,* the topoi remain the same: the virgin martyr is represented as a woman whose intact body is the source of an eloquence that is at once powerful and troubling.

It has been argued too that the image of the virgin martyr, which becomes more and more prominent in the sacred art of the high Middle Ages, in stained glass windows, in Gothic sculpture, perhaps most strikingly in Fouquet's wonderful and horrible illuminations for the *Heures d'Etienne Chevalier,* functions as a projection of the most brutal kind of rape fantasy.[43] This may be true, just as it appears to be true that Chaucer exploits the legend for its most absurd and even humorous elements. It is certainly true that devotional tracts and saints' lives written for women never explicitly encourage eloquence in their readers, recommending instead a modest silence that would have satisfied St. Jerome (if not Tertullian). But the examples of virginity they cite, Margaret, Agnes, Catherine, or Cecelia, are anything but silent; their speech is active, transformative, powerful, and explicitly rooted in their own, female bodies. This model of feminine speech clearly had an immediate and powerful impact on the lived lives of many medieval women, especially (although not exclusively) those who, like the virgin martyrs, rejected the traditionally silent role of wife and mother for a more or less militant virginity. Hildegard of Bingen, who was particularly devoted to St. Ursula, understood her gift of prophecy to be intrinsically linked to her virginity; not for nothing was she called the Sybil of the Rhine. Christina of Markyate's rejection of marriage deliberately mimics that of Cecelia (to whom Julian of Norwich was also devoted in her youth), suggesting just how specific a source of inspiration hagiography could be. And when Joan of Arc watched her sheep outside Domrémy, it was Catherine and Margaret who came to recruit her as a bride of Christ, and the last of the virgin martyrs.

King by Day, Queen by Night: The Virgin Camille in the *Roman d'Eneas*

Wendy Chapman Peek

Although Amazons are not always virgins, it is as virgins that they are most celebrated by medieval Christianity, for in this regard their militant vigilance against sexuality merits them the Christian honorific of "noble savages." Isidore of Seville facilitated this assimilation by linking the virgin to the virago etymologically, arguing that the two were joined in their "incorruptibility and capacity to resist feminine passion."[1] In some works, Amazons were even portrayed as the perfect women, because not only did they desire virginity but they also had the physical strength to defend it.[2] Yet Amazons have been put to literary ends other than the celebration of Christian virtues, and in some of these texts Amazon virginity becomes less a cause for praise than a source of anxiety. In this category is Camille, the virgin queen of the Vulcanes in the anonymous twelfth-century poem, *Le Roman d'Eneas*, a loose adaptation of Virgil's *Aeneid*, crafted with attention both to Virgil's text and medieval commentary on that text. In this work, most likely the second of the Anglo-Norman *romans d'antiquité* (including the *Roman de Thèbes* and Benoît de Sainte-Maure's *Roman de Troie*), virginity appears in a vastly different context than it does in works with religious salvation in mind. While militant virginity may be desirable in saints' lives, in romance it impedes the achievement of generic ideals, as it violates the genre's demands for heterosexual union. Devotion to virginity also violates another theme of romance: genealogical continuity, a theme that is especially prominent in the early romances associated with the court of Henry II.

Like many aristocrats of this period, Henry II traced his ancestral line back to Troy and the Trojan stories, drawing justification to rule from the textual corpus of the past. Not surprisingly, three of the most prominent literary works to issue from the Angevin court are revisions of the stories of Thebes, Troy, and Rome, as part of what looks to be a project associated with or perhaps even funded by

71

Henry II.[3] In R. Howard Bloch's analysis, this concern with aristocratic lineage marks in part the transition from a feudal to a monarchic state, wherein horizontal feudal bonds were displaced by vertical monarchic bonds that privileged rule by genealogical descent, the more noble and ancient the better.[4]

This political transition parallels the literary translation of epic into romance. The most marked feature of this translation is the expanded roles of some of the female characters, as is demonstrated in the representation of Lavine and Camille in the *Roman d'Eneas*. While the expansion of Lavine is not particularly surprising—after all, she is the romance heroine—the expansion of Camille is, as her fierce devotion to her Amazonic virginity contradicts all that is sacred to dynastic romance: love, marriage, and legitimate offspring. Yet rather than treating Camille and her radical virginity as a problem to be exorcised,[5] the medieval poet amplifies the character of Camille, expanding her 14-line description in the *Aeneid* (Book 7, 803–17) into two descriptions, the first 147 lines long (3959–4106), and the second 21 lines long (6913–6934).[6] In fact, the description of Camille in the *Eneas* is longer than the portraits of either Dido or Lavine. The *Eneas'* Camille also has two entirely new episodes associated with her: the encounter with Tarcon, and an elaborate description of her tomb after she is killed in battle. Why would a figure so antithetical to the ambitions of this emergent genre appear with such rhetorical amplification?[7]

A solution to this paradox is offered by the work of Julia Kristeva on the abject. Kristeva characterizes the abject as that which

> lies outside, beyond the set, and does not seem to agree to the latter's rules of the game. . . . It is thus not lack of cleanliness or health that causes abjection but what disturbs identity, system, order. What does not respect borders, positions, rules. The in-between, the ambiguous, the composite.[8]

The abject is figured as the thing that does not, and indeed cannot, comply with the "rules of the game"; it is that which must be expelled for the game to proceed.

In constructing this theory of abjection, Kristeva combines the discourses of anthropology and psychoanalysis to fashion a methodology that accounts both for the universality and yet the cultural particularity of abjection. As she points out, that which is classified as abject is not determined idiosyncratically, but is categorized as such across a culture. Thus, although the mechanism for abjection is universal, the forms that the abject takes are particular. For this reason, the category of the abject limns the boundaries of a given culture, demarcating the border between the pure and impure, the acceptable and unacceptable. In this respect, abjection and the abject are "primers of culture."[9] Kristeva's theory provides a means of interpreting the ambiguous nature of Camille, whose amplification and subsequent containment in the medieval poem result from her position as the abject, as she stands on the border of culture, threatening the terms that structure it. As the abject, Camille is the terrifying presence that discloses the ideological limits of the dominant culture.

A POLITICAL ROMANCE

The development of the character of Lavine is an important sign of the generic difference between epic and romance. Whereas in the *Aeneid,* women are presented as distractions who draw men's attention away from the male-to-male exchange of land and power (which they transact largely through battle), in the *Eneas,* Lavine is presented as a critical player in the exchange of land, a transaction that occurs through marriage as much as through battle, with a great deal of emphasis given to the former.[10] Although the plot of the *Eneas* does not change enough to allow Lavine to exercise any real control over her fate (she is still a pawn between three men, Latinus, Turnus, and Eneas), nevertheless the poet's introduction of Ovidian love themes (around l. 7857) gives such an emphasis to Lavine's erotic desires that the reader's sympathies are directed away from the heroes' conflict to the achievement of the heroine's romantic goal.[11] In the *Eneas,* it is not just the gods who demand that Eneas rule, but Lavine, and by metonymic logic Italy herself, who desires Eneas to be her master. In lines 8751–52, Lavine very clearly chooses Eneas according to her own desires: "o lui me tien, choisi l'en ai, ja mes d'amer ne li faudrai" [I have chosen Eneas and will hold with him. I will never cease to love him]. Whereas in the *Aeneid,* conquest cannot happen when romance is involved (as is clear from the encounter with Dido), in the *Eneas* conquest cannot happen unless romance is involved. No longer are women impediments to imperial conquest; in the romance they are essential for it.[12] As Christiane Marchello-Nizia writes, "In the medieval text, woman and land . . . are irrevocably linked, one would be nothing without the sign of the other."[13] The structuring logic of the *Eneas* is that empire results as much from sexual desire between a man and a woman as from violent conflicts between men.

This new emphasis on heterosexual love and marriage as the means to imperial acquisition is developed in several ways in the *Eneas*. When representing the terms of the conflict between Turnus and Eneas, the poet most often lists them as being, in order, "la femme et puis la terre" (6789; see also 4130–31, 6802; 7791–92; 9786–87), an additionally significant arrangement since most of these phrases are the medieval poet's additions and do not occur in Virgil.[14] The entry of women into what had been an exclusively male arena of feudal warfare is literalized by a significant gesture in the poem. When Lavine wishes to attract Eneas' attention, she does so by shooting an arrow at him, a strategy that signals her appropriation of the men's own military idiom and her entry into the conflict as a presence between them. Unlike the arrow exchanged between the combatants, Lavine's has a love letter attached. Thus, she gets Eneas's attention by masquerading as a man after his land when she is actually a woman after his affections.[15] At this point in the romance, battle becomes a metaphor for sexual relations (see l. 9067), so that the very meaning of "conquest" shifts in the romance, shading from the martial to the erotic.

Attention shifts from love of land to love of woman to such a degree that Eneas himself states that he loves the land *more* because of his love for Lavine, in a speech which begins with a surprising reference to Dido:

> "Never before was I in such distress. If I had such feeling toward the queen of Carthage, who loved me so much that she killed herself for love, never would my heart have parted from her. I would not have abandoned her for my whole life, if I had known so much of love as I have learned since yesterday morning. This land is now much more beautiful to me, and this country pleases me greatly."[16]

This speech is particularly interesting because it subsumes all the other reasons Eneas gives for his right to rule (namely his lineage from Dardanus) to the power of love. Alas! if only he had experienced that special feeling with Dido . . . a sentiment that, although touching, conveniently forgets the commands of the gods.

The emphasis on women and love as the means to acquisition of land relates the *Eneas* to changes in twelfth-century legal practice, wherein disputes were increasingly settled by public legal arrangements rather than private feud. As Christopher Baswell has recently argued, the *Eneas* shifts attention away from the military victories of the *Aeneid* to an emphasis on negotiation, which employs legal language and thus resembles judicial proceedings. As Baswell notes, this move to settle disputes through legal procedure worked to limit the power of individual nobles, who, in feudal times, could effectively indulge personal grievances by mounting private assaults, outside of the purview of any kind of legal system.[17] By subjecting disputes to the scrutiny of a centralized authority, kings were able to gain more effective control over potential disruptions in their kingdoms. These changes, which involved the keeping of written records, enabled the monarchy, as R. Howard Bloch observes, to "gain . . . mastery over the language as well as the institutions of law."[18] Henry II, in particular, widened the scope of the legal system, as he "extended the sworn inquest [the use of jury trial rather than battle to settle land disputes] by utilizing it to recover the lands and rights lost by Stephen."[19]

This new emphasis on legal negotiation as the solution to political conflict privileges marriage as yet another peaceful means of achieving imperial consolidation. Marriage was a prominent diplomatic tool in Henry's court, and was in fact the means by which Henry himself acquired so much power. Thanks to the skillful efforts of his grandfather, Henry I, who carefully negotiated the marriage between his daughter Matilda and Geoffrey, son of Count Fulk of Anjou, Henry was in line not only for the English throne but also eventually inherited possession of Normandy, Anjou, and Maine. Henry later added Aquitaine, Poitou, and Touraine to his imperial acquisitions through marriage with Eleanor of Aquitaine, and he cannily arranged ambitious marriages for his own sons and daughters, which extended his influence throughout Europe. As his entry in the *Dictionary of the Middle Ages* remarks, "almost to the end of his reign Henry outmaneuvered his opponents, sometimes by war but more often by diplomacy and marriage, his favorite weapons."[20] The medieval poet's refashioning of the *Aeneid* works well in endorsing Henry's political aims, for it both links Henry to the noble Trojan past and provides a sentimental endorsement of heterosexual marriage while touching only lightly upon the political benefits of such marriage alliances. This obscuring of the real motives behind imperial marriages has the effect of naturalizing shrewd political machinations so that they appear the products of private passions compelled solely by kismet. Although the *Eneas* in no way denies the political benefits of marriage, it does, however, suggest that good political marriages correspond fully to the intimate desires of the two partners, making such alliances a mutually beneficial proposition for all parties—men, women, and kingdoms. The idealization of marriage as the solution to even the thorniest diplomatic conflicts finds expression in the *Roman de Troie* of Benoît de Sainte-Maure (who was also commissioned by Henry to write the unfinished *Chroniques des ducs de*

Normandie), in which the impossible suggestion resonates throughout the poem that the Trojan War could have been peaceably resolved
if only the love between Achilles and Polyxena had resulted in official
union. This other antique romance offers the strongest example of
the idea that marriage was for the Angevin court a particularly important political and personal compact.

It would seem to follow that a genre that celebrates heterosexual
romance as the means to imperial acquisition must also repress
behavior that either violates the strict gender boundary between the
sexes demanded by heterosexual marriage in the twelfth century,
or at least, and probably more threateningly, suggests the radical
instability and contingency of that boundary.[21] Yet Camille thrives on
the margins of romance, this creature who defies the "compulsory
heterosexuality" (to use Adrienne Rich's phrase) demanded by the
romance plot with her self-sufficient androgyny. When first presented
to the reader, Camille is described as a woman who

> was marvelously beautiful and of very great strength. There was no other
> woman of her wisdom. She was very wise, brave, and courteous, and
> possessed great wealth, and she ruled her land wonderfully well. She
> had always been raised amid warfare, so that she loved chivalry greatly
> and upheld it all her life. She had no interest in any women's work,
> neither spinning nor sewing, but preferred the bearing of arms, tour-
> neying, and jousting, striking with the sword and the lance: there was no
> other woman of her bravery. During the day she was king, but at night,
> queen: no chambermaid or handmaid ever went about her during the day,
> nor even in the night did any man enter the chamber where she was.[22]

In this description, the gender difference that is so important to
the romance is collapsed in the figure of Camille. This beautiful
"meschine" ("maid") whose feminine beauty is carefully balanced
by her masculine power has it all: she represents the beautiful booty
as well as the courtly warrior, and, as her status as virgin queen
makes clear, she needs no Eneas to provide her with wealth, title,
or companionship. Camille's virginity stands for a self-sufficiency
anathema to the masterplot of romance, shaped as it is by an Aristo-
phanic drive for completion of the self through heterosexual union.

Yet in some ways it is not surprising that Camille is there, because
she embodies so many virtues dear to the heart of an aristocratic
culture that traces itself from the nobility of the past. For one thing,
she represents that past, as the embodiment of all its exotic antiquity.
As guarantor of the poem's ancient subject matter, Camille's presence in the poem authorizes the romance revision. In addition, she
conforms to contemporary chivalric expectations for she is an exem-

plary warrior, courageous and skilled, and, above all, loyal to her leader.

The double nature of this ambiguous woman emerges in other contrasts in her character, for not only is Camille both male and female but she is also a masculine virgin and a feminine sex object, a source of fear and attraction, simultaneously silly and deadly serious. Her resistance to traditional definition distinguishes itself by the non-referentiality of her description. Many critics have remarked on the absurdity of her portrait, pointing out its contradictions as evidence of the quaint medieval love of the fantastic, or the clerk's fixation on his own rhetorical powers.[23] Yet it is possible to see this rhetorical display associated with her as appropriate to her threat, which does not endorse a particular interpretation of her, but undermines the very certainty of any interpretation. For example, in the opening description quoted above, the poet describes Camille as a sex object ("She was marvelously beautiful"), yet the passage ends with a clear denial of her sexuality ("nor even in the night did any man enter the chamber where she was"). This kind of contrast occurs repeatedly in the poem; when the Amazons go into battle, for example, the poet writes:

> There he found Camille where she was waiting for him, fully armed. . . . The cape of the hauberk was made in such a way that she had drawn her blond hair outside, so that it covered her whole body. . . . Camille rode out to the tourneying, leading a hundred maidens with her, well clad in mail, each in a different armor; it was an extremely beautiful company.[24]

By focusing on Camille's beauty, passages such as this betray her desire to be admired as a warrior.[25] The effect of the description, then, is to turn the reader into a spectator of the worst sort, who not only admires the virgin's beauty but does so despite her desires—the highest form of voyeuristic pleasure. Yet the poem also works to thwart that pleasure, as observed in Tarcon's death. When Tarcon, spokesman for sexual difference, approaches Camille and addresses her as a sexual object, he is merely putting into words the kinds of erotic images encouraged by the description of her physical appearance.

> "Put down the shield and the lance and the hauberk. . . . This is not your calling, but rather to spin, to sew, and to clip. It is good to do battle with a maiden like you in a beautiful chamber, beneath a bed-curtain. Have you come here to show yourself off? I do not want to buy you. But nevertheless, I see that you are fair and blond. I have here four Trojan

deniers, all of a very good fine gold; I will give you these to have my
pleasure with you for a little while. . . . You will have a double profit from
it: the one in that you will have my gold, the other in that you will be
doing your pleasure."[26]

In this speech, Tarcon attempts to situate Camille in several different
traditionally feminine roles: she is not a warrior, but a housewife;
she is not a housewife, but a whore. In this scene, as with others in
the poem (most notably the description of Camille's outrageous
horse), one sees the failure of traditional linguistic categories to
name Camille. As Huchet remarks about these descriptions: "Her
excess dispels the possibility of a referent that could correspond to
the word."[27] Although the poet continually tries to locate Camille
within the categories of romance by featuring her as an object of
erotic desire, she evades that categorization by disclosing its limits,
most importantly by defying the distinctions so crucial to heterosexual romance. Not only is she a virgin but she is also equally masculine and feminine. The key to her unassimilable nature lies in the
name of her tribe, Amazon, coming from the Greek "amazōn" ("without breast"), a name that focuses not on an attribute possessed, but
on the absence of an attribute that would fix Camille and her sisters
in traditional categories of gender.

ABJECTION AS APORIA

This heterogeneity of Camille conforms to Kristeva's account of
the abject, wherein asymbolization (resulting from an excess of
meaning) is a symptom of the fear of the unknown. The linguistic
excess associated with the abject results precisely from the lack of
a proper object on which to fix meaning and so satisfy the fear; it is
"a *drive economy in want of an object.*"[28] Rather than fear of an
object, it is fear of the loss of an object that gives rise to the abject,
so that the abject is a "metaphor . . . taxed with representing *want
itself.*"[29] In Kristeva's account, the phobic response to the abject
masks the fear of separation from the maternal body, a fear that must
be overcome for the narrative of subjectivity to be written. Even before the oedipal stage occurs, the infant begins to break away from
the mother's body to identify with the Imaginary Father.[30] Yet this
separation is difficult because the mother is, up to that point, constitutive of the child's identity. As Lacan argues in "The mirror-stage as
formative of the function of the I," the image of the maternal body
is the mimetic template that the child uses to imprint its own iden-

tity.[31] To facilitate that difficult though necessary separation, the child begins to figure the mother as abject, eventually associating her with the bodily zones she monitors (ingestion and digestion—hence taboos against pollution by certain foods and excrement). Yet because of the ambivalent feelings about the maternal body at this point in development, the abject remains as attractive as it is threatening. Hence the phenomenon of the "two-faced woman," the simultaneously hated and idealized female figure. This ambivalent woman (though it is really only the child's sentiment that is ambivalent), a woman who can "wreck the infinite" in Céline's phrase, is at once appealing and disturbing, for while capable of giving life, she is also capable of taking it. As Kristeva writes, "the Célinian mother is Janus-faced, she married beauty and death."[32] This ambiguity is the central signifier of the abject.

The abject, then, stands for that which is repelled in order to underwrite the subject, a process that involves both departure from the intimacy of the maternal body and an initiation into the world of language, culture, and the father, the Symbolic.[33] Because it is constructed to be the antithesis of culture, the abject stands in opposition to the superego. As Kristeva writes, "To each ego its object, to each superego its abject."[34] For this reason, her account of the nature of the abject applies to the constitution of both cultural and subjective (as in the psychoanalytic subject) histories. For as much as abjection is part of the founding fiction of subjectivity, it also constitutes the founding fiction of culture, revealing how an individual culture marks and maintains the borders of the Symbolic.[35]

Because the abject is born out of the pre-oedipal union with the mother, its appeal cannot be understated, for although it stands for the thing repulsed in the construction of subjectivity, it is also the reminder of that Edenic dyad before the entry into the Symbolic. Because of its power, it continues to reappear and to replay its threat, especially in literature. These reappearances occur, argues Kristeva, when there is a failure of the paternal signifier. But this is not a failure that could necessarily be restored. The failure of the Symbolic to banish the abject completely parallels its inability to foreclose all aporia. Because the dominant culture founds itself on essentialist fictions, it must be ever vigilant to guard against the exposure of those fictions as such.

Although the abject can resurface at any time, it seems particularly appropriate that it reappears in a moment of transition from an old regime to a new, when Henry's Angevin empire is in the process of constituting itself through both law and letters. Henry and his court were seen to be ushering in a new age, after the disastrous reign of

Stephen. (The limits of Stephen's monarchy are curtly noted by Walter Map: "He was a man distinguished for skill in arms, but in other respects almost a fool, save that he was rather inclined to the side of evil.")[36] Henry's reign, by contrast, was marked by aggressive political and legal reforms. He rebuilt castles destroyed by the civil war, stabilized relations with the Welsh and Scottish, gained control of Ireland, and instituted trial by jury.

Henry also worked actively to consolidate his power. As Amy Kelly notes, "In the first lively years of their reign Henry Plantagenet and the Countess of Poitou were the hammer and anvil of a single enterprise—to weld the widespread and individual provinces that were theirs by conquest and inheritance into a massive domain, and to plant thereon a dynasty."[37] Sometimes this was achieved in small ways, such as in 1173 when Henry added the phrase "King by the grace of God" to his official title in an effort to forestall clerical opposition to divine right of kings.[38] His efforts were also aided by the genre that flourished within his court. As well as rewriting the past to point to the Angevin present, and doing so in a language accessible to many, these romances subtly sketched their revised epic heroes on the model of Henry. As several critics have pointed out, Henry and Eneas bear an uncanny resemblance to one another: both gained land with a wife, both restored an older house when they took the throne, and both attempted to rule through legal manipulation rather than armed conflict.[39] The suggestion is that Henry, like Eneas, was a romantic leading man, building an empire by breaking away from earlier models of aristocratic rule.

Yet, just as Camille marks the ideological limits of Eneas' empire building, so in turn will she be limited by the narrative devoted to celebrating such empires. Accordingly, the poet fashions for Camille a spectacular end. Though she dies a warrior's death (reaching down for booty she is struck from behind), her tomb commemorates her abjection, her position between two opposed poles. One hundred eighty-seven lines compose the description of this tomb (longer than either of the descriptions of the living Camille), an oriental wonder of engineering. Camille's body is to be preserved in the tomb, but only as long as certain precise conditions are maintained:[40]

> Over the tomb, directly in the center, hung a chain of gold swung from a pulley overhead, and descending with great art. At one end of the chain hung a lamp, full of a very rare oil so that it threw a very bright light. It will never fail in its fire, but will always burn, everlasting, if it is not broken or struck. . . . The other end of the chain, which held and supported the lamp, went across to a pillar. There a golden dove, fixed to

the cornice of the pillar, held it in its beak, wholly at rest in the tomb. The lamp would never fall as long as the dove held it; and it would hold the chain forever if it were not for a single thing. There was an archer in another part of the room, sculptured with great care, and facing the dove on a block of dark marble. He held his bow stretched and looked straight toward the dove. The arrow was nocked and was so directed that it would strike the dove immediately, as soon as it left the bowstring. . . . At a breath all would be lost; if someone blew the snare it would loose the bow immediately, and the archer thus would shoot straight at the dove and hit it. Then the chain would be broken and the lamp wholly destroyed.[41]

The construction of the tomb parallels the representation of Camille, for just as she is between man and woman, encompassing both, so does her tomb draw together life and death (in the anerobic presentation of her body) and movement and stasis (in the continual menace of the archer's stance).[42]

Also preserved in this tomb is the anxiety surrounding her character. For though this tomb memorializes Camille so that she will live still, she is also literally stilled within the monument (in the paradox of "stillness" explored by Keats), left behind by a narrative that cannot afford to linger over the alternative vision she offers.[43] To do so would endanger the narrative mission of fashioning heterosexual desire as the cornerstone of empirical consolidation.[44]

The conditions of Camille's preservation stand as a testament to her abject virginity by mirroring the conditions of that virginity; though she rests inviolate, the threat of violation is perpetually staged by the posture of the archer, whose arrow, already nocked and mounted, stands ever ready to penetrate the dove. This tableau is a fitting metaphor for Angevin designs, which, while preserving the fantastic charms embodied by Camille, stage in perpetuity their containment.

A Genre is Born

It is possible to read the birth of the romance genre as paralleling the birth of subjectivity. Both births must come through separation from a sponsoring body, either the maternal body or the classical text of the past. In the *Eneas,* these two bodies coincide in the figure of Camille—the beautiful emblem of the past who must be killed off for the romance to live. Camille is a virgin cast as the abjected maternal body, repulsed to make way for the new order of the Father, an order introduced by Henry and his busy scribes. It is not surprising, then, that Camille is killed just before the medieval poet makes his most dramatic departure from his sponsoring genre; the *Eneas* becomes a romance—that is, the Ovidian monologues begin—a mere 150 lines after Camille's death and entombment.

By killing Camille, the Symbolic authority of heterosexual romance effectively defends itself against the threat of the lack of sexual differentiation. In this context, the entombment of Camille can be read as a purification ritual, whereby the abject is removed from the community and put in its proper place.[45] Yet the enduring appeal of what Camille represents is also honored in the elaborateness of the tomb.

The appeal/threat of Camille, then, partakes of and combines two narratives: one about the institution of a new hegemonic discourse out of an old and the second about the constitution of the subject within specific ideological structures. Camille is the figure who links the shared instabilities in the fictions of self and empire, revealing the aporia of personal and political histories.

Diana's "Bowe Ybroke": Impotence, Desire, and Virginity in Chaucer's *Parliament of Fowls*

Kathryn L. Lynch

> "For ever warm and still to be enjoy'd,
> For ever panting . . ."
> —Keats, "Ode on a Grecian Urn"

I

The *Parliament of Fowls* is a spectacularly disunified poem. Beginning with a confusion over love and art, rapidly succeeded by a summary of a famous Neoplatonic political dream, followed by the narrator's crazyquilt vision of Venus's Temple and Nature's garden, where in turn a perplexing parliament of birds fails to find a mate for a female eagle, this love-vision, if that is its genre, cannot even seem to decide whether its narrator is a mere rhetorical effect or the focus of the poem. Indeed, the most remarkable facet of the history of *Parliament* criticism may be that readers once found adequate closure in the poem's circularity, its lyricism, and its polished surface. In recent years, at least, critics have been much more likely to acknowledge the significant gaps and fissures that scar that surface.

At the same time, the most cursory survey of essay titles hints at a powerful drive underlying the multiplicity of readings, a drive to uncover the secret theme that unites all its disparate parts: "Aesthetic Order and Individual Experience," "Antithesis as the Principle of Design in . . .," "The Genre of . . . ," "The Center of . . .," "Structure and Meaning in . . . ," "Artistic Conclusiveness in . . . ," "A Philosophical Interpretation," "The Harmony of Chaucer's *Parlement*."[1] Even such a tendentious moniker as "The Harmony of Chaucer's *Parlement*: A Dissonant Voice" or "The Question of Unity and the *Parlement of Foules*," where the question is answered with a decided negative, gives testimony to the persistent critical need to bring under control the evocative and provocative disorder of this text, to settle the question of its artistic form once and for all.[2] As shown by a recent analysis of three manuscript collections in which the *Parliament* appeared, even the poem's earliest scribal critics were powerfully motivated to "disambiguate" this disruptive poem by placing it near other texts, about politics or romantic love, that would dispose its readers towards one interpretation over another.[3] The *Parliament of Fowls,* in other words, demands editorial control; it offers a tantalizing disarray of human needs and motivations, of speculations about love, procreation, and fulfillment, to which the superficial unity of plot and birdsong seems simply unequal. The poem's failure to control its material adequately, a failure acknowledged in the final lines, invites our attempts, which can by definition only be attempts *at* attempts, since the narrator himself never discovers that "certeyn thing" (line 20) that will cause him to "fare / The bet" (lines 698–99).[4]

But, if we suspend the effort to discover the unity of the *Parliament*—that is, to determine its conscious principle of design—where does that put us? Are we left, like Robert Jordan, admiring "a poem without a centre," organized by principles of display and analysis alien to the post-romantic sensibility?[5] Or may there be another way into the poem, one that honors the deep psychological demands of the *Parliament*'s disunity and that questions the poetic motivations that prompted this disharmonious *concordia discors?* A recent essay by Russell Peck suggests an alternative approach to the poem as a record of "the naive dreamer's coming of age," which explores the asymmetries between private erotic love and its translation into the public world of political negotiation and war.[6] This psychological avenue into the poem's politics suggests a disjunction between its ideological framework and its personal motivation, between its outcome and its negotiation of the psychologically fraught transition from the private fantasies of childhood to the full possession of manly virtue. In this essay, I will explore this disjunction by examining the poem's attitude toward the female figures upon which the narrator's masculine power finally rests, especially focusing on the psychologically ambiguous figure of the virgin, and will finally look closely at the way that the narrator's profound ambivalence about women prevents him from fully assuming the mantle of his masculinity.[7] In this way I want to locate some of the sources of the *Parliament*'s ragged power without reducing the poem to a single discursive statement or even to one thematic approach.

II

At first, the *Parliament of Fowls* may seem to have little to do with virginity.[8] The formel eagle in Chaucer's poem, though a prospective bride, is after all only a bird, and nothing is explicitly made of her avian virginity. Indeed, many other species of bird in the poem pair off easily. Yet the formel is confronted with what turns out to be an undesired marriage, putting her in the classic position of numberless reluctant maidens in the Middle Ages. Chaucer himself explores her dilemma in several other poems, including the Knight's Tale, the Physician's Tale, and the Second Nun's Tale, in all of which the besieged virgin resists her male suitor, with a variety of outcomes. Of course, in keeping with the tone of this poem, the eagle's "heroics of virginity"[9] are a comically diminished version of what one might find in hagiography or romance. Rather than threatening suicide, self-mutilation, or martyrdom, she asks only for a year's delay, ostensibly to help her make a choice among three eligible bridegrooms.

But the eagle is, nonetheless, described in terms that evoke courtly maidenhood with its peculiar blend of sensuality and aloofness, coquetry and modesty. Our first glimpse of her—brief though it is—reveals a creature "of shap the gentilleste" (line 373), who combines moral virtues ("the moste benygne and the goodlieste" [line 375]) with physical allurements. Nature herself has "showered" her with "divine adoration";[10] the goddess cannot keep from looking at the bird, and, with a delicate homoeroticism, "ofte hire bek to kysse" (line 378). Later, after listening to the first tercel eagle's passionate declaration of love, the young formel blushes gracefully, her silence through most of the poem clearly the result of a sweet and pleasing virginal restraint:

> Ryght as the freshe, rede rose newe
> Ayeyn the somer sonne coloured is,
> Ryght so for shame al wexen gan the hewe
> Of this formel, whan she herde al this;
> She neyther answerde wel, ne seyde amys,
> So sore abasht was she.

(lines 442–47)

However lightly and facetiously represented, the formel eagle's virginity lies near the center of this lopsided poem. Although her sexuality is rendered harmless by her well-bred silence, and indeed by the very incongruity of her maidenly birdness, her presence hints at a

sexual awakening that can have disastrous and chaotic consequences (as it does for the similar eagle whose courtship is re-
counted in the Squire's Tale). The poem's marriage plot, indeed,
explicitly seeks her sexual inauguration. The chief (if silent) object
of desire, she is balanced by the fecund Lady Nature, on whose arm
she perches, and Nature's even more ominously luxuriant counterpart, Venus, "naked from the brest unto the hed" (line 269). It is this
threat of active and possibly overwhelming female sexuality—and
not, as Elaine Hansen argues, female indifference[11]—that I think mo-
tivates the narrator's behavior in the *Parliament of Fowls.* Faced with
this unholy trinity of females, the male response in Chaucer's poem
wavers between the perpetual tumescence of Priapus, "with hys scep-
tre in honde" (line 256), and the voyeuristic withdrawal of the narrator, would-be poet of love, who despite his hesitancy to participate
nonetheless "liketh hym at wrastlyng for to be" (line 165).

The allusion to Priapus itself raises the specter of virgin seduction,
which Chaucer chooses to foreground by inserting the reference to
Priapus's embarrassment in his pursuit of a virgin between the sighs
of jealousy and the portrait of Venus herself. Although Ovid recounts
Priapus's story in the *Fasti* twice, Chaucerians have focused virtually
exclusively on his first telling, in *Fasti* I, when a braying ass disturbs
Priapus in his pursuit of the nymph Lotis.[12] But Chaucer is almost
certainly following his immediate source, Boccaccio's *Teseida,* in
referring to Ovid's retelling of the story in *Fasti* VI, where it is the
celebrated virgin Vesta whom Priapus is about to violate when the
braying catches him out.[13] Boccaccio is clear about the identity of
the maiden "Vesta whom Priapus desired not a little and toward
whom he was advancing,"[14] as is Ovid, who entertains the possibility
that Priapus conceived his "obscene hope" (*spes obscena*) in full
knowledge of the lady's identity, perhaps even because of it. Indeed,
the entire context in Boccaccio underlines the importance of Vesta's
virginity, for Palaemon's personified prayer to Venus that travels to
the garden of love in the *Teseida* will soon be followed by Emilia's
sacrifice to Diana to preserve her virginity, a sacrifice whose ill success is foreshadowed by the broken bows of Diana's luckless devo-
tees, described by Boccaccio in the stanza that directly follows his
description of Priapus. In the *Parliament,* the broken bows are post-
poned for twenty lines, so that Chaucer can position the vivid if
languid picture of the goddess of love herself directly following Priapus's embarrassment, as if to imply that proximity to the powerful
and seductive female is somehow related to Priapus's impotence
and diminishment (in stature if not in size). Venus and Diana are
thus linked, and Priapus's disgrace is compounded by Vesta's famed

chastity. Through her connections with Nature and Venus, then, and obliquely with the endangered virtue of the virgin Vesta, the female eagle possesses a vivid if repressed sexuality.

Her unapproachable sexuality suggests that she may invoke the famous "taboo of virginity," which reflects a deep male fear of the untouched female.[15] This taboo is based on the important reality that the virgin simultaneously repels and attracts. In response, the narrator's hesitation at the gate of Nature's park reflects "the male's hesitation between fear and desire, between the fear of being in the power of uncontrollable forces and the wish to win them over," which Simone de Beauvoir has argued, for reasons I will explore shortly, "is strikingly reflected in the myth of virginity."[16] In the obscure logic of the psyche here, the forces of Nature, genetically aligned with the virgin, are precisely those primitive maternal forces that draw the male narrator in but that also, because they remind him of his finite origins, threaten to annihilate him.

To be sure, the most powerful image of virginity during the Middle Ages was a fiercely positive one, especially for women.[17] Patriarchal societies, in which property is transferred along the male line, require close guardianship of female purity and a high value on chastity both before and within marriage. Even the Prologue to the Wife of Bath's Tale, an extended, blasphemous call to feminist arms, in many ways depends on the writings of such Church Fathers as Jerome and Augustine, enforcing the Pauline recommendation of virginity: "he heeld virginitee / Moore parfit than weddyng in freletee" (lines 91–92); "Virginitee is greet perfeccion, / And continence eek with devocion" (lines 105–6). The wife's lusty rejection of virginal perfection indeed has meaning only within a tradition that placed its highest premium on female sexual restraint.

And yet at the same time the Wife's meditation also takes place in a context that acknowledges the power of female sexuality and its connection with both life-giving and life-destroying forces. Her query, "certes, if ther were no seed ysowe, / Virginitee, thanne wherof sholde it growe?" (lines 71–72), is one that was actually demanded of such clerical writers as St. Ambrose, who had to defend himself against the argument that virginity depleted the population.[18] But sexuality is nonetheless only uneasily linked to fertility. Despite her appeal to the argument of procreation, the Wife herself has no children in evidence, and her later reported dream of a bed "ful of verray blood" (line 579) in which her lover seeks to kill her evokes the most terrifying and contaminating aspects of female sexuality, including menstrual blood, the blood of childbirth and, I would add, the blood of virginity lost in the marriage bed, all reminders of universal human mortality.[19] Even within the Christian tradition, virginity participates fully in all the terrors and contradictions of female sexuality. That sexuality, as John Bugge has pointed out, was in the early gnostic tradition both cause and effect of original sin: "The explanation of death lay in a primordial and cosmic derangement of a sexual nature. . . . [S]exuality is the means of replenishment of life *because*, ultimately, it is the cause of death."[20] Regarded as the antidote to the death that Eve introduced into Eden along with sexuality, Mary's virgin purity recalls Eve's corruption.

Like many cultural values, then, virginity invokes its opposite. The virgin is the young girl before deflowering; her unplucked sexuality is in tantalizing bud. Chaucer's Apius loves Virginia for the sweet chastity he longs to destroy, just as Shakespeare's Angelo craves Isabella "to sin in loving virtue": Angelo asks wonderingly, "Can it be / That modesty may more betray our sense / Than woman's lightness?" (2.2.168–70).[21] The answer, no surprise, is yes. The "virtuous maid" (2.2.185) and the "strumpet" (2.2.183) lie on a continuum; the one evokes, promises, even demands, the other. Eve and Mary shared one thing—their virginity—however differently they chose to employ it.[22] Similarly, Diana/Artemis, the ancient goddess of chastity, was in addition both the goddess of childbirth and Hecate, who ruled the forces of the underworld. Even today, in the Nepalese cult of the virgin Kumari, the young virgin idol is dressed in red, painted with elaborate makeup, and worshipped for the access she provides to the sexually mature and demon-destroying goddess Taleju Bhavani. As anthropologists speculate, "pre-menstrual, virginal girls combine in their persons the seemingly irreconcilable values . . . of purity, reproductivity and destructive capability."[23] To return to Simone de Beauvoir, "the virgin would seem to represent the most consummate form of the feminine mystery; she is therefore its most disturbing and at the same time its most fascinating aspect."[24] Poised uncertainly between withdrawal from and participation in the ceaseless natural alternation of death and life, the virgin invites man simultaneously to transcend and to acknowledge his mortal weakness. She is seduction itself, alluring and dangerous.

This paradoxical combination is well-reflected in the medieval myth of the poison damsel, or as Danielle Jacquart and Claude Thomasset call her, "the venomous virgin."[25] The most common exemplar of her story occurs in the widely known *Secretum Secretorum,* the compendium of Aristotle's advice to King Alexander, where he recounts saving Alexander from the deadly ministrations of a beautiful maiden reared up by a rival king or sometimes queen on poison until the maiden is fatal to the touch. But the story can also be

found in works as various as one Italian edition of Brunetto Latini's
Il Tesoretto[26] and the famous tale-collection the *Gesta Romanorum.*[27]
Depending on the version, the poison-damsel's embraces kill slaves
or condemned men brought into her presence for the purpose of
testing her true nature, or she is simply unmasked by Aristotle, who
explains to Alexander that "thy deth shold have come to the thurgh
the ardure that thow sholdest have in flesshly delyng with her."[28] As
this warning makes clear, it is the virgin's peculiarly potent sexuality
that is to be feared. The story of the poison-damsel thus relates to
more general male fears of female, and especially virgin, sexuality
that have been recorded cross-culturally—in tribes, for example, that
require defloration, either surgically or by an approved holy man,
before consummation of a marriage, to protect the groom from the
evil emanations of his bride's intact sexuality. In Rome, the virgin
bride sat on a stone phallus of Priapus in a symbolic violation that
reminds us of Chaucer's allusion to Priapus's pursuit of Vesta.[29] In
medieval Tibet, reports Marco Polo, "no man would ever on any
account take a virgin to wife."[30] Instead, the Tibetans make their
daughters available to passing travellers, whose gifts and trinkets
demonstrate her desirability and safeness as a lover. As Polo remarks
mildly, "Obviously the country is a fine one to visit for a lad from
sixteen to twenty-four."[31] Similarly the fourteenth-century Sir John
Mandeville describes an unnamed island where, despite an overall
strictness about female sexuality, the custom of premarital defloration is still carried out. Here, the young men required to perform
the act are in such a desperate circumstance that they are called
"*Gadiberis,* that is for to say, fol[s] dispered":

> They seyn there and affermyn it for soth that it is a ful perilous thing
> to takyn a virgyne maydynhed; for they seyn ho so doth, he disposith
> hym to peril of deth. And yif the husbonde of that woman fynde here a
> maydyn in the nyght aftyr . . . thanne here housbonde shal han his acci-
> oun to hym byforn the iuge, as meche as he hadde slayn his fadyr.[32]

This tradition of the venomous or poisonous virgin, to quote Simone
de Beauvoir, expresses "the idea that the feminine principle has the
more strength, is more menacing, when it is intact."[33] Even the
charming medieval story of the virgin and the unicorn includes, as
Tom Moore observes, "deception and death."[34] After attracting the
all-too-phallic unicorn by exposing her uncovered breast, the virgin
makes the beast vulnerable to the hunter, who has the option either
of taking the unicorn alive or of slaying him.

But it is not just the lulling enchantment of maidenhood that is feared. The virgin is actively threatening; she must be defanged, as it were. The apocryphal Book of Tobit tells the story of seven bridegrooms who perish on their wedding nights, until Tobit's son Tobias approaches the bride with the aid of a charm arranged by an angel.[35] This tale is apparently related to the motif of the vagina dentata, which itself comes from stories of serpents hiding in the woman's sex organs prepared to bite her unsuspecting partner unless he is assisted by a "kindly spirit."[36] As Mandeville historicizes the isle of the poison damsels,

> I, Ion Maundeuyle, askid hem what was the cause and the skil whi that swich customys weryn vsed ther. And thei seidyn me that in olde tyme some men in the cuntre weryn dede for they refte yynge maydenys of here maydynhed, for they haddyn withinnyn hem, as longe as they were virgynys, nederis, and therfor they heldyn that custome in that contre.[37]

It is but a (small) step from such stories to the deep dread of women articulated by modern psychoanalysis as anxiety about impotence and castration.

Indeed, whatever the source of his disease—and I will have more to say about this in a moment—our narrator in the *Parliament* does seem to be struggling with a kind of impotence. Freud's description of those victimized by psychical impotence—"Where they love they do not desire and where they desire they cannot love"[38]—might almost be a translation of this dreamer's Boethian plaint: "For bothe I hadde thyng which that I nolde, / And ek I ne hadde that thyng that I wolde" (lines 90–91). He exists in a state of frustrating arrest, unable to succeed in art or love, unable to discover even the object of his yearning, the "certeyn thing" that we saw him seeking in line 20 and that he still has not found at the poem's end. What is the dreamer looking for? And why can't he find it? How is it that he finishes the poem in such frustration? In what ways is his frustration related to that of the formel eagle or her suitors? Or to the satisfaction in love achieved by the birds who mate and sing the Valentine's Day roundel? Why does he look in books for answers to questions that seem to have more to do with life? To find our own answers, we will need now to turn back to the poem itself.

III

The second main section of the *Parliament* (lines 85–294), which details the beginning of the narrator's dream and encompasses first his hesitancy to enter the garden and then his initial impressions of its beauty and its danger, constitutes, as Russell Peck notes, "both the most ignored portion of the poem" and possibly "the most important."[39] Although, as Peck acknowledges, bits of this section frequently find their way into commentary, the passage is rarely read as part of the poem's total "experiential plot," despite the fact that here "Chaucer rehearses in miniature the whole process of coming to knowledge, of moving from narcissism to politics."[40] But, one must ask, does this passage or the poem as a whole, as Peck implies, ever achieve a political standpoint, or is its achievement merely a standoff? Rather than rehearsing the dreamer's "coming of age,"[41] the second two hundred lines, with their complex alternation of attitudes towards the female principle, might be said effectively to prevent the narrator's embrace of a straightforward, masculine politics. The female, who must be dominated and repressed fully to invoke the patriarchal transcendence recommended by Africanus, intrudes, interrupts, and asserts her potency, so that by the end of the poem the only version of polity we have is a cacophony of bird voices that blur the "natural" hierarchy of gender (the female turtle dove, for instance, debates the male cuckoo, and many birds remain unspecified as to gender). Nature, "vicaire of the almyghty Lord" (line 379), presides, but she seems cut off from her ultimately masculine source of authority. By considering the initial description of Nature's garden in the context of the entire poem and by providing a psychoanalytic framework for the impasse the narrator experiences when he first confronts Nature and Venus, I hope to explain why the gap between common profit and courtly love is so difficult to bridge in this poem and why the narrator finds himself at the end stranded on the far side of the chasm.[42]

In a classical Freudian analysis, the *Parliament* narrator would be one of those unfortunates whose inability to negotiate the oedipus complex has led him to substitute for adult heterosexual love "the performance of an act which normally is but an introductory . . . one . . . in looking . . . or in watching the other person's most intimate doings."[43] Excluded from the ranks of Love's servants—"this writyng nys nothyng ment bi the, / Ne by non but he Loves servaunt be" (lines 158–59) he assigns himself the role of voyeur—"Yit that thow canst not do, yit mayst thow se" (line 163). Pursuing this role, the dreamer confronts Venus by coyly observing of her partial undress:

> And naked from the brest unto the hed
> Men myghte hire sen; and, sothly for to say,
> The remenaunt was wel kevered to my pay,

Ryght with a subtyl coverchef of Valence
Ther was no thikkere cloth of no defense.

(lines 269–73)

As A. C. Spearing notes, "The impersonality of 'Men myghte hire sen' is not kept up for long; what is revealed underlying it is '*my* pay', the watching Chaucer's pleasure."[44] Even the narrator's eagerness as a reader—"the longe day ful faste I redde and yerne" (line 21); "To rede forth hit gan me so delite" (line 27)—can be seen as a kind of voyeuristic intensity.

In normal development as outlined by Freud, oedipal fantasies of supplanting the father and possessing the mother are suppressed by fear of the father's castrating law, which itself is ultimately internalized as the individual achieves a new psychic, heterosexual integration. But the narrator of the *Parliament* seems unable to move forward toward that integration, for reasons that remain obscure both within Freudian analysis and also within this poem. Indeed, what the Freudian (or even Lacanian) analysis leaves out, with its emphasis on the phallus and the father's threat of castration, is the part played by the seductive and transgressive female in inhibiting induction of the male into full heterosexual participation. As Jane Flax has written, Freud "displaces and lessens preoedipal fears of annihilation by transforming them into oedipal ones (castration). He evades the centrality of the preoedipal mother-child relationship by insisting that the oedipal struggle is the crucial event in the life history of an individual and culture. . . ."[45] Chaucer's poem suggests why emphasis must be replaced on the feminine and maternal in human psychosexual development.[46]

The key contrast in the *Parliament* is between the male-dominated civilization of Africanus ("culture," in a word), with its world-transcending philosophy, and the female-dominated love-garden of Nature and Venus ("nature"), with the painful ambiguities and complexities of living in a place where the perpetual replaces the eternal and where death and reproduction stand in for the survival of the personal-I outside of time. In these terms, the poem's structure is regressive. Beginning with the law of the father—literally the grandfather—in the person of Africanus, its bookish, oracular vision of political grandeur and universal order capable even of containing and reforming "likerous folk" (line 79) gives way to an *insomnium* of feminine disorder and chaotic coupling. We have here what Jane Flax would call "the return of the repressed mother world."[47] The Didonian Carthage, from which such specular distance had been achieved by Africanus, suddenly swings back into close, full view.[48]

Rather than "regressive," "retrospective" might offer a better description of the poem's structure. More precisely, the *Parliament of
Fowls* chronicles what John Brenkman calls "the oedipal moment,"
not exactly the same thing as the oedipal stage itself in early childhood, but the time later when the young man is initiated into full
possession of the privileges of manhood in a patriarchal society and
so must retroactively revise his attitude toward women and specifically toward his mother.[49] Seen now for the first time as the goal of
heterosexual desire and the subject of male dominance (both roles
mediated through the figure of the father), the mother appears suddenly not as the real-life mother, the ambiguously nurturing figure
of early childhood, but as an object of fantasy and prohibition, split
into the dichotomous "mother/whore," "the tabooed and the model
object."[50] In this analysis, the threatening female, the "mother/
whore," is not, as Brenkman argues, "a 'primary' object" but one
who has "been worked up through the eyes of the father and through
the symbols, institutions and roles of the society."[51] Hence, we have
the father Africanus's introduction of the narrator-poet to the feminized garden of love after laying out a vision of masculine polity,
and hence also that garden's display of femininity as a perilous opposition of overt sexuality and civilized forms of hyper-restrained courtship. Full adult masculine sexuality, which includes the marriage
choice, will not be available to the dreamer until he accepts and
internalizes this new contradictory attitude towards women and love,
an event that never happens within or after this dream. Indeed, of this
dream one cannot even say what Macrobius wrote of the essentially
insignificant *insomnium*, that "The lovere met he hath his lady
wonne" (line 105).[52] The narrator-poet Chaucer represented here is
no lover, and the amorous pursuit represented in his dream has no
clear outcome, but only an uneasy alternation of impatience and
delay.

Behind it all, the narrator is stymied by a fear of sexual engagement, of being fragmented and reabsorbed into a pre-oedipal unity
with the mother, a fear everywhere related to the poem's pervasive
concern with time and mortality. What he feels is essentially an
apprehension of sacrificing identity to union with the Other; an anxious longing for the mother and her womb, which is simultaneously
a terror of annihilation. In the complex calculus of this poem, a
number of disparate anxieties are drawn into the equation: commitment to eros threatens annihilation; commitment to a defined poetic
program does as well. Commitment on any of life's fronts feels indeed like a move towards oblivion, a violation, a loss of virginity. As
R. Howard Bloch has suggested in a recent analysis of the Physician's

Tale, Chaucer "deflowers at the very instant he depicts."[53] To represent anything, but especially to represent love and womanhood, is to embody it, to bring it before the reader's and the author's eyes, to limit it by giving it flesh, to bring it into time and so to destroy it. An idea is more purely entertained as an idea; once it has descended, it is subject to death. Even in the first stanza of the *Parliament*—with its famous opening line, "The lyf so short, the craft so long to lerne"—the narrator conflates anxiety about mortality with dissatisfaction about poetry's ability to conquer death; he confuses both with eros—"Al this mene I by Love" (line 4)—a force that threatens to dissolve his identity if he cannot find some point of control outside it. In both the formel and the narrator, then, the poet explores the complex of fears and desires associated with virginity: fear of mortality, of the contaminations of the flesh, desire for purity, permanence, transcendence.

The dream proper continues to explore the poet's concern with mortality and his quest to find a way to exist outside the circle of time. It replicates a version of the conflict between transcendence and immanence—between the taut aspiration of the father and the warm seduction of the mother—in its own terms. Here a vision of love as personal self-gratification, which confirms the endurance of the singular self, proceeds to a vision of love as procreation, which includes the succession of generations and the relentless march of time. The uncanny stillness of Venus's corner ("No man may there waxe sek ne old" [line 207]) is cancelled out by the energetic activity of Nature's realm, suggesting that even the sublimations of romantic love cannot defeat the horrors of maternal sexuality. Like the lovers on Keats's urn, the figures the narrator sees painted on the wall of Venus's temple—Dido, Isaude, Helen, et al.—are static images. But they are no less threatening for their artistic suspension. To be sure, in their current aesthetic form, these figures stand off from involvement with time, but they are destroyed by their love nonetheless. Diana's bow is broken (line 282) merely by being spoken, and the desire she arouses leads only to heartache and death (line 294).

IV

Given how sharp and disabling the conflict is between Scipio's glimpse of common profit and the courtly birds' venereal quest for personal satisfaction, a quest encouraged by both Nature and Venus, it is surprising to find that critics frequently do not judge the conflict between the public male world and the private female one to be the chief opposition in the poem. But Mother Nature does not square off against Father Africanus in scholarship nearly so often as she does against her sister goddess Venus. In fact, arguably the most common critical strategy for unifying the *Parliament* consists of demonstrating the Chartrian Nature's affinity for the common good; that is, Nature's neoplatonic harmony with Africanus. Robert L. Entzminger, for example, sees the work as a "reconciliation of Africanus' Stoicism with Alain's exaltation of the created world."[54] Rather than the term that disrupts the narrator's progress to full masculinity, Nature is thus more often seen as the unifying term, whose plenitude and harmony make possible the compromises that give this poem its happy ending.[55] As Charles O. McDonald observes succinctly, "Nature plays the role of a tolerant mediator between apparently contradictory points of view."[56] And even when, as is commonly the case nowadays, Nature's unity is conceived as having "limitations," hers is nevertheless still an attempted unification that merely falls short.[57] In such a reading, Nature is sanitized by separation from the purely selfish and venereal. As Robertson and Huppé put it, when all is said and done, "only the worshipers of Venus remain unsatisfied and sterile."[58] This critical maneuver is not unlike the psychological one we noted earlier, to save the good mother (the "madonna") at the expense of the bad (the "whore").

Of course, the fact that it mimics a move from within Chaucer's poem does not invalidate this interpretation of Nature's and Venus's opposition. On some level of intention, Chaucer may well have meant to line Nature up with Africanus and to demonstrate the deep continuity of their philosophical positions. He probably did. But to ignore Nature's even deeper implication with Venus, whose temple her garden literally surrounds, is to miss something extremely important about the sources of this poem's psychic energy. To quote John Fyler, "there are not two gardens, any more than there are two gates."[59] Nature/Venus represent a complex of conflicting reactions that the male experiences when he confronts the necessity of subordinating the matrix of female power in order to assume his own privileged role in society: desire and fear; love and alienating pride; admiration and loathing. The eagle who sits on Nature's hand and inspires Venus's followers links these two goddesses and joins them to Diana, whose own virginal indifference and intactness, as we have seen, epitomize the threat of the female. And at least temporarily Diana is victorious; her triumph is thus completely consistent with the loud and enthusiastic coupling of the lower fowls. It is the triumph of the principle of female power, of the repressed pre-oedipal mother.

According to the proportions of this poem, Scipio's brief vision of universal harmony stands against the fertile chaos of Nature's garden, and loses. Likewise, the dreamer can find no point of engagement either inside or outside of the garden, no way to jump into the game of love, unlike the impetuous and expressive male eagles, who are frustrated by forces outside their control. And so, the narrator at the end of the *Parliament* stands on the brink of commitment. In this respect at least he is similar to the formel eagle; he is consecrated neither to a tradition of poetry that celebrates the love of common profit nor to one that cherishes romantic or sexual love. One might say that, in her aloofness and delay, the virgin bird has moved from being the object of desire to an aspect of the narrator himself. And he, returned to the intimacy of the mother world, seeks in her his very identity. Even here, though, he is rebuffed, while she is returned to a position of power. The narrator's aesthetic distance, what Elaine Hansen calls his "magisterial indifference," does not constitute for him an "enabling difference" from the female bird.[60] Any difference, in fact, proves crippling. The man's position, in the end, is less secure and effective than the bird's, for he does not actively choose his marginality, but is instead a virgin by default. This is the true measure of his impotence. Despite the productive distance from the oedipal drama that permits the observing poet to turn life into art, the narrator within the poem ends searching restlessly through his books (lines 695–99) because life remains beyond his grasp.

Menaced Masculinity and Imperiled Virginity in the *Morte Darthur*

KATHLEEN COYNE KELLY

> To men a man is but a mind. Who cares
> What face he carries or what form he wears?
> But woman's body is the woman.
> —Ambrose Bierce, *The Devil's Dictionary*

> I write woman: woman must write woman. And man, man; it's
> up to him to say where his masculinity and femininity are at.
> —Hélène Cixous, "The Laugh of the Medusa"

> It is the hymen that desire dreams of piercing, of bursting, in an
> act of violence that is (at the same time or somewhere in be-
> tween) love and murder.
> —Jacques Derrida, "The Double Session"

MALE VIRGIN?

IN the discourse of our profession, and inscribed into the texts we read, the female body has figured prominently as site, as meeting-place for ideological conflict. The male body, on the other hand, has been often and emphatically constructed literally, a thing in and of itself. For example, when Thomas Laqueur speaks of the "problematic, unstable female body" and the "unproblematic, stable male body" as they were constituted in the medical discourse of antiquity, he describes not only a historically attested way of figuring difference, but his own construction of difference as well.[1] However, in the past few years, in the wake of feminist readings of the female body, and under the rubrics of gender studies, gay/lesbian studies, and the study of masculinities, scholars have begun to challenge such monologic representations of the male body.

My interest in the male body grows out of a larger project on virginity as something to be tested, measured, and verified, both in medical and gynecological treatises of antiquity and the Middle Ages

97

and in medieval vernacular romance (magical proofs and ordeals of chastity can be found in almost all Arthurian romances.) Early on in my research, it became clear to me that when we talk about virginity, we have a tendency—unconscious, as it were—to mark the virgin body as female. Virginity is thus made a naturalized feature of gender difference.[2] Tertullian's *De Virginibus Velandis* (*Virgins Must be Veiled*, c. 211) serves as an example of (if not origin for) this idea. When Tertullian refers to *viri autem tot virgines*, "so many men-virgins," he demonstrates his awareness of the shortcomings of Latin to describe the new social categories created by Christianity.[3] He must appropriate the Latin word *virgo*, grammatically and denotatively feminine, in order to specify the male virgin—a category, I would argue, that had to be stipulated not only in Tertullian's day, but also in the Middle Ages, and even today. As Monique Wittig puts it, "the mark of gender" is always feminine, never masculine.[4] Laqueur describes the mark of gender in the following way:

> it is *always* woman's sexuality that is being constituted; woman is the empty category. Woman alone seems to have "gender" since the category itself is defined as that aspect of social relations based on difference between sexes in which the standard has always been man.[5]

As such, male sexuality has remained unmarked and underexamined. Female sexuality, on the other hand, has been historically so overdetermined that Shirley Ardener argues for the linguistic term "back-formation" to describe the process of applying terms of female sexuality to "similar" facts of male sexuality.[6] In the same way that contemporary expressions like "male model" and "male nurse" foreground certain expectations about gender roles, Tertullian's qualifier in the phrase "male virgin" reveals a number of gender-driven assumptions about virginity that are still in force today.

Virginity, or the lack thereof, was crucial to female sexual and gender identity in medieval Western Europe. But what role did virginity play in male identity? What sort of narrative strategies were available to an author who wanted to represent or dramatize male virginity? Spiritual/physical purity is usually listed as one of the knightly virtues, but how does one know if a man possesses these qualities? If the "fact" of a woman's virginity could be subjected to a test or ordeal—a motif found throughout world literature across a wide range of cultures and time periods—what about a man's?

There is, I realize, a hint of a whine in that last question, partly because it is too easily answered: a man's virginity is normally not discussed or tested. In fact, male virginity hardly exists as a secular

cultural concept—let alone a physical one. Patriarchy, in which assured paternity and secured lineage and property are so crucial,
depends upon maintaining *female,* not *male,* virginity and marital
fidelity. Thus the female body has been constructed as a *readable*
body, subjected to endless explication, while the male body has been
figured as exempt from interpretation. As I suggested above, this is
true of both the texts that we read and of the critical approaches
that we bring to them. I hope to show that such a concentration on
the female body reflects—as well as reproduces—certain narrative
strategies designed to protect the male body from scrutiny, for to
focus on the male body dislodges masculinity from its privileged
position as the sign of the subject.[7]

One such narrative strategy is found in Thomas Malory's *Morte
Darthur,* in which the female body is fetishized in such a way that
we do not—cannot—look at the male body. In this text (which so
problematizes late medieval codes of knighthood) it is the masculine
body, functioning as a metonym for the social body chivalric, which
must be preserved intact and inviolate at all costs. I will argue that,
when the male body is threatened with penetration and fragmentation (words taken from the rhetoric of menaced female virginity), a
feminine and feminized body takes its place within the narrative
frame. Nor is substitution the only strategy activated to protect the
male body: we can also discern a pattern of transformation of the
masculine into the feminine for precisely the same reason—the feminized masculine body preserves the body chivalric from any real
critique.

Not only are we encouraged to look *at* the female body and *away*
from the male body, we can also look *through* the male body to
discover another man. As I read it in the *Morte Darthur,* this homoso-
cial/homoerotic line of sight is a feminizing gaze, and thus implicated in the bait-and-switch game to which I have alluded.[8] (I should
note that I am using the terms *female body* and *male body* to denote
the essentialized notion of sex in the *Morte Darthur,* and I reserve
the terms *feminine body* and *masculine body* to describe gender as
a social category; i.e., positions that are not naturalized and fixed
but negotiable and unstable. However, both ways of looking at bodies
are realized in the text—sometimes simultaneously.)

WHOSE BODY?

Male virginity in Malory's *Morte Darthur,* I had assumed, would be
most visible when it is under attack, which is when we usually see

female virginity foregrounded in romances and saints' lives. Several hagiographical legends develop a similar pattern: first, the conse- crated virgin's physical beauty is emphasized; second, as a result of her beauty (enhanced, apparently, by her unavailability), a pagan official or suitor attempts to seduce her; third, once the virgin refuses, she is stripped (or otherwise humiliated) and threatened with rape. In such a narrative, one cannot avoid "looking." When we consider the various temptations and seductions that the Knights of the Round Table face in the *Morte Darthur,* it is the female body that once again captures our attention—this time, not as menaced virgin, but as menacing seductress. Under cover of the feminine, the male virgin/ male body fades into the background.

For example, after Gareth (disguised under the name of Bew- maynes) arrives at Persaunte's castle, Persaunte commands his (un- named) daughter to visit Gareth in bed. He gives her very specific instructions: "'And lye downe by his syde and make hym no strange chere but good chere, and take hym in your armys and kysse hym and loke that this be done, I charge you, as ye woll have my love and my good wylle.'"[9] Gareth awakens to find Persaunte's daughter beside him. She tells him that her father sent her. He asks, "'Be ye a pusell [maiden] or a wyff?'" (315). His own behavior, apparently, will depend on her answer—her *body*—and not on any commitment to his own chastity.

In fact, when Persaunte's daughter says that she is indeed "'a clene maydyn,'" Gareth asks her to leave. She then reports his behavior to her father. His response: "'Truly . . . whatsomever he be he is com of full noble bloode'" (315). Obviously, it is not chastity, or, more accurately, it is *more* than chastity that is being tested here. Larry Benson would call this episode an example of "proof-of-knighthood," in which the term "knighthood" subsumes a number of different qualities, of which chastity is only one.[10] In this light, one might conclude that the subject of this "test" is Gareth's allegiance to the guest-host relationship. However, if we look again, we might detect Persaunte lurking behind his daughter's body in Gareth's bed. Using a paradigm quite different from Benson's, we can read this scene as an enactment of homosociality, in which male-male desire is "con- ducted" through the body of Persaunte's daughter.

Malory is always circumspect when it comes to scenes in which women and men lie "abed togydirs," and this scene is no exception.[11] But while the bedroom episode has no erotic content, the same cannot be said of Persaunte's speech to his daughter. Persaunte's words have a certain forbidden and ambiguous allure: he seems to commit a kind of verbal incest on the one hand, and to express a homoerotic desire on the other. And how are we to interpret the order to make "no strange chere but good chere"? We can translate this to mean simply "do not be shy" (i.e., reserved, distant, aloof). Yet in Malory's English, as in modern English, *strange* also connotes that which is alien, foreign, unfamiliar—even abnormal.

I am not saying that Persaunte's interest lies in incest or, to use the language of fifteenth-century England, in sodomy. However, this episode has the effect of destabilizing the normative relationships between daughter and father, guest and host, man and maid. And in this murkiness, what gets lost is Gareth. His body, his virginity, remain invisible, unreadable, while the virginity of Persaunte's daughter is openly displayed—though refused. And Gareth's refusal opens up a line of sight through the daughter to Persaunte, away from his own body, and thus to another relationship altogether: a relationship between men.

The female body diverts the gaze elsewhere in the *Morte Darthur*, in two parallel episodes involving Bors and Percivale as they seek the Grail. An unnamed lady begs Bors to lie with her, saying, "'I have loved you longe for the grete beauté I have sene in you and the grete hardynesse that I have herde of you'" (965). When he refuses, she threatens suicide—and murder, for she will take her twelve ladies with her. In spite of the women's pleas and threats, Bors remains steadfast. The women cast themselves down from a tower. As they do so, Bors "blysse[s] hys body and hys vysayge"—that is, blesses the very thing that we ought to be looking at, but aren't—and everything disappears in a great rush of noise (966). Apparently, that was no lady.

Percivale meets a woman who claims that she is a "'jantillwoman . . . diseryte'" (917). She invites him to her pavilion for a feast. After drinking strong wine with the lady, Percivale

> was chaffett [heated] a lityll more than he oughte to be. With that he behylde that jantilwoman, and hym thought she was the fayryst creature that ever he saw . . . [Percivale] profird hir love and prayde hir that she wolde be hys. Than she refused hym in a maner whan he requyred her, for cause he sholde be the more ardente on hir. And ever he sesed nat to pray hir of love. (918)

She makes him promise to be her "'trew servaunte.'" He swears, appropriately enough, "'by the feythe of my body.'" She has a bed made up, and lies down "unclothed." Percivale also lies down "naked," which may mean that he removes all of his clothes, or, simply, that he disarms (918). He happens to glance at his sword, which is also "naked"; i.e., out of its scabbard. As he gazes upon the crucifix in the pommel, he begins to have regrets, and makes the sign of the cross. The lady, the devil in disguise, departs on the wind, "rorynge and yellynge" (919).

Both episodes represent a well-known and well-documented misogynist intertext in which female desire is demonized—here literally. Moreover, in both instances, the devil, indicated as masculine in the text, is the real body in woman's dress and flesh—the homoerotic with a whiff of brimstone. More important still is the larger "body" that is being tested through Percivale and Bors: the secular body chivalric, the code that bonds knights in service to another man—namely, Arthur. And, of course, the sacred body chivalric is at stake in the Grail Quest, undertaken on behalf of Jesus Christ himself.

When I first began to look closely at these and other episodes involving Gareth and Launcelot, it seemed to me that my own line of sight—*my* temptation, perhaps—was directed toward the female body and away from the male body.[12] As the passages I cite reveal, it is not anything overt in the text that would cause me to read this way. Instead, I had assumed that the appropriate point of view would be a naturalized male one, and therefore I looked *with* Gareth, Bors, and Percivale. One can recover the textual and critical context for such an immasculated reading when one considers the classical, patristic, medieval, and modern discussions of virginity, its temptations, and its proofs. As noted in the introduction to this volume, patristic and medieval descriptions of chastity and virginity include a range of emphases, from the simple fact of physical intactness to a more capacious notion of spiritual integrity. As we read from Tertullian to Aquinas, from *Hali Meiðhad* to The Physician's Tale, virginity is commonly inflected as feminine. We can trace the origins of this development back to the consolidation of the Christian Church in late antiquity and the early Middle Ages. Briefly, what is at stake here is not just the virgin and her body, but the thing that they have come to represent: the body of the Church. These two bodies are equated many times in patristic texts. For example, Jerome says that "no vessel of gold or silver was ever so dear to God as the temple of a virgin's body."[13] Ambrose says the virgin is a living *templum Dei*.[14] Historian Peter Brown, in his reading of Jerome and Ambrose, calls the early virgins of the Church "human boundary-stones," whose presence marked a "privileged, sacred space."[15] A violation of a consecrated virgin was emphatically a violation of the Church. Thus virginity became essential to the construction and continuance of the Christian Church.

This is not to say that women and only women marked the boundaries of the Church through their bodily and spiritual chastity.[16] However, in the hierarchy that evolved in the early Church, male celibacy
acquired its own distinctive historical and discursive power.[17] When
we talk about male virginity in the Church, it is useful to distinguish
between, first, the history of clerical continence; i.e., chastity in the
context of the evolution of a Christian priesthood in which compulsory virginity eventually became the norm, and, second, the personal
commitment to virginity that any Christian man or woman was invited
to make. It should be added, however, that in making such a distinction we artificially separate the private and public functions and va-
lences of virginity, which, in reality, are historically interrelated. Its
deficiencies aside, this distinction between types of virginity allows
us to see that while clerical continence continued to be a subject
of sometimes acrimonious debate within the Church, the praise of
virginity-by-choice remained constant even as its realization took
different forms at different times. John Bugge, for example, traces
out what he calls the "sexualization" of virginity in the monastic
culture of twelfth-century Western Europe—"the irretrievable identification of virginity with womankind," as he puts it.[18] This association
of the feminine with virginity (at its most obvious, a way to exert
control over the unruly and dangerous female body) proved to be
quite a productive trope for the remainder of the Middle Ages and
beyond.

In addition to what we find in patristic writings and the medieval
commentaries on them, the concept of virginity/chastity is also (and
predictably) constructed as feminine in medieval medical and scientific treatises and in their classical antecedents. In their almost exclusive focus on the female/feminine body, medical texts succeed in
making the male body disappear. The rhetoric of virginity, no matter
the discourse, is always overtly feminized; therefore, as I attempt to
examine male virginity in the following pages, I often must do so by
analogy, using female virginity as the standard by which male virginity may be identified or verified.

DO MEN HAVE A HYMEN?

The question "Do men have a hymen?" is a facetious one if we think
strictly in terms of anatomy, but it is a serious question in the context
of social roles and how such roles have been historically marked,
measured, and regulated.[19] Yet we must also ask: do *women* have a
hymen? The answer, from a medical standpoint, is "Only some-

times."[20] Today, the primary physiological "sign" of virginity in women is considered to be the "unruptured" or "unbroken" hymen; "proof" of first intercourse is the flow of hymeneal blood. I use scare quotes here to emphasize that even at the end of the twentieth century, the hymen is commonly figured in ways that do not coincide with the known medical facts: the ridge of venous tissue that typically constitutes the hymen can vary so much from woman to woman that the hymen is not very useful as an indicator of virginity. In fact, in medieval medical texts, the presence of a hymen was recognized as but one of many physiological signs of virginity.

The hymen hardly exists as a concept in classical texts (it is discussed once, only to be dismissed),[21] and is mentioned only rarely in medieval medical texts; however, this does not mean that virginity was thought to be untestable or undiscoverable. For instance, some medieval physicians acknowledge that there may be bleeding at first intercourse, and that this is useful information to have. But a urine test is much more reliable: if a woman's urine is clear, white, and sparkling, she must be a virgin. If it is cloudy and dull, she is not. If her private parts are narrow, she is a virgin; if not, she is not.

In some medieval medical texts, most notably in the thirteenth-century gynecological treatise known as *The Secrets of Women*, at the very moment it is asserted that virginity can be tested, it is recognized that virginity can be faked.[22] A dove's bladder filled with blood, inserted into the vagina, and designed to break at the climactic moment, is one such circumvention of proof of virginity.[23] Taking a warm bath infused with certain herbs (to tighten the muscles of the vagina) on the wedding night is another. There are no virginity tests or prescriptions for faking virginity for men in these medical treatises.

Literary texts also contain a number of tests of chastity for women. These typically involve some sort of magical object—a drinking horn, for example, from which only chaste women may drink without spilling a drop. Most women fail the test. In the Italian version of the Tristan legend, *La Tavola Ritonda*, six hundred and eighty-six women fail the horn test.[24] Medieval romances also include tales of women who fake their virginity or their fidelity to their husbands, or who survive an ordeal or a test through some verbal legerdemain. Iseut is the example *par excellence* of the equivocal oath in Béroul's *Romance of Tristan* (twelfth century) and its retellings.

These and other tests and ordeals of female chastity are clearly labeled and foregrounded in the romance plot. As a result, the reader cannot avoid thinking about and imagining the female body and its purported secrets. There are no narratives in which the male body is subject to speculation and no explicit attempts to ascertain male virginity. I would argue, however, that there are many narratives in which the questioning or proofing of male virginity is implicit. In these cases, the test, such as it is, is submerged in the plot, the masculine body a mere Derridean trace.

MENACING LAUNCELOT

Let us consider how Launcelot is "tested" throughout the *Morte Darthur,* in one-to-one combat and in various encounters with ardent maidens. Both kinds of tests bear similarities to the more fully articulated chastity tests to which women in romance are subjected. In the *Morte Darthur,* the Grail Quest is the supreme test of chastity and of knighthood. In the end, Launcelot is denied the full vision and experience of the Grail because of his sin—however, the exact nature of this sin is left open to interpretation. Is it lust of the body, or pride? Devotion to Gwenyver that exceeds his devotion to God? A fondness for killing?[25]

I am particularly interested in the manner in which Launcelot passes numerous tests of chastity and of knighthood when it would appear to the reader that he shouldn't. The text oscillates between demonstrating that Launcelot is invincible because he is pure and furnishing us with evidence that he is not so pure. It has been argued that Launcelot remains a virgin until he is tricked into having intercourse with Elayne (approximately halfway through the *Morte Darthur*), and that the first time that he has sex with Gwenyver is after Mellyagaunce abducts her.[26] However, I believe that the *when* and the *how* of Launcelot's virginity is deliberately left ambiguous in the *Morte Darthur.*[27] Recall that Launcelot, like many a consecrated virgin before him, possesses certain healing powers. Launcelot cures the wounded Melyot de Logrys in the adventure of the Chapel Perelus. Later, Launcelot is the only knight who is able to heal Sir Urré. In fact, as if to emphasize Launcelot's unique gift, Malory lists the names of one hundred and ten knights, including Arthur, who had attempted to cure Urré, but were unable—or unworthy—to do so.[28] This episode, apparently original with Malory, follows immediately after "The Knight of the Cart"—that is, after Launcelot clearly and explicitly has had intercourse with the queen.

Consider further that Launcelot is able to defend Gwenyver against numerous accusations, regardless of the status of his bodily and "social" virginity (and regardless of the queen's fidelity, of course). In theory, Launcelot never fails Gwenyver—as Bors reproachfully puts it to the queen, "in youre ryght nother in youre wronge" (1052). First,

Launcelot defeats Sir Mador in a judicial trial-by-combat after Gwenyver is accused of poisoning Sir Patryse. While Gwenyver is indeed
innocent of this crime, she and Launcelot *are* guilty of adultery. In
theory, Launcelot lacks the ritual purity necessary for such a trial-by-
combat. The question of Launcelot's virginity, and the consequences
of that virginity, are left ambiguous. Second, Launcelot (fresh from
the queen's bed, as it were) triumphs over Mellyagaunce in another
trial-by-combat, a battle that he should have lost by reason of his
own impurity. Finally, and most spectacularly, Launcelot saves Gwenyver from burning after he is ambushed in her bedchamber. In the
latter two episodes, Launcelot makes a series of equivocal statements
about his and Gwenyver's innocence that, while they may be techni-
cally true, reveal a distinct gap between *verbum* and *res.* Consider
what Launcelot says after the ambush: "I shall . . . prove hit uppon
ony knyght . . . that my lady, quene Gwenyver, ys as trew a lady unto
youre person *as ys ony lady lyvynge unto her lorde,* and that woll I
make good with my hondis" (1188, emphasis mine). Does that mean
that Gwenyver is faithful absolutely? Or simply as faithful as anyone
might expect; i.e., faithful in comparison to other women? It follows
that Launcelot is *just as* "trew" as Gwenyver.

Throughout the *Morte Darthur,* it seems that Launcelot's prowess
is not tied to the "fact" of his virginity, but nevertheless his prowess
can be interpreted as "proof" of his virginity. It is not that Launcelot
is exempt from the rules—secular *and* sacred—that seem to govern
chivalric behavior in the *Morte Darthur;* rather, chivalry and its reali-
zations are always already flawed, contradictory, and relative. It
seems that perfected knighthood, like perfected virginity, resists
representation.

Nacien the hermit is the first critic to supply us with a (postmodern) reading of Launcelot, telling Gawayn that Launcelot "ys nat stable" (948). Nacien seems to recognize that "Launcelot" is a site of
contradictory and often ironic meanings, whether he happens to
represent the man who is Arthur's best knight or the very ideals of
knighthood. He is both chaste and an adulterer; he is worthy enough
to see the Grail and yet not. Launcelot's virginity is both affirmed
and denied in the *Morte Darthur,* and this single contradiction illustrates in small not only how the text resists any sort of closure, but
also how virginity itself resists final resolution.

In order to compare the testing of female chastity with that of male
chastity/knighthood, let us look at a very explicit test of women's
chastity that occurs at King Mark's court in the *Morte Darthur.* Morgan

le Fay sends a magic drinking horn to Arthur, but Lamerok intercepts it and sends it to King Mark instead. Malory describes it as

> a fayre horne harneyste with golde, and the horne had suche a vertu that there myght no lady nothir jantyllwoman drynke of that horne but yf she were trew to her husbande; and if she were false she sholde spylle all the drynke. (429)

Queen Isode and one hundred of her ladies drink, and "there were but four ladyes of all tho that dranke clene" (430). Mark swears that Isode and the others will be burned at the stake, but his barons overrule him, saying "playnly they wolde not have tho ladyes brente for an horne made by sorcery.... For that horne dud never good, but caused stryff and bate" (430). The infidelity is thereby erased, and blame is transferred from the women to the now-maligned and untrustworthy horn—and away from any critique of the men and their relationship to Mark. This transference is necessary, of course, for if the very bonds holding society together are destroyed—namely wives, sisters, and daughters—the "stryff and bate" would be unbearable.

According to the same logic, if men could not "pass" the test of knighthood, if Launcelot were not able to furnish proof-of-knighthood upon demand, then all that Arthur's Round Table stands for would be nullified. The male body (like a woman's virginity) is of value only in paradox: when it is at once inviolate *and* sacrificable. Extremes, such as the absolutely unassailable body or the irreparably wounded and broken body, would leave no game to be played at all. What is needed is a body that breaks and heals, breaks and heals over and again, and Launcelot becomes the paradigm for such a body.

So far, I have been arguing that, to the degree to which female virginity is overdetermined, male virginity is underdetermined, and can be made intelligible only by reference to an elaborate feminized and feminizing signifying system. Such a system allows another, but related, story to emerge in the *Morte Darthur,* as we shall see.

THE PLEASURES OF THE HOMOEROTIC

As the knights of the Round Table make their vows to find the Grail, Arthur says:

> "nevyr shall I se you agayne *holé togydirs,* therefore ones shall I se you *togydir* in the medow, all *holé togyders!* Therefore I woll se you all *holé*

togyder in the medow of Camelot, to juste and to turney, that aftir youre
dethe men may speke of hit that such knyghtes were here, such a day,
holé togydirs." (864, emphasis mine)[29]

The Grail Quest will indeed sunder the body chivalric, fragmenting
it irrecoverably. Arthur's lament emphasizes the importance of communal integrity, and, through its very excess of repetition, reveals
its fragility.

The word *togydirs* also links this passage with two distinct but
parallel moments repeated over and again throughout the *Morte
Darthur*: first, the times a knight and a lady lie "abed togydirs," and
second, the times when two knights, spears at the ready, rush "togydirs" at one another in the first heat of battle.[30] Fellowship, sexual
intercourse, and the *pas d'armes* become points on a circle, part of
a tautological tangle.[31]

While seduction troped as battle is overt enough in medieval
texts—the assault on the Rose in the *Roman de la Rose* comes
immediately to mind—battle troped as seduction is a more subtle
phenomenon. Still, it is possible to recover moments when spears
and swords substitute for, and perhaps extend, the phallus/penis. We
can discern a pattern in Malory (and in other medieval romances)
in which bed and battlefield stand in chiastic relation to each other.
There is, however, one difference: on the battlefield, the Other—so
often figured as female—is male.[32] In the clash between the hero
and this male Other, "virginity" of a different sort appears to be at
stake, while the imagery remains essentially the same: the imagery
of submission, penetration, and triumph.

I would argue that such imagery underwrites a common discourse
that constructs descriptions of one-to-one combat *and* intercourse
in the *Morte Darthur*, a discourse in this instance that figures the
homoerotic in terms of heterosexual coupling. Thus the more threatening end of the homosocial continuum, i.e., male-male desire, is
suppressed in one part of the text only to surface elsewhere, in the
ritualized "courtship" of battle.

We find a rather bizarre enactment of the homosocial/homoerotic
(in which blood takes on a feminine valence) in the triangle that
develops between Tristram, the unnamed wife of Segwarydes, and
King Mark. Mark attacks Tristram out of jealousy—he himself is attracted to Segwarydes's wife—and seriously wounds him. Tristram
rides from this encounter to tryst with Segwarydes's wife, and "eyther
halsed other in armys" (394). (Tristram puts down one set of arms
to take up another.) However, "in hys ragynge [Tristram] toke no
kepe of his grene wounde that kynge Marke had gyffyn hym, and so

. . . bledde bothe the over-shete and the neyther-shete, and the py-lowes and the hede-shete" (394). Segwarydes comes home to find "hys bedde troubled and brokyn." Segwarydes concludes—though the text does not explain how—that only a wounded knight could have left such blood, the sheets serving, then, as a sort of knightly Veronica's veil.

In a comparable episode, Launcelot enters into Gwenyver's chamber in Mellyagaunce's castle. In his eagerness, he lays hold of the iron bars on the windows and cuts his hand "thorowoute to the bone." He goes "to bedde with the quene and toke no force of hys hurte honde, but toke hys plesaunce and hys lykynge" (1131). As a result, "all the hede-shete, pylow, and over-shyte was all bebled of the bloode of sir Launcelot" (1132). Mellyagaunce, who apparently shares with Segwarydes a talent for reading sheets, assumes Gwenyver has slept with "som" of the wounded knights who lie near her bedchamber—the very knights who were wounded in their heroic attempt to rescue the queen. Here indeed is an excess of fellowship—or, at least, fellowship as it is imagined by Mellyagaunce, who has already tried, unsuccessfully, to crash the Arthur-Gwenyver-Launcelot triangle.[33]

In "Symbolic Sexual Inversion and the Construction of Courtly Manhood in Two French Romances," Gary Ferguson suggests that the blood on the sheets is multivalent, evocative of menstrual blood, hymeneal blood, circumcision—and even the "blood" of lineage.[34] This is a productive way for us outside the text to "read" the bloody sheets. In effect, both Tristram and Launcelot reverse gender roles: no longer readers of feminine bodies, they are instead made readable by the bodily fluids they leave behind.[35]

Yet I am more interested in how the blood on the sheets is read *within* the text. After all, the significance of the blood seems to be clear to Segwarydes, Mellyagaunce, and, apparently, to all of Gwenyver's knights who crowd her bed for a look at the sheets. Granted, Gwenyver is surrounded by ten wounded knights, so Mellyagaunce's conclusion makes some sense. But there are no wounded knights in the Tristram episode, apart from Tristram himself. One could explain this episode away by describing it as one of the many instances of doubled plot (here imperfect) that characterizes the *Morte Darthur.* However, what the two episodes have in common is that the interpreters of bloody sheets make the woman—usually conveniently and obviously inserted between men—a conspicuous absence.

I see these two acts of interpretation—reading bloody sheets—as radical examples of slippage in the text. The knights read past the feminine to gaze directly upon the masculine, which is just the opposite of the way that I was reading the stories of Bors and Percivale earlier. The knights cannot "see" the woman in these scenes because in the homosocial relationship, she has no originary power or agency. The blood on the sheets is read *by* men as saying something *about* men because they have so completely appropriated the feminine that it is here reconstituted as a sign of the homoerotic. Just for a moment, the true relationship between men is exposed. Gwenyver is then hastily reinserted into the story, charged with treason, and sentenced to burning at the stake. And as we have seen, Launcelot passes a test he ought to fail when he successfully rescues the queen—in spite of both their guilt.

The case of Segwarydes's wife is more complicated. The episode is apparently designed to highlight Mark's enmity and jealousy, providing one more reason for the craven Cornish King to hate Tristram. Yet the episode also sends ripples through the text in quite another direction. The triangle, in which the (unnamed) lady finds herself between Mark and Tristram, expands to a quadrangle when the lady's lawful husband sees the sheets. Then the quadrangle becomes a pentagon when Sir Bleoberys comes to court and asks Mark to give him "'the fayreste lady in your courte'"—who turns out to be, in Bleoberys's estimation, Segwarydes's wife (396). Tristram decides to stay out of any rescue attempt (it's a matter of honor, he says [397]), until he hears how badly Bleoberys has beaten Segwarydes. He then rides after Bleoberys. They meet and fight to a standoff. The wife of Segwarydes is told to choose between the two combatants, and she picks Bleoberys, for, she says, Tristram had abandoned her. He is therefore a shameful knight. Bleoberys and Tristram himself agree with this assessment, and Bleoberys decides to give the lady back to her husband. Now I think that one would be hard put to find a more blatant example of the commodification of women or of the primacy of the homosocial bond anywhere in the *Morte Darthur*. Yet this sequence of exchanges—in which the lady is so speedily passed from one knight to another—seems to parody homosociality, not to affirm it, and opens up a space for a critique of the body chivalric within the text.

In the world of the *Morte Darthur*, social roles are radically constrained by gender, and are continually reproduced as binarized, exclusionary positions. As Joan Cadden puts it, "in spite of the possibility of middle terms admitted by medical theory" in the European Middle Ages, we find a relentless drive toward a "binary typology."[36] In other words, one "must" be either masculine or feminine—which is not to say that the *Morte Darthur* succeeds in realizing such an imperative, but only to acknowledge the resulting tensions from any attempt to do so. This dynamic allows for the possibility that it is not two "men" who are engaged in battle in the text, but, in effect, one "man" (the triumphant knight) and one "woman" (the defeated knight). The body chivalric remains intact, because, once again, "women" are consigned to its margins.

HYMENEAL PERFORMANCES

I want to return to a scene that I have suppressed in my reading until now: what Percivale does after his diabolical lady vanishes. At this point, Percivale moves clearly into our line of sight as he draws his sword, and declares, "'Sitthyn my flessh woll be my mayster I shall punyssh hit'" (a comment original with Malory). The narrator takes over at this point: "And therewith he rooff hymselff thorow the thygh, that the blood sterte aboute hym" (919). As the blood flows from his wound, Percivale laments: "'How nyghe I was loste, and to have lost that I sholde never have gotyn agayne, that was my virginité, for that may never be recoverde aftir hit ys onys loste'" (919).[37] The thigh is a common enough euphemism for the genitals; thus it seems that Percivale intended to make an eunuch of himself, "for the sake of the kingdom of heaven" (Matthew 19:12). However, taking a cue from Peter Brown's discussion of Origen's reputed self-castration,[38] I'd like to suggest that castration is too dangerous and too extreme a remedy, for it calls into question what it means to be a man, and therefore destabilizes the premises of the homosocial bond. Within the context of a homoerotic constructed by a feminine/masculine binary that consistently feminizes the "other" knight, a different reading of this self-mutilation is possible.[39] Percivale enacts on his own body what an Other, demon lover, would have done, effectively taking his own maidenhead in a ritualized enactment of intercourse. Being feminized (or feminizing oneself) assures social and sexual difference more safely than castration, which consigns the castrated to a place outside difference.

Thaïs E. Morgan's remarks on transvestite female impersonation have relevance here:

> I regard female impersonation in any context as suspect *for women*—potentially misogynist because it too often turns out, upon closer analysis, to be a mockery and expulsion of the feminine in men by men. . . . At the same time, I see female impersonation as liberating *for men*—potentially disruptive of normative heterosexual masculinity.[40]

Morgan adds, "the sex-gender system . . . often operates *not despite but through* gender crossing" (emphasis mine).[41] In other words, when the strict binaries of feminine/masculine, female/male are to some degree destabilized and subverted, such subversions do not free up these polarities, but lock them into place. It might be said that, when a knight is defeated on the battlefield and forced to take a submissive posture, he switches social categories and is feminized. He simply cannot "be" masculine *and* "be" defeated simultaneously. Such a transformation guarantees the working of the body chivalric by keeping at least one man on top.

So men do have a "hymen," a cover that effectively shields, not the individual man, but the idea of manhood. The hymen that culture has imposed on the feminine body, on the other hand, reveals an obsession with (or perhaps a fear of) fragments and fragmentation. It is a metonym that reduces a woman to less than the sum of her parts. The masculine hymen, however, is generalized to cover the entire body chivalric; as such, it is metaphoric, and greater than the sum of his—their—parts.

GALAHAD "YS A MAYDE"

In his essay, "The Double Session," in a now notorious move, Derrida appropriates the hymen, which he describes as "a closeness and a veil," as

> first of all a sign of fusion . . . It is not only the difference (between desire and fulfillment) that is abolished, but also the difference between difference and nondifference.[42]

Derrida, of course, is fully aware of the masculine/feminine binary that he has created. He goes on to collapse the masculine/feminine together in order to arrive at hymen, and then reconstitutes the binary *in* hymen. One result is that the hymen functions as/is figured as both an opening and a cover. In Malory's *Morte Darthur*, this contradiction is embodied by Galahad.

When we compare Galahad to the other knights of the Round Table, we see that he is the only man whose virginity is foregrounded. A hermit tells Gawayne that Galahad "'ys a mayde and synned never, and that ys the cause he shall enchyve where he goth'" (891). And Mordrayns says to Galahad: "'For thou arte a clene virgyne above all knyghtes, as the floure of the lyly in whom virginité is signified. And thou arte the rose which ys the floure of all good vertu, and in colour of fyre'" (1025). Galahad makes a well stop boiling, described as "a sygne of lechory that was that tyme muche used. But that hete myght nat abide [Galahad's] pure virginité" (1025). He also heals Mordrayns, who is said to have waited four hundred years for the Grail Knight—and, of course, he heals the Maimed King. Most important, and most famously, he is the only knight who is able to behold the Grail without impediment.

Yet in spite of these accomplishments, Malory's Galahad remains a curiously static character. The battles he fights do not help Galahad grow into knighthood in any way (as, say, Gareth's adventures do by helping him enter into homosociality). Alone among the knights of the Round Table, Galahad is not tested: he is simply affirmed in his monumental monologism. From start to finish, Galahad escapes penetration and dismemberment; he dies intact, his soul translated into heaven.

In short, Galahad never enters into the homosociality that so often drives Malory's *Morte Darthur*. He does not participate in any exchange; he never circulates or is circulated. Galahad exists outside *any* sociality; in fact, he prevents sociality from ever becoming fully realized, even before he comes to Camelot: the Syege Perelous is a rupture, a site that predicts the final destruction of the Round Table. Galahad's very place at the Round Table (itself rather like the hymen) is a breach.

Galahad is the "sygne" *par excellence* of the threatening feminine that Arthur's knights work so hard to suppress.[43] More accurately, he is in excess of this sign, more feminine than the feminine itself in his inviolateness. Virginity, constructed as it is in the realm of the social, always carries within it the potential for its own loss—a paradox not lost upon the early Church Fathers. They were so concerned about the fragility of chastity that they insisted on sequestering the virgin to protect her from prying eyes and lascivious thoughts, either of which could lead to the loss of her chastity/virginity. Similarly, Malory's Galahad is shielded from bodily and spiritual penetration, both within the text, in that he remains unscathed by sword and temptation, and outside the text, in that he resists any final or complete reading.

In this essay, I have tried to imagine how the hymen—a phantom body part—might serve as a sign for the male virgin. Yet, as the figure of Galahad demonstrates, the male virgin seems to have no place in the *Morte Darthur*'s system of signification; he is an impossibility, just as a male virgin equipped with a hymen is an absurdity. However, it is necessary to invoke such a figure in order to make visible a narrative in which masculinity and virginity are equally threatened by the feminine. (Why else do Jerome, Ambrose, and others masculinize the virgin in the first place, if not to save her from her own nature?) Menaced masculinity in the *Morte Darthur* looks very much like imperiled virginity, because at the moment of crisis on the battlefield, loss is gain: as the masculinity of the weaker knight begins to destabilize, it reemerges in a new, more powerful form in the figure of the triumphant knight.

Part II
Virginity in the Renaissance

Il Trionfo della Pudicizia: Menacing Virgins in Italian Renaissance Domestic Painting

CRISTELLE L. BASKINS

VERGINE, Onesta, Casta: injunctions to women in early modern Italy to guard their chastity as the highest form of feminine virtue appeared everywhere from sermons and preaching to treatises devoted to the management of the family and from debates over the equality of the sexes to advice offered to exceptional women humanists.[1] The monotonous repetition of the theme sounds from Francesco da Barberino to Torquato Tasso and beyond. In Paolo da Certaldo's *Libro di buoni costumi* (fourteenth century), for example, a woman's reputation for chastity is compared to a beautiful flower and a husband's crown.[2] Francesco da Barbaro urges wives in his "On Wifely Duties" (1416) to be, "or at least seem to be, chaste in that sort of temperance from which chastity is derived . . . lust and unseemly desire are harmful to their dignity and to their husbands, even when they later say nothing about it."[3] Giannozzo, one of the male participants in Leon Battista Alberti's dialogue, *Della Famiglia,* composed in the 1440s, tells his wife that, "nothing is so important for yourself, so acceptable to God, so pleasing to me, and precious in the sight of your children as your chastity. The woman's character is the jewel of her family . . . her purity has always far outweighed her beauty."[4]

The speakers in Baldasssare Castiglione's dialogue, *Il Cortegiano* (1528), move beyond rhetorical comparisons of chastity with flowers, jewels, and crowns to ponder the construction of exemplary female chastity in the service of men. Giuliano de'Medici challenges the misogynistic Gasparo: "But if you will acknowledge the truth, you surely know that of our own authority we men have arrogated to ourselves a license, whereby we insist that in us the same sins are most trivial and sometimes deserve praise which in women cannot be sufficiently punished unless by a shameful death or at least a perpetual infamy."[5] Whether or not *Il Cortegiano* wages an effective critique of patriarchal social organization, the dialogue presented there registers much of the ambivalence and contradictoriness of what Stephanie Jed has recently called "chaste thinking."[6] In Jed's formulation, the conflation of textual/sexual purity by early humanists like Coluccio Salutati results in an endless cycle of castigation so that every gesture towards purification of the text or the body risks further contamination and pollution. Virginity emerges in Renaissance discourse, then, as both an idealized and overdetermined state of feminine virtue and as a site for the exercise of misogynistic assumptions about women's limited capacity for sexual restraint.

While early modern men, women, and their families may have taken for granted the concept of conjugal chastity, it is worthwhile to pause over this construction of legally and spiritually sanctioned sexuality. Again the figure of Giannozzo from Alberti's *Della Famiglia* offers revealing advice to his young wife: "see that you never want another man to share this bed but me."[7] But Giannozzo's admonition to his wife to observe conjugal chastity does not address the transition a young bride must make from virtuous virginity to conjugal sexuality. How did Renaissance brides imbued with "chaste thinking" make that shift from maiden to matron—how did they learn to pay the marital debt? In those negotiations concerning marital chastity, as Elizabeth Cohen reminds us, the language of debt, payment, and exchange makes virginity a commodity.[8] Fifteenth- and sixteenth-century wedding furniture, including elaborately painted and historiated *lettucci* (beds), *cassoni* (dowry chests), and *spalliere* (wainscotting), is a domestic commodity employed in conspicuous consumption; it also offers an opportunity to examine Renaissance marriage ideology through the visual imagery geared for the primary spectatorship of brides and grooms.[9]

By the late fifteenth century in Florence grooms of the elite patrician class customarily redecorated a chamber within the family residence destined for the new couple's use.[10] The commissioning of decorations in anticipation of an imminent marriage frequently marked the beginning of a man's artistic patronage; the initial purchase of decorated wedding furniture might be followed by commissions for religious pictures and sculpture as well as by *deschi da parto* (painted birth trays) presented to parturient mothers.[11] The groom normally contracted with a shop specializing in domestic pictures, but we know too little about actual commissions to ascertain how and by whom the subject matter was chosen.[12] We can assume that given the considerable expense of wedding furniture and the connection to marriage, which represented not only a critical life-cycle event but also a social and political one, that the selection of subject matter was not casual. Imagery displayed in the nuptial chamber probably aimed to edify by means of example and perhaps even more concretely to inspire the conception of children and thus the expansion of the patriline.[13]

One of the most frequently illustrated subjects in Renaissance domestic painting is the poem cycle, the *Trionfi*, composed by Francesco Petrarca in the 1340s.[14] In a dream vision the *Trionfi* narrator describes Cupid/Love being vanquished by Laura/Chastity, who is in turn defeated by Death. Fame overtakes Death, but Time conquers Fame, and the ultimate victory is granted to Eternity.[15] Of the six triumphs, the only physical combat occurs between Cupid/Love and Laura/Chastity. The parade format of the six sequential chariots tends to emphasize smooth transition rather than conflict; in manuscript illuminations, maiolica, tapestries, and paintings the *Trionfi* always appear as a series of personifications riding triumphal chariots in imitation of the triumphal procession granted to victors in ancient Rome.[16]

The *Trionfi* illustrated on wedding furniture complimented Renaissance brides who themselves went on a ceremonial procession from their father's to their new husband's home. Contemporary moralists like San Bernardino inveighed against the pomp and vanity of the bridal cavalcade, costume, and jewelry. But social historians today note the temporary nature of such triumphs; the festive welcome of the finely dressed and bejewelled bride soon faded to memory as new duties and regimens of the household taught a young wife her place.[17] Jewelry might be pawned, showy garments sold, and dowry money used without a wife's consent according to the needs of her new husband and his family.[18]

A fifteenth-century Florentine bride would have viewed Petrarchan *Trionfi* on painted wedding furniture with a particular set of expectations and associations; her own temporary triumph in the form of a bridal procession prefaced the conquest of her virginity and transformation into a sexually active spouse. Yet, the Petrarchan *Trionfi* trace a development from physical, sexual love to the renunciation of Cupid, just the opposite course of the itinerary followed by contemporary brides. For them the state of chastity must be overcome but only by a chastened and disciplined conjugal love, not by the irresponsible, unpredictable passion inspired by Cupid. Just as the notion of conjugal chastity reveals contradictions within its construction, so too the display of Petrarchan *Trionfi* on wedding furniture must work to conceal the lack of fit between occasion and subject and thus, to blur the distinction between compliment and coercion. Domestic pictures illustrating the *Trionfi* simultaneously must encourage the bride to abandon her fiercely maintained chastity to the needs of the patriline and yet to renounce illicit, physical passion;

such pictures have to convert the menace *to* virginity into the menace *of* virginity.[19]

Of the dozens of examples of *Trionfi* commissioned for domestic display, the most extensive treatment of the battle between Cupid and Chastity as described by Petrarca appears in a series of *spalliere* attributed to Gherardo del Fora and dated to the late fifteenth century.[20] This cycle, intended for an unknown patron, originally consisted of three panels each 90 to 100 centimeters in length. Scanning the first panel from left to right we see the abandoned chariot of Cupid flanked by his exemplars, followed by the central scene of the *Battle between Cupid and Chastity,* and further to the right a group of personified Virtues. The second panel opens with the *Castigation of Cupid* followed by the triumphal procession of Chastity, her celebrated followers and the captive Cupid. A late nineteenth-century description records the composition of the third panel, now lost. Accompanied by Scipio, Chastity leads Cupid in chains to the Temple of Chastity, which is guarded by Joseph and Hippolytus, and there she deposits her laurel crown.

Gherardo del Fora is exceptionally attentive to the text of Petrarca's poem, unlike other Renaissance artists who invent visual details to fill in the scanty imagery of the *Trionfi*. In the first panel the chariot of Cupid, drawn by four white horses and led by Jupiter, encourages the viewer to look to the center of the composition, where Gherardo del Fora positions the battle between Cupid and Chastity as a symmetrical, gracefully choreographed assault. Cupid appears as an adult nearly-nude male with only a flutter of drapery artfully concealing his genitalia; this is not the childish Cupid bound to make errors and indulgently reprimanded by his mother, Venus.[21] Rather, as in Petrarca's *Trionfi,* Cupid and Chastity are well-matched warriors. Each figure advances toward the center on opposing legs, drawing the free leg back as if in a *pas de deux*. Cupid's left arm mirrors Chastity's own shield-bearing left arm; their opposing arms pull back or upward in a complex compositional *contrapposto* suggesting both variety and resemblance.[22]

Petrarca opens his account of the battle with epic imagery:

> As when two lions roaring in their rage / together crash, or blazing thunderbolts / plunge downward, riving air and earth and sea, / So I saw Love, with all his armaments, / Moving to capture her of whom I write, / Swifter than flame or wind in her defense. / And far more terrible than the mighty sounds / Of Aetna shaken by Enceladus, / or Scylla and Charybdis in their wrath, / Was the first clash of the two combatants—/ the outcome of the dread assault unsure—/ Nor have I words to tell of it aright.

Gherado del Fora, *The Battle of Cupid and Chastity*. *Center:* London, National Gallery (photo courtesy of the Trustees of the National Gallery). *Left and right:* author's photos, locations of originals unknown.

Gherardo del Fora, *Triumph of Chastity*. *Left and center:* author's photos, location unknown. *Right:* Turin, Galleria Sabauda (photo courtesy of Alinari/Art Resource, N.Y.).

As the narrator piles up bestial, meteorological, and seismic similes, the individual protagonists come to represent elemental forces of nature. Despite Cupid's rapid and fierce attack, like that of a leopard, Chastity fends off his arrows like a "fencer" or a "ship's pilot" equipped with valor and honor (49–51).

Gherardo del Fora presents Chastity expertly using her shield to deflect the arrows of Cupid; the pointed central boss and flaring scalloped edge of the shield suggest aggression, as well as optical fascination. The elaboration of the surface of the shield with its floral inlay and glinting highlights equates feminine ornament with martial display. The shield also conceals Chastity's face from Cupid's gaze, thus doubly protecting her from physical as well as optical assault.[23] Petrarca's narrator adds that this is the very shield that Perseus employed to bring Medusa to her death; thus, the impenetrable barrier of the shield frustrates but also protects the male viewer. In confronting the threat, Cupid and his stand-in, the male viewer, also experience a thrill, a *frisson*, of reassuring manhood.[24]

One of Cupid's arrows appears to break mid-flight and others litter the ground between the two opponents: "His gilded shafts, lit with the flame / Of amorous beauty, and in pleasure dipped, / Were by the coldness of her honor quenched" (67–69). Despite Cupid's impossibly close aim and determined stance, his exertions have no effect on his female opponent. In addition to the shield, Chastity wields "a chain once dipped in Lethe's streams— / A chain of diamond and topaz, such / As women used to wear, but wear no more" (121–23). Only this chain forged of the hardest precious stones and infused with infernal strength will be able to render Cupid a captive in the Temple of Chastity. The narrator of Petrarca's *Trionfi* engages the rhetoric of sumptuary display when describing the chain just as he had previously done in describing the shield; he implies that while women once possessed adamantine chastity, they now require moral as well as sartorial discipline.[25] Alberti echoes this sentiment in his equation of jewels and a woman's pure character. If Chastity carries glittering, jewel-like weapons, she is the exceptional woman who proves the rule; the majority of women adorn themselves with jewelry out of an immodest and immoderate love of finery and male attention, rather than as armor against unwanted sexual advances.

The prominent display of Chastity's chain invokes not only feminine ornament but also martial fury of the kind displayed in Antonio Pollaiuolo's nearly contemporary engraving, conventionally titled *Battle of the Ten Nude Men*. It has been argued that the chain linking Pollaiuolo's pair of opponents not only plays on the slippage between *vinco, vincire* (to fetter) and *vinco, vincere* (to conquer) but that it also connotes more generally bondage to the flesh and mortality.[26] If so, a Florentine spectator might see in Chastity's chain not only the power to conquer Cupid/Love but also the unchaining of the soul through the death of the body. In any event, Gherardo del Fora's extraordinary display of the *Battle Between Cupid and Chastity* draws on a host of visual sources in order to suggest the seriousness of the conflict and its consequences and to mystify the battle of the sexes. Equipped with a shield and chain, the menacing virgin Chastity defends herself only too well; her deft employment of masculine weaponry will prove more successful than the phallic arrows of Cupid, which fail to hit their mark or shatter on contact.

Chastity's victory, like that of other weapon-wielding women, the Amazons or Judith, provides an extreme example both of feminine virtue and masculine renunciation. Actual women were constantly encouraged to be modest in their glance, decorous in their movements, and to avoid vigorous, athletic, or strenuous activities.[27] Violent women whose behavior was deemed criminal were especially abhorrent in early modern Florence and subject to punishments including public whipping, hanging, and burning.[28] And domestic violence, widowhood, and prostitution led to the establishment of charitable organizations increasingly put under bureaucratic state supervision.[29] Against this social and cultural background the violent defense of Chastity and the defeat of Cupid emerge more clearly as projections rather than prescriptions for actual behavior. Through Petrarca's association of Chastity with the ferocity of lions, thunderbolts, and earthquakes, Florentine patrician men could excuse a temporary surrender before the force of nature itself. At the same time, a woman's refusal to marry and her resistance to conjugal sexuality called forth not praise so much as pressure to conform with patrilineal family strategy. Granting power to women, in terms of their vigilant maintenance of chastity, simultaneously justifies the exercise of control over women, the need for discipline and surveillance.[30]

In the *Trionfi* the narrator describes Chastity's conquest of Cupid as "favored by Heaven" and rewarded by a "thousand shining palms of victory . . . wrested from his hands." The narrator detects fear, grief, shame, and wrath on Cupid's face but soon his words fail: "I leave untold things glorious and great / That I beheld and dare not tell" (115–16). The moment of masculine defeat at a woman's hands is literally unspeakable. When the narrator resumes speech he takes up the theme of the castigation of Cupid by Chastity's exemplars. As in Petrarca's text, Gherardo del Fora's second *spalliera* foregoes the climactic conclusion of the battle and instead features the post-defeat scene at left margin: "Lucretia and Penelope were first, / For they had broken all the shafts of Love / And torn away the quiver from his side, / And they had plucked the feathers from his wings" (132–35). The nude, seated figure of Cupid is surrounded by a group of women who secure his arms behind his back, scatter and destroy his weapons, and tear the feathers from his detached wings.

If Florentine painters rarely depicted the *Battle between Cupid and Chastity,* as Gherardo del Fora's unique version suggests, the *Castigation of Cupid,* in contrast, appeared frequently in domestic painting. In the roughly contemporary *Triumph of Chastity* by Jacopo del Sellaio, four women riding atop the triumphal chariot similarly break Cupid's bow and arrows and tear the wings from his back while Chastity stares ahead, unconcerned with her adversary's humiliation.[31] Gherardo del Fora's *Triumph of Chastity,* which follows the castigation scene, resembles Sellaio's treatment of Chastity in her chariot, shield and laurel branch in hand, with a captive Cupid riding at her feet. A Sienese contemporary, Girolamo di Benvenuto, devotes an entire *desco da parto* (birth salver) to the chastisement scene; the nude, blindfolded Cupid yields to Lucretia, Penelope, and the other chaste exemplars who confiscate his weapons and pluck the pink and yellow feathers from his wrists, ankles, and back.[32] The women, whose figures are attenuated and delicate, nevertheless apply themselves vigorously to their task while the kneeling figure in the foreground exposes a surprisingly deep decolletage.

Perhaps the most violent chastisement of Cupid appears in a cycle of fresco decorations commissioned for the 1509 wedding of Borghese Petrucci and Vittoria Piccolomini in Siena.[33] The Casa Petrucci *Castigation of Cupid* by Luca Signorelli features a kneeling Cupid whose arms are in the process of being tightly bound by an extremely muscular and vigorous follower of Chastity. Her counterpart on the left is just about to snap off the plumes from Cupid's wing while another woman uses her knee to break his bow into two pieces and render it useless. The background vignettes illustrate the moments before and after the foreground event. In the left background, the followers of Chastity dash headlong like Maenads; two women wrestle with Cupid, one bending down to bite his calf while the other crushes him at the waist in a devastating stranglehold. The physical assault here resembles nothing so much as the airborne defeat of Antaeus by Hercules; in order to conquer him, Hercules had forcibly to separate Antaeus from contact with the earth that gave him strength. Likewise Cupid's power is no match for the strength of the maidens who stop him in his tracks, tripping and crushing the god of

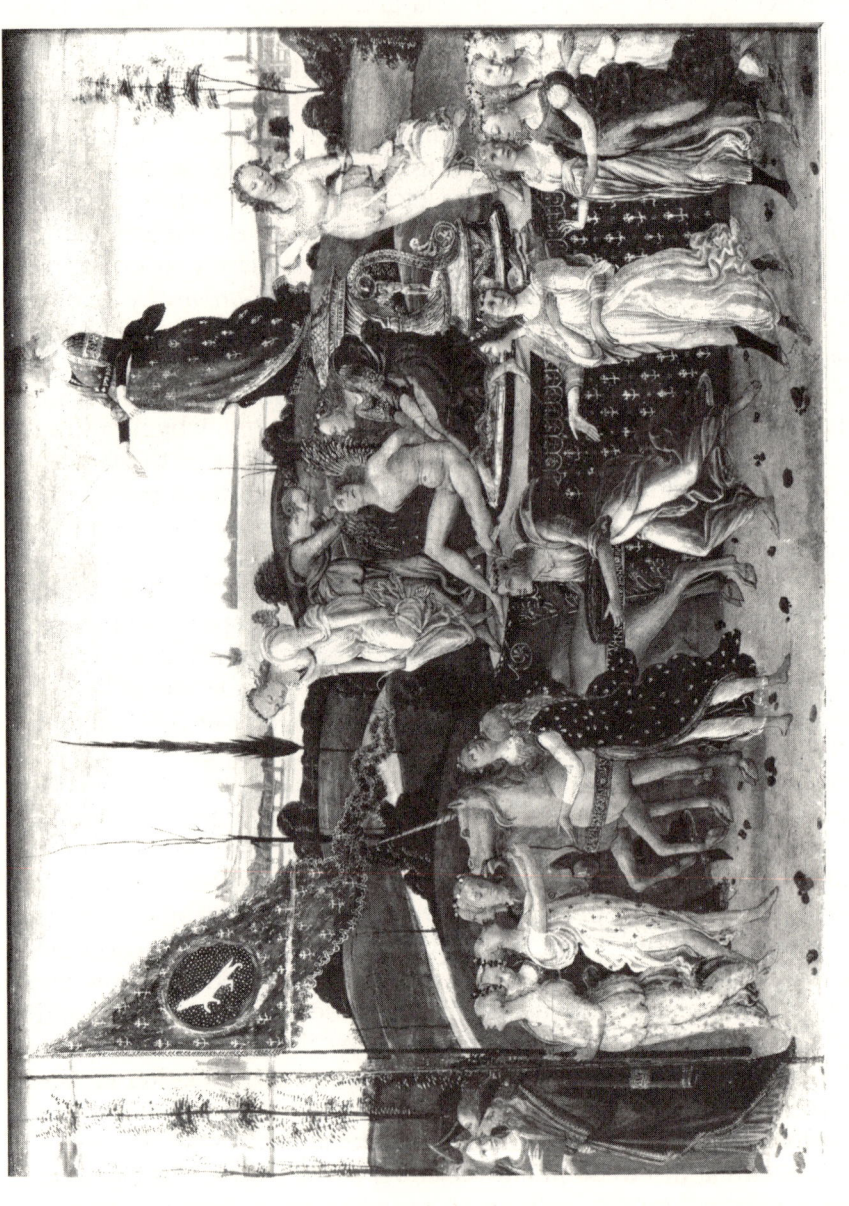

Jacopo del Sellaio, *Triumph of Chastity*. Fiesole, Museo Bandini (photo courtesy of Alinari/Art Resource, N.Y.).

Girolamo di Benvenuto, *Castigation of Cupid*. New Haven, Yale University Art Gallery, James Jackson Jarves Collection (photo courtesy of Yale University Art Gallery).

love in mid-stride. In the right background Chastity and her followers parade in triumph with Cupid in tow.

Renaissance spectators of these images of the *Castigation of Cupid* could be expected to read the compliment to vigilant chastity as well as to gauge the irony of such representations of feminine violence. In Francesco di Giorgio's panel of *The Defeat of Cupid and Cupid Led Captive to the Temple of Chastity* for the 1464 marriage of a Sienese couple, Gabbriello di Paolo Gabbrielli and Portia di Giovanni Luti, the followers of Chastity not only bind the arms of Cupid behind

Luca Signorelli, *Castigation of Cupid and Triumph of Chastity.* **London, National Gallery (photo courtesy of the Trustees of the National Gallery).**

his back but they also burn his chariot and beat to death the white horses who had once conveyed the god of love in splendid pageantry.[34] On the left side of the panel, a unicorn pulling the chariot of Chastity and her followers menaces Cupid's backside with his horn. Cupid, nude among the lavishly costumed exemplars of Chastity, is further isolated from the other figures by his position at the head of the procession. His facial expression conveys Petrarca's list of competing emotions: fear, grief, shame, and wrath. Is it fanciful to see in the solitary figure of Cupid an echo of the groom, relatively ignored in nuptial events in comparison with the pomp and display accorded to Renaissance brides? Blindfolded and bound, but still in possession of his golden wings, Cupid approaches the Temple of Chastity where he will be chained to a jasper column and guarded by Joseph and Hippolytus. Chastity wears a transparent veil on her head and holds her shield as she rides toward the temple; "there the fair victress spread her glorious spoils / and there she left the crown that she had won, / the sacred laurel crown of victory" (184–86).

The ornamented temple appears to have two entrances, one on axis with the defeated god of love and the other oriented toward the frontal plane; the spectator, rather than Cupid, has the privileged view of the entrance to the temple. The new bride and groom, spectator-recipients of this picture, are encouraged to focus on the altar and the temple interior soon to become Cupid's prison.[35] The threshold of chastity thus appears as a penetrable space and as a container walled in by the low parapet surrounding the structure; the architectural analogy between the closed virginal body of the bride and the husband who will cross that privileged threshold is explicit in a variety of vernacular sources as well as in Renaissance architectural treatises.[36]

Gherardo del Fora's lost panel, the climax of his ensemble, is known only through a description, which conforms in general with Francesco di Giorgio's version of the scene: "The second panel represents Cupid, nude, chained up in front of the chariot conducted by women, entering a temple with a portico and carved columns. In the distance another group of women may be seen near a marble column topped with a statue. In the foreground two young men are seated near the chariot and two unicorns."[37]

Although the appearance of Laura as Chastity and her many female adherents encourages an association of that virtue with women, male figures other than the defeated Cupid also march in the procession of chaste exemplars. Luca Signorelli and Francesco di Giorgio include the male figures mentioned by Petrarca in their compositions; by concluding the Triumph of Chastity with Scipio, Joseph, Hippolytus, and Spurrina, Petrarca implies that men are the rightful recipients of the laurel crown of victory as well as the guardians of the temple. In the Petrucci fresco of the *Triumph of Chastity,* Scipio can be identified as the armor-clad soldier who looks toward Cupid and grasps his dagger as if contemplating a death blow. The other soldier presumably represents Hippolytus and the young, dark-haired figure at the right margin should be Joseph. In Francesco di Giorgio's picture Scipio and Hippolytus face front and link arms below the seated figure of Chastity, while Joseph moves against the direction of the procession; Joseph's red cloak not only ripples with his motion but it also reminds the viewer that Potiphar's wife makes her accusation of adultery by means of the cloak left behind when Joseph flees her sexual advances. Francesco di Giorgio positions the nude, bound Cupid in vertical alignment directly above the head of Scipio as if to

Francesco di Giorgio, *Triumph of Chastity*. Los Angeles, J. Paul Getty Museum (photo courtesy of the J. Paul Getty Museum).

indicate the bipolar possibilities of masculine sexual behavior, lust and continence.

These male heroes of chastity engage varying degrees of ambivalence; Scipio achieves fame for returning a female prisoner of war to her rightful fiancé rather than deflowering her himself, Hippolytus kills himself to avoid the sexual overtures of his stepmother Phaedra, and Joseph barely escapes the charge of adultery made by Potiphar's wife. The Tuscan youth, Spurrina, mentioned by Petrarca but not illustrated, scars his face so that women will have nothing to "fear" from his beauty. Each example of male chastity takes place against the very threats to feminine sexual purity supposedly guaranteed by Chastity's triumph and Cupid's imprisonment: rape, incest, adultery, and uncontrollable passion. If Scipio's prisoner of war plays no part in the struggle over who claims the right to her virginity, Phaedra and Potiphar's wife actively pursue illicit sexual gratification. And the Tuscan women can only control their fearful desire once Spurrina disfigures his face. While it may be supposed that chaste men threatened by unchaste women provide a symmetrical counterpoint to the female exemplars of Chastity, Petrarca positions the men at the culminating point of the triumph and he leaves Cupid in their supervision. Within a few lines of the next triumph Chastity will die when Death plucks a "single sacred golden strand of her hair" (114–15); the weapons that once proved successful against Cupid are useless against Death.

If Borghese Petrucci and Gabbriello di Paolo Gabbriello commissioned their respective domestic pictures in order to celebrate the virtue of their brides and to stimulate conjugal chastity, the very imagery employed reminded viewers of the commodification of virginity in a culture driven by dowry exchange and patrician alliance. The figure of Cupid may have encouraged male viewers temporarily to relinquish control during nuptial festivities and newlywed dalliance, but the chaste male heroes also reminded the new husband of his duty to guard the temple of chastity: i.e., his wife, since his own crown of honor and reputation ultimately rested there. For her part the young bride could identify with the vigilant maintenance of chastity illustrated by Chastity's followers, but her claim to virtue would be undercut by the reminders of lustful women and wayward wives like Phaedra and the wife of Potiphar, who beset exemplary chaste males.

Renaissance domestic pictures with their conventional, formulaic iconographic types and personifications conveyed the most nuanced of double messages, transforming the menace *to* virginity into the menace *of* virginity. Such pictures suggest that what haunts patriarchy is not so much the sexually available or insatiable woman as the resistant, impenetrable body of the virgin conjured into being only in order to be disavowed.

Metaphor and the Mystification of Chastity in Vives's *Instruction of a Christen Woman*

Nancy Weitz Miller

> Socrates . . . affirmed that the greatest fortresse and defence that
> nature had given to a woman for the preservation of her reputa-
> tion and honour was Chastity. . . . So that woman which is
> adorned with Chastity, is safely armed against all inordinate affec-
> tions whatsoever.
> —Robert Greene, *Penelope's Web*

> All richest Pearles, Gold, Jewels heere below,
> Are nothing to this Gem of Chastitie.
> —Robert Aylett, *Peace with her Foure Garders, viz.*
> *Five Morall Meditations*

> The accomplishment of the aim of biology has been entrusted to
> the aggressiveness of men and has been made to some extent
> independent of women's consent.
> —Sigmund Freud, "Femininity"

Eᴀʀʟʏ modern conduct books for both sexes are founded upon the
notion that one's outward behavior directly reflects one's inward
state. There is a notable difference, however, between the way the
manuals for each sex present their subject matter and, consequently,
how their advice may have been received by their readers: the advice
encoded in conduct literature for girls and women is deceptively
vague in stark contrast to directives intended for boys and men. *De
Civilitate Morum Puerilium*, Erasmus's grammar school manual for
boys, explicitly connects social conduct with the project of education
and contains practical advice for controlling bodily functions, achieving pleasant table manners, and conducting polite discourse: "Let
him close the fart under color of a cough"; "To lick thy fingers greasy
or to dry them upon thy clothes be both unmannerly; that must rather
be done upon the boardcloth or thy napkin"; "To interrupt any man
in his tale before it be ended is against manner."[1] Although female
conduct literature developed as an offshoot of the humanist educa-

132

tional project that sought to teach intellectual, moral, and social virtues together, girls were largely excluded from the curricula of formal study established for boys.[2]

Humanist educators did, however, develop regimens intended to improve the moral sense of the "weaker" sex. A few years before Erasmus wrote *De Civilitate,* Juan Luis Vives published his compendious *Instruction of a Christen Woman.* This conduct book for girls and women thoroughly avoids such graphic, physical advice, insisting instead upon the importance of chastity and the presentation of a modest demeanor without explicitly describing how to achieve such ideals. Originally written in Latin in 1523, *Instruction* was commissioned by and dedicated to Catharine of Aragon as an educational manual for her daughter Mary Tudor, though *Instruction*'s readership extended far beyond these royal patrons: the book was widely published throughout Europe in thirty-six English, Castilian, French, German, and Italian translations. Moreover, the first English translation (around 1529) by Richard Hyrde, a tutor in Thomas More's household, ran to eight complete editions by 1592.[3] Indeed, the book attempts to formulate a general and broadly applicable regimen for rearing and educating women.[4]

The advice contained in *Instruction,* with its overarching concern for the retention of female sexual purity throughout the entire span of a woman's life (as untouched virgin, faithful wife, and celibate widow) codified a way of thinking about women and their relationship to sexuality that rapidly dispersed through the middling and upper classes of the female populace. But the seemingly simple message to remain chaste that Vives exhorts to his female audience is founded upon an inconsistency that would make it impossible for his readers ever to approach his ideal of moral excellence. Hidden below the layers of abstract and figurative discourse that Vives employs to convey his message with eloquence and authority lie tensions that stem from an attempt to justify the Neoplatonic belief in the appreciation of physical beauty as inherently good, while perpetuating the traditional popular misogyny that condemns women for leading men into vice.[5] These battling ideologies simultaneously objectify and subjectify women, who are at once the passive objects of male desire and the agents that create that desire. The juxtaposition of two conventional metaphors to represent chastity signals this ideological clash as *Instruction*'s rhetoric conveys to its readers the "mystery" of chastity; this strategy aims to contain the virtue textually and evade its contradictions by maintaining Manichean oppositions. In effect, Vives locates the impetus for male sexuality in women and then instructs those women to become asexual, a quality that is supposed to deter lust and inspire "holy" love. Thus *Instruction* holds women responsible for male desire *in toto,* even in the extreme case of rape.

The sheer length of the work somewhat belies Vives's prefatory comment regarding the simplicity of a woman's need for instruction: "a woman hath no charge to see to but her honesty and chastity. Wherefore when she is informed of that, she is sufficiently appointed" (sig. B2).[6] Janis Butler Holm offers a possible explanation for Vives's copiousness on this mandate for chastity when she writes, "Vives's practice of *copia* could be viewed as decorous, as effecting a masterful elaboration of a simple social formula while attempting to compensate for the insufficiency of that formula, its failure to be definitive."[7] Yet, not only does this social formula fail to be definitive, it also fails to be inherently, logically stable, which could very well impel the author to write at length, forcing the concept to hold still under the sheer weight of words. Instead of the practical "dos and don'ts" that Erasmus's pupils receive, *Instruction*'s readers are lectured, wheedled, goaded, and frightened into keeping their chastity always foremost in their minds through a variety of examples and maxims that prove contradictory under close scrutiny.

Although it would have been a relatively simple matter for Vives to instruct convent-bound women to remain chaste, his task here is a more difficult one: the women he addresses are and will continue to be intimately connected to men for most of their lives in both sexual and nonsexual relationships. Vives insists, "this I would not that only maidens should think spoken unto them, but also married women and widows, and finally all women" (sig. G3ᵛ). Even Book One, which addresses the rearing of young virgins, constructs a chastity that is contingent upon virginity's temporary state (surprisingly, this pre-Reformation text does not refer to a woman's choice to remain virginal in a monastic life): the chastity of the virgin delineated in *Instruction* is intended to lead to marriage and is thus always-already compromised by the specter of sexual activity. The virgin must achieve that careful balance between drawing the attention of one man (her future husband) and maintaining asexual purity to discourage other men, a dilemma addressed by a series of patristic and Neoplatonic dualistic distinctions between "true" virtues, which can be known by certain signs, and "false" virtues that are evil masquerading as good.[8] Of particular interest are the distinctions between true and false beauty and sacred (spiritual) love and profane (fleshly) desire. Vives's *Introductio ad Sapientiam* (1524) establishes his thoughts on human nature, which consists of a divine soul, containing the seats of intellect and passion, and an animal body, all of which must retain their proper order. Sin comes from disorder—the rebellion of the animal passions—and wisdom consists in recognizing the "true" value of whatever appears to be "good."[9]

In *Instruction*, Vives endeavors to construct chastity as a barrier, impenetrable from both sides, that separates a woman from sexual passion and saves her and the men with whom she comes into contact from the dangers of lust. Chastity also becomes the locus for the entire gamut of positive attributes that define feminine perfection, subsuming all other qualities into and beneath it: "Chastity is as the queen of virtues in a woman, and that two inseparable companions ever follow it, and that of shamefastness cometh soberness, of which two cometh all the other sort of virtues belonging unto woman" (sig. M2). In this genealogy of virtue, chastity begets shamefastness, which begets soberness, and other virtues (e.g., frugality and devotion) stem from these last two scions of the reigning matriarch. As such, no other virtues can exist in a woman if chastity is not initially in residence, and once gone, the others vanish with it. This, of course, is tantamount to claiming that there are no other female virtues; qualities such as shame and soberness are smaller building blocks that help to erect the chastity monolith.

The success of such a monolith depends upon mystification, which lends it an aura of divinity and makes incomprehensible the ideology that drives it. Vives's use of figurative language mystifies by cloaking the contradictions lurking within his construction of chastity, and this project is largely dependent upon metaphor to initiate a chain of deferral, facilitating the signifier's drift further and further away from the signified.[10] Despite its copiousness, *Instruction*'s precise definition of chastity remains elusive, as its metaphors both define and defer: they seem to clarify and concretize the abstract concept, yet they also inflate the definition to encompass contradictory significations. These metaphors signal that a gap indeed exists in the apparently seamless logic of the text. Two categories of metaphor dominate the discussion: the economic metaphor, likening chastity to a "treasure" or "prize," constructs the virtue as a desired commodity; and the martial metaphor, the "armor" or "fort" of chastity, highlights the perception that male sexuality seeks to conquer a resistant woman and chastity is the power that allows her to resist that assault. Used in conjunction, as Vives does, the metaphors produce a conflict in internal logic: chastity is simultaneously a defensive force protecting women from injury and a defenseless object itself in need of protection from theft. Both metaphors also turn the virtue into an object distinct from the bearer of the virtue.

The economic metaphor transforms chastity from an innate quality, a mode of being or behaving, into a material object that a woman carries enclosed within her body. This transformation gives a woman agency—in fact, sole responsibility—for whatever may befall her, as it allows Vives to heap blame upon women who "lose" their chastity. The virtue is thus, in the language of the economic metaphor, a woman's most important possession, her greatest treasure or prize: a maid "hath within her a treasure without comparison" (sig. F2^v); "thy price cannot be esteemed if thou join a chaste mind unto a chaste body" (sig. F4). As the receptacle of a woman's entire social value, nothing could be worse than to lose this prize:

> She that hath once lost her honesty should think there is nothing left. Take from a woman her beauty, take from her kindred, riches, comeliness, eloquence, sharpness of wit, cunning in her craft; give her chastity, and you have given her all things. And on that other side, give her all these things, but call her a naughty pack; with that one word, thou hast taken all from her, and hast left her bare and foul. (sig. G4^v)

Without this treasure, a woman is empty of all that belongs to her sex, and, as the protective vessel is meant to remain sealed until marriage, the loss of her prize requires an intentional opening of her body. Yet, "one word" spoken against her chaste reputation can strip her of her treasure, and according to *Instruction*, only the truly ignorant or thoughtless virgin would allow such a self-negating loss: "The ungracious maid doubteth not to lose that which . . . she shall by no means recover again when she hath once lost so great a treasure that ever she had" (sig. G2).

Moreover, the economic metaphor correlates with the notion of a wife's function in marriage as a "keeper" of that which her husband brings home: "Aristotle saith that in housekeeping the man's duty is to get, and the woman's to keep. Wherefore nature seemeth to have made them fearful for the same purpose, lest they should be wasters, and hath given them continual thought and care for lacking" (sigs. I2^v–i3). *Instruction* asks the virgin always to have her future function in mind: "If a woman remember, it shall cause her to take better heed and to be a more wary keeper of her goodness, which alone, though all other things be never so well in safety, so lost, all other things perish together therewith" (sig. G4). Only the "wary keeper," the woman who understands her economic role, is a fit marriage partner, will perform her wifely duties properly, and truly deserves the appellation "woman."

Vives's mystification of chastity also relies upon the often chaotic movement from one economic metaphor to another in both precepts and examples, tacitly befuddling the reader and undermining her attempt to fix upon either a definition or a logical course of action. While positive examples are sprinkled throughout the book, Vives expends much of his rhetorical force in creating negative examples— a pedagogy of fear—to frighten the maid into retaining her prized chastity. The consequences of engaging in premarital sex, he suggests, are shame and community ostracization. The grand style of this dire warning resonates with language that objectifies chastity and makes the virtue material:

> Everyone shall think themselves dishonested by one shame of that maid: what mourning, what tears, what weeping of the father and mother and bringers up. . . . What cursing will there be of her acquaintance, what talk of neighbors, friends, and companions, cursing that ungracious young woman; what mocking and babbling of those maidens that envied her before; what a loathing and abhorring of those that loved her; what fleeing of her company and deserting, when every mother will keep not only their daughters but also their sons from the infection of such an unthrifty maid. (sig. G2^v)

The rhetorical strategy works on the fear that other young women (and men!) can in fact "catch" unchastity from the unfortunate young woman who has "lost" her virtue. The economic metaphor is here disrupted by an image of pollution: a woman who engages in adultery is *ipso facto* polluted by that sinful act.[11] It is not so much the absence of chastity but the presence of sin that leads to pollution: the notions of retention and loss obvert into a paradox in which the absence of chastity is necessarily the presence of sin (and vice versa). The presence of sin consequently destroys a woman's value. *Instruction* offers several examples of men who have seen fit to kill their unchaste female relatives:

> I know that many fathers have cut the throats of their daughters, brethren of their sisters, and kinsmen of their kinswomen. . . . In Spain . . . two brethren that thought their sister had been a maid, when they saw her great with child, they dissembled their anger . . . but as soon as she was delivered of her child, they thrust swords into her belly and slew her, the midwife looking on. . . . Histories be full of examples and daily ye see. (sigs. G2^v–G3)

As the sole purpose of the young woman's life is to be married well, the unchaste woman is a worthless commodity. She is common, cheap, easily attained, a contagion or blot to her community, unable to enhance her family's social status, unworthy to live: "If it be well considered, women be worthy these punishments, and much worse, that keep not their honesty diligently" (sigs. G3^v–G4).

The keeper of such an insecure object (the loss of which leads to pollution) must therefore find ways to preserve it, not only to shield it from possible theft but, more crucially, from her own desire to give it away, not only as a passive object, but as a desiring subject must she be constrained. The contemporary misogynistic discourse that represents women as vice-loving, sensuous creatures without a dependable faculty of reason to rein in their desires is at the heart of this necessity to protect women from themselves. Vives's *De Officio Mariti*, a marriage guide for men, attests to the author's opinion that women are naturally defective in passion control, and, while women can be improved by male guidance, they cannot be profoundly changed.[12] Thus much of *Instruction* aims to get virgins to protect their chastity from their own sexuality, as young women are susceptible to lust: "When they begin to grow from child's state, hold them from men's company, for that time they be given unto most lust of the body" (sig. G4^v). Vives's method of instruction here has little to do with the conduct or behavior of the maid herself: his answer is external control and prohibition, as he supports the custom of sequestering virgins within the confines of the house: "A maid should go but seldom abroad because she neither hath any business forth and standeth ever in jeopardy of her chastity, the most precious thing that she hath" (sig. K4).[13] This custom serves not only to keep men away from the virgin, but to keep the virgin away from men.

In keeping with the Neoplatonic hierarchized relationship between soul and body, Vives's Manicheism constructs chastity as double-natured, "the pureness both of body and mind" (sig. F2^v). Thus even a virgin in body may be polluted by her fleshly desires:

> Be not proud, maid, that thou art whole of body if thou be broken in mind, nor because no man hath touched thy body, many men have pierced thy mind. What availeth it thy body to be clean, when thou bearest thy mind and thy thought infected with a foul and an horrible blot. O thou maid, thy mind is withered by burning with man's heat. (sig. F3^{r-v}).

The sight of men brings on the burning heat of desire, a form of penetration that, despite the virginal body, infects the soul.[14] The fire imagery, heavily laden with connotations of hell, also draws from contemporary physiology: when her humors are properly balanced, the virgin is cool and moist.[15] The penetration of dry masculine heat leads to her physiological imbalance and a sickness of the soul. Yet sin is a form of disease that is brought upon oneself, not innocently encountered. Responsibility for sin lies entirely with the maid who allows herself to "bear" a mind "infected" by gazing upon men: the maid's subjective gaze opens a conduit between her and men that actively invites penetration.

As her physical beauty is a danger to herself, it brings ruin upon the men who see her as well. This dual endangerment creates a tension between subject and object (between the desirer and the desired) and between object and object (chastity and beauty), as *Instruction*'s discussion is subtly undergirded with the idea that whether through negligence or determination, women are fundamentally responsible for the reaction that men have to them: "What guard of chastity can there be where the maid is desired with so many eyes, where so many faces looketh upon her, and again she upon many. She must needs fire some, and herself also be fired again if she be not a stone" (sig. P1ᵛ–P2).[16] To see and be seen is to desire and to be desired (and lose a firm hold on chastity), and such negligence is morally indistinguishable from the deliberate will to reject the virtue. A maid's appearance to the male beholder (when she cannot avoid venturing out into public) must therefore be carefully controlled. To go abroad clothed in costly and beautiful apparel— to adorn the body to catch the eye—is to be deliberately unchaste:

> If thou array thy body sumptuously and go gaily forth abroad, and entice the eyes of them that behold thee, and draw the sight of young men after thee, and nourish the lust of concupiscence, and fire and kindle the smell of sin, insomuch that though thou perish not thyself, yet thou shalt cause others to perish, and make thyself as a poisoner and a sword unto them that see thee. Thou canst not be excused as chaste in mind; thy evil and unchaste raiment shall reprove thee. (sig. K2ᵛ)

In a reversal of the usual power-relationship between the gazer and the object of that gaze (where the process of being objectified removes agency from the object), the object is here entirely responsible for "enticing" the sight and "drawing" the eyes of men. A virgin whose appearance draws the male gaze is an agent of destruction to the soul of the man who sees her and is attracted to her: she is responsible for the gazer's response to her. In a monstrous inversion of the proper order (as Vives would see it), the visible maid penetrates the mind of the gazer, "like a sword." In addition, her body, and the way she adorns it, is an enemy to her prized chastity; simply by existing, the body that houses the treasure endangers it.

Vives's solution to this problem is to erect a barrier between the maid and the gazer, between the treasure and the thief. To do so, he calls on the very thing that he (so forcefully) insists needs guarding. Alongside his figuration of chastity as a treasure that needs protection, Vives figures the virtue as itself a protective power through his use of the martial metaphor. By extending the argument above, we recognize that the maid's attractiveness necessarily brings her into the danger of enticing lust in a man who may be unable to control his passionate response, who may in fact take her by force. The martial metaphor suggests that the chaste maid is fully furnished with shield, armor, and weapon to fend off the possibility of physical attack.

The martial metaphor derives from the Pauline "armor of faith," and, like the economic metaphor, while it provides a material analogue to the abstract concept, its principal image is that of shielding or veiling the woman, principally from the desiring gaze. A chaste woman is a type of defender of the faith, one of the *milites Christi*, doing battle against evil. She must arm herself with "holy chastity," the quality that allows her a measure of divine protection against the "darts" of evil lust:

> Before she go forth at door, let her prepare her mind and stomach none other wise than if she went to fight. . . . Some thing shall chance on every side that shall move chastity and her good mind. Against these darts of the devil, let her take the buckler of stomach, defended with good examples and precepts, and a firm purpose of chastity and a mind ever bent toward Christ. (sig. N3)

Instruction's portrait of the warrior virgin resonates with the legends of medieval virgin martyrs, wherein the virgin's chastity is the source of her resistance to the lusty devils that threaten her.[17] In much medieval thought, as the devil's power manifested itself through the sexual organs, a Christian's power to resist the flesh and the devil lay in his or her virginal integrity, spiritual self-containment.[18] This idea supports Vives's ability to make chastity the crucial link between body and spirit.

The visible face of chastity, the quality that opposes the allure of the adorned body, is "shamefastness," the source of "true" beauty. This companion virtue works with chastity's armor, protecting the woman's virtue by veiling the body and replacing the woman's physical image with an image of the purity of her chaste mind:

> She cannot be chaste that is not ashamed, for that is as a cover and a veil of her face. For when nature had ordained that our face should be

open and bare of clothes, she gave it the veil of shamefastness wherewith it should be covered, and that for a great commendation, that who so did look upon it should understand some great virtue to be under that cover. (sig. L4ᵛ–M1)

Shame works to keep a woman constantly aware of her body, the part of her being that remains associated with pollution, while her soul, or "mind," is the potentially purifying agent. Sumptuous raiment notwithstanding, simply to allow a man to look upon her bare face is for the maid to act as an agent for evil: "Her face doth inflame young men's minds unto foul and unlawful lusts, whom she knoweth not whether she can withstand" (sig. O1). As her body is a threat to both her own chastity and the soul of the gazer, the spiritual covering of the veil of shamefastness offers the only protection: "They say that the holy virgin, our lady, was so demure and sad that if any man cast a wanton eye upon her, that foul heat was all quenched as though a man had cast a firebrand into the water" (sig. N3ᵛ). Shamefastness, by presenting the image of cold chastity, defends against the heat of lust inspired by viewing the physical body.

If the truly shamefast virgin can quench the fires of lust so successfully, what happens to the concept of rape in Vives's philosophy of chastity? Sixteenth-century definitions of "rape," which include both a sense of seizing and carrying away and of sexual force, reveal how directly that concept is implicated in the mystification of chastity.[19] A conflation of theft and sexual force is bound up with the concept of rape that obtained in England contemporaneously with the publication of Hyrde's translation of *Instruction:* the woman herself is perceived as a commodity stolen from her male guardian—she as victim is a neutral object of male conflict. *Instruction*'s economic metaphor constructs rape in accordance with that primary definition—theft as opposed to bodily injury—but in terms that shift blame onto the victim: the object of value is stolen from the woman, which in turn destroys her value, none of which could occur, however, unless the victim were a negligent keeper.

Moreover, the martial metaphor does away with the problem of rape altogether by so mystifying the protective properties of the virtue that the truly chaste woman is by definition fully shielded from ever becoming the object of sexual assault in the first place: only the unchaste can be so victimized. Vives claims that the virgin's pure condition is universally cherished: "How pleasant and dear to everybody is a virgin. How reverent a thing, even unto them that be ill and vicious themselves" (sig. G1). This insistence that even the vicious are awed by the power of chastity sets up a situation in which

the virgin can only be self-defiled. By combining the chastity metaphors, Vives implies that no man would attempt to steal that virginity,
which itself is so divine that even the word, the mystifying sign,
inspires dread:

> How much then ought that to be set by that hath oft times *defended*
> women against great captains, tyrants, and great hosts of men? . . . We
> have read of women that have been taken and let go again of the most
> unruly soldiers, only for the reverence of the name of virginity, because
> they said that they were virgins. For they judged it a great wickedness for
> a short and small image of pleasure to diminish so great a *treasure,* and
> every of them had liefer that another should be the causer of so wicked
> a deed than himself. (sig. G2, my emphasis)

When approaching the issue of rape, Vives appears unable to describe the virtue without a logical inconsistency: the use of both
economic and martial metaphors in the same passage highlights
their contradictory nature. Apparently, even the most hardened man
of war is deterred from assaulting a young woman because of the
mystery contained in her virginity, which is both protection and treasure, both deflective and attractive. Likewise, the ardent lover will
refrain from his attentions:

> For there is none so outrageous a lover if he think she be a virgin, but
> he will always open his eyes and take discretion to him and deliberation,
> and take counsel to change his mind. Every man is so sore adread to
> take away that which is of so great price that afterward neither can they
> themselves keep nor restore again. (sig. G2)

Whereas a maid may "keep" her chastity, the man who "takes" it is
left with nothing: materiality dissolves the moment the "prize" is
transferred from its rightful owner to the thief. Vives generously attributes discretion and reverence for a woman's virginity to all men,
making no exception for either the heat of a lover's passion or the
violence of a warrior's rapaciousness. Yet, he does not bestow the
same measure of discretion upon the virgins themselves, who are
always in danger of letting their passions rule them and so need to
be consistently reminded of their duty to their chastity.

Indeed, it is the virgin's only responsibility (and hers alone) to
protect herself from sexual assault by remaining pure of mind and
body in expectation of her prospective spouse. She is, in fact, given
an exaggerated amount of agency and attributed with far too much
power over others, as if she alone could entice or repel any man, as
if she were in complete control of all men's desires as well as her

own. The loss of her virginity before the marriage night is also her responsibility and hers alone, regardless of the manner of its loss. In *Instruction,* there is no possibility of forced coition; the woman is always willing, and only the most vicious maid would toss this treasure aside: "Oh, cursed maid and not worthy to live the which willingly spoileth herself of so precious a thing, which men of war that are accustomed to all mischief yet dread to take away" (sig. G2). Thus, rape is impossible. The truly chaste woman is defined by her protection from lust, and a woman who cannot repel sexual assault is clearly not chaste: "It is an evil keeper that cannot keep one thing well committed to her keeping and put in trust to her with much commendation of words, and especially which no man will take from her against her will, nor touch it, except she be willing herself" (sig. G4). In no uncertain terms, Vives asserts that a man will not assault a woman; she is always complicit in the loss of her virginity, the act is always consensual.

The virgin's chastity is really, according to Vives, only kept by her in trust until the proper time for her to turn her "treasure" over to its rightful owner: on her marriage night she surrenders her virginity to her husband. She must marry the man whom her parents approve, a man ostensibly discriminating enough to recognize and love the truly virtuous woman, and such a union is dependent upon sexual consummation. The virgin's chastity is certainly the first quality to recommend her to her prospective spouse: "If she have [chastity], no man will look for any other [virtue], and if she lack that no man will regard other" (sig. L4ᵛ). Her untouched nature makes her social capital: valuable, elite, exclusive.[20] Her chastity is also what makes her truly beautiful, in contrast to the false lures of clothing and jewelry: "It is to be judged of chastity in women that she that is chaste is fair, well-favored, rich, fruitful, noble, and all best things that can be named, and contrary, she that is unchaste, is a sea and treasure of all illness" (sig. L4ᵛ). Vives, who follows the Neoplatonic formulation that the soul is naturally drawn to beauty, explains in *De Anima* how we can recognize true beauty:

> As we judge inward goodness from outward deeds, so too we think that the face is an image of the soul and are naturally inclined to love beautiful people. . . . The most enticing looks are not the pretty ones but the graceful, the pleasant, those enhanced by modesty and admiration. Such looks are proof of a properly formed mind.[21]

The "true" beauty of shamefastness, besides veiling the body and quenching the fires of lust, attracts a kind of pure love: "No man should see [her face] covered with that veil, but he should love it, nor none see it naked of that, but he should hate it." (sig. L4^v–M1).[22] In fact, the chaste woman's entire body is so covered, beneath which veil she is abominable:

> You wives, when you put off your smocks, put upon shamefastness, and keep always—both day and night, both in company of other men and of your husbands, both in the light and in the dark—that most honest veil of nature. Let never God, let never angels, let never your own conscience espy you bare of the cover of shamefastness. For there is nothing more foul and loathsome than you be, if you be naked of that cover. (sig. F1)

The removal of this image of female humanity produced by chastity renders a woman beastly. The necessary relationship between the moral quality of the soul and the consequent beauty of the body is a problematic one, as Vives insists there is a distinction between "desire," which seeks union with the beloved only for selfish reasons, and "love," which seeks union with the beloved simply because the soul naturally craves what is good and beautiful.[23] The question is whether the male gazer's desirous response to the chaste woman can indeed be distinguished from his response to the unchaste woman.

The kind of marriage that appears in *Instruction* is founded upon a pure craving for union with the beloved that is not sexual in nature, presupposing that procreative sexuality is indeed distinct from lustful sexuality. The holy love that the ideal husband feels for his wife is described by Vives as producing a moderate and reasonable coupling only for the purpose of engendering children rather than the irrational and ultimately fruitless desire of lust. *Instruction* consistently attests to a profound distrust of sexuality as beastly and "unworthy of the soul," even in marriage.[24] Husbands are admonished with Paul's directive, "they should have their wives as vessels of generation in holiness and not in unlawful concupiscence or immoderate, as the pagans do that know not God"; likewise, wives are told, "Let them not defile the holy and honest bed of wedlock with filthy and lecherous acts" (sig. E4). How then, one asks, can we recognize which sexual acts are "holy and honest" and which "filthy and lecherous"? Men must, presumably, conduct a thorough examination of their own motives. Though male desire is dualistically (and problematically) constructed in terms of that which is inspired and sanctified by spiritual holiness and that which is generated by evil bodily lust, women are simply to be devoid of all desire whatsoever. Zenobia (despite her "pagan" status) exemplifies this perfect state:

> [She] was of so great chastity that she would not lie with her husband without she had proved before whether she . . . had conceived, and if

she had not, then was she content to suffer her husband's will again. Who would think that this woman had any lust or pleasure in her body? This was a woman worthy to be had in honor and reverence, which had no more pleasure in her natural parts than in her foot or her finger. (sig. E4^{r-v})

For Vives, the companionship of marriage is clearly a holy alliance of the souls, whereas procreation requires an essential, if distasteful, union of the body. To compensate for this necessary sexuality, Vives formulates a moderate, divinely inspired love on the part of the husband for his chaste, utterly undesiring wife, who accedes to the act in proper compliance with her husband's will and in order to fulfill her whole duty as wife and mother.

Ultimately, *Instruction* sets out to desexualize women, who had long been thought too weak in reason to competently resist the powerful animal urges of the body. By concentrating on chastity as the single most important physical, moral, and spiritual virtue that a woman can possess—by worrying it, enlarging it, and mystifying it— Vives becomes a new and powerful voice on the eve of the Reformation in the struggle to maintain a degree of Christian asceticism while accounting for the Renaissance celebration of physical beauty, which so often leads to sexual desire. By locating the root of sexual sin in women, Vives absolves men from the greater share of responsibility for their own sexual desires, leaving them free to contemplate beauty without being tainted by lust. Vives's problematic representation of the ideal woman would be read and digested by a large readership throughout the sixteenth century, and whether or not they were directly responding to *Instruction,* writers of conduct and imaginative literature alike would explore the concept of chastity in ways that resonate with the image presented by Vives.

Figuring Chastity: Milton's Ludlow Masque

Lauren Shohet

> . . . To him that dares
> Arm his profane tongue with contemptuous words
> Against the Sun-clad power of Chastity;
> Fain would I something say . . .
> —The Lady, *A Mask Performed at Ludlow Castle*

> A harlot . . . is full of words.
> —Barnabe Rich, *My Ladies Looking Glasse*

Barnabe Rich's concatenation of whorishness and verbosity represents a commonplace of early modern misogynist discourse: women who speak freely also give freely of their bodies. As Peter Stallybrass, Catherine Belsey, Suzanne Hull, and others have shown, the three cardinal feminine virtues of chastity, silence, and obedience are commonly figured to depend on one another.[1] In this context, Milton's 1634 *Mask Performed at Ludlow Castle* (also known as *Comus*) presents a paradox. Here, a chaste Lady eloquently defends the principle of Chastity, traducing the conventional link between chastity and silence. This is not to say that Milton's text is anomalous in representing the speech of chaste women. Such sixteenth-century figures as Spenser's Britomart certainly articulate their chastity; moreover, a reevaluation—however ambivalent—of women's speech, literacy, and indeed social position may be seen as one of the rare consistent factors linking such diverse strands of seventeenth-century English culture as the court of Queen Anne (culturally if not politically semi–independent of King James's purview) and the startling feminist positions of the largely plebeian Ranter sect that flourished mid-century.[2] Furthermore, Milton's *Mask* does not unequivocally embrace the possibility of chaste female speech: in the lines just prior to my epigraph, the Lady asks "Shall I go on? / Or have I said enough?" (779f).[3]

146

But Milton's *Mask* does not engage "chastity" merely as a feminine imperative; nor does it stop with a Reformist rearticulation of chastity in more inclusive gender terms (although, as I shall discuss, this is an important part of Milton's project). Rather, astonishingly, Milton takes up the issue of chastity *in a masque:* the very genre that Puritan critics most explicitly indict as "wanton." Lucy Hutchinson, for instance, associates these costumed, choreographed, musically embellished moral "entertainments"—performed on special occasions by courtiers or members of aristocratic households for the instruction and delight of their peers and patrons—with "fornication," "incest," and "adultery." Hutchinson proposes masque and sexual lewdness to be linked signs of impending (revolutionary) apocalypse: "To keep the people in their deplorable security, till vengeance overtooke them, they were entertained with masks, stage plays, and other sorts of ruder sports. Then began murder, incest, adultery, drunkenness, swearing, fornication, and all sorts of ribaldry, to be no concealed but countenanced vices."[4]

Hutchinson's critique is typical of anti-theatrical invective in broadly denouncing masque as one among several targets (here including "stage playes," other "ruder sports," and general "ribaldry"); indeed, it is masque's position at the intersection of three different cultural categories that (over)determines its status as "wanton."[5] First, masque epitomizes those aspects of general dramatic practice that are most virulently attacked by an anti-theatrical tradition concerned with what the London City fathers term theater's "hurtfull corruption of youth with incontinence and lewdness."[6] William Prynne, for instance, compounds "effeminate mixt Dancing . . . Stage-Playes, lascivious Pictures, wanton Fashions, Face-painting . . . amorous Pastoralls, lascivious effeminate Musicke . . . [and] Mummeries" as "wicked, unchristian pastimes."[7] Structurally dependent on the unfolding of an emblematic conceit or "device" through the mixed media of song, speech, and symbolic visual spectacle, masque intrinsically embraces *all* of Prynne's detested practices (whereas contemporary public theater encompasses most of them only contingently, if at all); moreover, masques culminate in masquers' "taking out" the spectators for equally inevitable "mixt Dancing." The second transgressive characteristic of masque is its permitting women to appear in dramatic spectacles at a time when their exclusion from public acting is similarly sexualized: in the words of John Rainolds, the display of women on stage would be a "disgrace to the feminine sense of shame and modesty."[8] Third, insofar as masque devices body forth figurative or allegorical abstractions, masque might be seen as the embodying quintessence of "figurative" rhetoric, in that *figurae* can connote rhetoric assuming a human "figure." Thus not only the costumed bodies that present masques but also the type of rhetoric on which masque depends constitutes an abomination in some Puritan eyes. Intriguingly, some rhetoricians invoke this third scandal—of figurative language—not in general or abstract terms but once again, as Patricia Parker has elucidated, in the same lexicon of female sexual propriety wielded in the first two types of masque critique.[9] Thus Dudley Fenner cautions that when "one word is drawn from his first proper signification to another," "this change of signification muste bee shamefest, and as it were maydenly, that it may seeme rather to be led by the hand to another signification, then to be driuen by force vnto the same."[10]

Hence, I want to consider two paradoxes together: the near-oxymoron of a Chastity who speaks, and the more traditional critical problem of an incipient Puritan and eventual Commonwealth secretary writing a text in a form so opulent, so aristocratic, and so traditionally Royalist as masque. As Maryann McGuire comments, "*Comus* is a Puritan masque[;] there is an insistent paradox in the term."[11] I think it crucial to remember that however typical of *Milton* the *Mask*'s complexities might be—the deferrals of conclusion, the corresponding subtlety of allegorical import—these characteristics are exceptional for the genre of masque. For part of the point of masque is that all present at these elite gatherings know how they are meant to go about reading the masque's pageantry. Masque relies on the interpretability of the spectacle, both on the level of "insider knowledge"—which masqued figure alludes to which guest, say, or what recent political policy the masque action invokes—and in the more exalted terms of the Neoplatonic world view that justifies elaborate (and expensive) visual spectacle as a means of contemplating the Ideal reality that lies beyond the material sphere.

By taking chastity as the central device of the Ludlow masque, Milton undertakes, I believe, to explore the challenged chastity both of his Lady and of masque figuration itself. The Ludlow masque displays two formal anomalies: first, the drawn-out question of "what's going to happen," within a genre predicated on the self-evidence of virtue and the ineluctable triumph of good; second, the principal masquers' need for the supplemental figure of Sabrina to effect closure. I shall argue that these elements reflect the complexity of the unprecedentedly interwoven strands of Miltonic "chastity."[12] Even denser than the intersection of representational and sexual categories in the anti-aesthetic construct of "wantonness" sketched out above, Miltonic "chastity" comprises personal chastity as necessary precondition for composing poetry; chastity as ethical process; chastity as mode of figuration; and chastity as epistemological and interpretive principle. The *Mask* distinguishes true chastity from three misleadingly similar foils: first, the easy recognizability of virtue in contemporary court masque; second, overly *exclusive* abstinence; and third, overly *inclusive* "charity." The *Mask*'s deferrals of resolution serve to rigorously delimit the definition of Miltonic chastity.[13] By refining various misunderstandings and erroneous half-understandings of "chastity," the *Mask* involves spectators in a figurative and interpretive process that scrupulously examines and purifies its own foundations. I shall argue that the hermeneutic of chastity this produces reconceives masque figuration as a tool that enables the masque community to undertake the characteristic Miltonic *agon* that alone can lead to truth.

Analyzing the process of chastity my reading suggests, I propose a link between the *Mask*'s model of chaste figuration, which depends on a degree of allegorical indecipherability, and the historical shift in representational practice described by Michel Foucault as the move from "analogy" to "signification": from a premodern world in which the name of a thing, ordained by God, shares the thing's essence, to a modern world in which the names of things are arbitrarily assigned by human language.[14] To conclude, I contrast the *Mask*'s logic of figuration to twentieth-century disavowals of using sexual violence as a trope, suggesting that the Freudian- and Marxist-inflected modern redefinition of "the figurative" as a symptom (the return of the repressed) presses contemporary feminism into a curious recapitulation of the very suturing of rhetorical, sexual, and ethical categories that appears so alien in Puritan attacks on representational practice.

*   *   *

In 1634, when Milton was an unknown twenty-five-year-old, the Egerton family commissioned from him a text for Henry Lawes's masque production celebrating the installation of Sir John Egerton (Viscount Brackley and the Earl of Bridgewater) as Lord President of Wales (an administrative role) and President of the Council of the Marches (a primarily judicial function). The masque was performed the evening of Michaelmas Day 1634. Bridgewater had actually assumed the duties of office previously; the formal celebration in late September marked the arrival of his wife and younger children at Ludlow Castle, also following the tradition of installing public officials on Michaelmas Day. Performed by three of Bridgewater's children and Lawes (their music tutor), among others, the Ludlow masque depicts a chaste Lady (Alice Egerton), separated from her two younger brothers in a dark wood, importuned by the hedonistic Comus to join his unchaste revelers. When she refuses, Comus immobilizes her in a magic chair and threatens her with a forced draught from his cup of hedonism. Both the captive Lady and the brothers who seek to rescue her assert the invulnerable power of "true virginity," but the fact that the Lady remains in danger through several attempted rescues compromises the masquers' claim for virginal potency. Guided to her by an Attendant Spirit disguised as a shepherd (Lawes), the brothers shatter Comus's cup of magic liquor and scatter his band. Since they neglect to break his magic rod, however, the Lady remains transfixed. The Attendant Spirit then calls on Sabrina, nymph of the nearby Severn river, who breaks Comus's spell to free the Lady. At this point the masque scene changes to reproduce Ludlow Castle, where all three children are presented to their parents. The masque's major themes thus gesture to salient aspects of its occasion: reunion of family members, celebration of chastity (in the person of the fifteen-year-old Alice), and the judicious evaluation of evidence necessary in the *Mask* for the Lady to penetrate Comus's seductive rhetoric and in the Welsh Marches for Bridgewater to competently discharge his newly undertaken duties of hearing appeals to local legal decisions.[15]

CHASTITY AND VIRTUE

Although the Egertons' commission was undoubtedly a vocational and social coup, Milton's attempting a masque remains surprising in light of his stated objections to spectacle and emblem in both political and religious life—expressions that certainly run counter to contemporary claims for masque representation as a privileged way to edify spectators and participants. Written in rebuttal of Stuart apologies for monarchical absolutism, Milton's *Eikonoklastes* singles out the masque-like iconicity of Stuart kingship as dangerously deluding to ruler and subject alike. Suggesting sycophantic Royalist masque to be a metonymy for monarchy itself, Milton sarcastically equates Stuart authority with the manipulation of theatrical "court-fucus" [cosmetics] and "painted feathers."[16] Such "quaint Emblems and devices," Milton warns, "will doe but ill to make a Saint or Martyr" (*CP* 3.343). Where *Eikonoklastes* argues that rational discourse rather than icons must underlie legitimate government, *Of Reformation* criticizes analogous ritual pageantry in the religious sphere. Repudiating the rich liturgical symbolism advocated by Anglican Archbishop William Laud, Milton claims that spectacle obscures spiritual truth: "*Faith* need[s] not the weak, and fallible office of the Senses, to be either the Ushers, or Interpreters, of heavenly Mysteries" (*CP* 1.519–20). For Milton, ornate Laudean ritual constitutes a repulsive "new-vomited Paganisme of sensuall Idolatry" (*CP* 1.520); a bitter pun in *The Reason of Church-Government* recasts the celebratory *masque* of such sacred practices as deceptive *mask:* "Do not, ye Church-maskers . . . cover and hide [Christ's] righteous verity with the polluted cloathing of your ceremonies . . . ye think by these gaudy glisterings to stirre up the devotion of the rude multitude; ye think so, because ye forsake the heavenly teaching of S. *Paul* for the hellish Sophistry of Papism" (*CP* 1.828). Milton thus rejects the didactic theory of spectacle espoused by such secular masque scriptors as Ben Jonson, who explains in the preface to *Hymenaei* that munificent spectacle makes the masque community "not onely studious of riches, and magnificence in the outward celebration, or shew; (which rightly becomes them) but curious after the most high, and heartie *inuentions,* to furnish the inward parts . . . which . . . should always lay hold on more remou'd *mysteries*."[17]

By contrast, Milton does not believe the didactic ends of ornate spectacle to justify the bedazzling means. Rather, he uses these seductive means to draw participants into a masque experience whose implicit critique of conventional masque hermeneutics emerges— like the error of Satan's arguments in *Paradise Lost*—only after spectators have begun engaging the masque. Where contemporary court pieces like Thomas Carew's *Coelum Britannicum* employ masque figuration to mystically celebrate the status quo by rehearsing moral allegories whose resolutions are immutably intertwined with the ascendancy of the aristocrats and royals who portray the masque's most important virtues, the Ludlow masque plays *off* of traditional masque expectations. Although Leah Marcus's focus is political, her description of the *Mask*'s relationship to its genre illuminates its epistemological implications as well: "Milton deliberately arouses generic expectations about masquing structure and political strategy only to subvert them."[18] The epistemological basis of Stuart court masque lies in the static, Neoplatonic self-evidence of virtue, power, and error: the masquer in Jonson's *Mask of Beautie* who asks another to identify the king ("Albion") is chided: "What ignorance dares make that question? / Would any aske, who MARS were, in the wars?"[19] But in the Ludlow masque, new problems keep arising, changing the shape of the challenge at hand. Each time the masque approaches a resolution, the masquers discover that this interim point is insufficient: the Lady thinks she has found succor in the

rustically disguised Comus, but he transforms into an urbane seducer; the humanist Elder Brother successfully navigates a philosophical conundrum, but realizes this has failed to locate his missing
sister; the brothers locate the Lady and break Comus's cup, but find
the Lady still transfixed. The masque's title itself constitutes a refusal
of masque convention about establishing meaning: by titling the
piece after the place of performance instead of after its "device" or
theme, as is standard for Stuart (although not Elizabethan) masques,
Milton presents the masque community with the initial challenge of
discovering just what its central concern might be. As several readers
have noted, moreover, the Lady is vulnerable to Comus precisely
when she relies on traditional masque epistemology in which appearance equals reality, taking him on first encounter to be a "gentle
shepherd" (271)—the trustworthy leader of the masque proper—
rather than the antimasque villain whose convincing disguise and
spurious but beguiling arguments must be exposed.[20]

When Jonson didactically explains that masque spectacle should
inspire philosophical inquiry "after the most high and heartie *inuentions,*" his tone leaves little doubt that participating in the masque
experience will bring the "remou'd mysteries" it illuminates to hand,
refreshing faulty memories in familiar wisdom. Milton, by contrast,
exploits the ornate spectacle of masque to imbricate spectators and
masquers alike in a far more difficult struggle for truly reliable knowledge, as distinct from the intermediate easy answers the masque
periodically proffers. The poetry, music, and visual tableaux of
Comus's invitation to debauchery, undeniably appealing, entice
spectators into a world that *resembles* Royalist masque but here
constitutes the *antimasque:* the scenes of disorder, performed by
professionals, that contrast to the celebrations of order in the masque
proper. Similarly, the anticlimax when the brothers' swordplay, fan-
fares, and heroic declamation fail to liberate the Lady is viscerally
disappointing to the spectators (who remain equally seat-bound until
the masque is complete), drawing them into the brothers' failure.
Such experiential involvement of spectators in the logic of the antimasque, followed in each case by the revelation of its error, enacts
for spectators the masque's thesis that fully realizing Chastity—freeing the Lady so that she may return to the rest of the masque community—entails looking beyond the conventional masque epistemology
that here constitutes the morally spurious antimasque of Comus'
enticements.

Chastity and Abstinence

Since "chastity" acts throughout Milton's early oeuvre as a synecdoche for virtue in all aspects of life, his Protestant insistence on a

distinction between chaste living and mere (Catholic) abstinence expresses not only an apology for married sexual love but an analogous engagement of other kinds of experience as well.[21] Milton's understanding of chaste love as the embracing of properly directed desire (towards the lawful spouse and through him/her to God) draws closely on Britomart and her ideological sisters; for instance, commenting in the *Apology Against a Pamphlet* on St. Paul's admonition that those who are "defil'd with women" will never apprehend "celestiall songs," Milton claims that Pauline "defilement" "doubtlesse meanes fornication: For mariage must not be call'd a defilement" (*CP* 1.892–93).[22] But unlike the sixteenth-century Anglican Spenser, the seventeenth-century Reformist Milton engages the wider-ranging notion of chastity that follows from Calvinist rearticulations of the virtue. As explained in the *Institutes of the Christian Religion,* "chastity" for Calvin is the worldly category through which Christians express their passionate relationship to God.[23] Thus all virtuous uses of God's gifts—good husbandry, broadly understood—constitute chastity. The opposite of chastity is not the specifically sexual "whorishness," in such texts as William Ames's 1627 *Medulla Theologiae,* but the more general "luxury." In Milton's *Mask,* the Lady's retort to Comus's *carpe diem* celebration of wordly pleasures (706ff) indicates the wide compass of chaste living:

> . . . [Nature], good cateress,
> Means her provision only to the good,
> That live according to her sober laws,
> And holy dictate of spare temperance:
> If every just man that now pines with want
> Had but a moderate and beseeming share
> Of that which lewdly-pamper'd Luxury
> Now heaps upon som few with vast excess,
> Natures full blessings would be well dispens't
> In unsuperfluous eev'n proportion.
>
> (764ff)

Sobriety, temperance, moderation, and fair distribution of goods all contribute to the "pure cause" (794) of chastity.

Just as sexual chastity for English Protestants dictates discriminate engagement rather than ascetic abstinence, so too do other aspects of chaste living entail judicious enjoyment rather than utter refusal: measured but joyful partaking of Nature's "full blessings."

Although this understanding of chastity is common to Reformist thought generally, it seems to have had a particular resonance for the young Milton, as commentators have remarked of the meditations on chastity common to the *Mask* and the *Apology Against a Pamph-*

let.[24] In this 1642 polemical pamphlet, Milton recapitulates images from the 1634 *Mask,* distinguishing the "charming cup" of virtue that is true Platonic "chastity and love" from the "thick intoxicating potion which a certaine Sorceresse the abuser of loves name carries about" (*CP* 1.891, 892). No doubt the defensive emphasis on chastity in the *Apology* arises in part from aspersions cast by the Smectymnuus writers. Beyond this, the *Apology* not only defends the chastity of Milton's personal conduct but also invokes his indoctrination in chaste virtue as part of his literary autobiography. Milton first writes generally of apprehending the connection between moral judgment and literary worthiness:

> having observ'd them [the great poets, orators, and historians] to account it the chiefe glory of their wit, in that they were ablest to judge, to praise, and by that could esteeme themselves worthiest to love those high perfections which under one or other name they took to celebrate, I thought with my selfe by every instinct and presage of nature . . . that . . . with more love of vertue I should choose . . . the object of not unlike praises. (*CP* 1.889f)

Studying letters of chaste virtue inspires both chastity and writing, the quality of the writing being linked to the praiseworthiness of its subject. Specifying his models, Milton comes to admire above all others two poets who write chastely of love, Dante and Petrarch:

> [I] preferr'd the two famous renowners of *Beatrice* and *Laura* who never write but honour of them to whom they devote their verse, displaying sublime and pure thoughts, without transgression. (*CP* 1.890)

Milton does not value writers who avoid "transgression" by eschewing love, but rather those who enter into love sublimely and with purity.

The masque's argument for broad engagement as opposed to hermetic withdrawal informs its implied representational theory as well, albeit in a more ambivalent and perhaps symptomatic way than its judiciously structured responses to other issues. This part of the masque's semiotic structure becomes apparent through examining the position of the nymph Sabrina, the figure whose "chast palms moist and cold" alone can dissolve the "gumms of glutenous heat" welding the Lady to Comus's chair (917f). Sabrina's centrality is anomalous for three reasons. First, as Cedric Brown remarks, the subgenre of the dynastic masque to which Milton's piece belongs characteristically celebrates the efficacious potency of the feted family—not its inability to solve a problem without outside assistance.[25]

Second, other masques clearly distinguish the function of aristocratic masquers (realizing order) from the professional antimasquers' task (enscening disorder). Third, as I have remarked, masques are not wont to be obscure in their figuration—but just what Sabrina represents is far from self-evident.

In considering Sabrina, I propose shifting the critical focus from what she might figure specifically to what her presence suggests *structurally*. That is, perhaps the interpretation of what Sabrina represents—variously proposed to be autochthonous Welsh culture, classicism, nature, art, divine grace, government by principality, and vulnerable femininity—is less important than, first, the necessity that the Spirit turn to the nymph; second, the very multiplicity of suggestive possibilities regarding her meaning.[26]

Invoking Sabrina, the masquers turn to a figure who signifies in a very different way from the Lady, brothers, and Spirit. As members of the aristocratic household (although Lawes himself is not, of course, an aristocrat), the latter participate in conventional masque representation. In this mode, the persona a masquer assumes is neither an opaque disguise nor a transparent presentation of the real-life person, but rather a translucent figuration of the masquer's real-life identity. As Rosemond Tuve remarks, "masque devices do not just fasten sets of classical or abstract names upon James or Charles or Anne; they turn all the latter . . . into *figures for* the virtues, powers, or situations presented."[27] Masque's didactic authority depends on "Jove" or "Virtue" or, for that matter, Ludlow's "Thyrsis" constituting more than a sycophantic compliment; masque's aesthetic effect as well as its ideological potency derives from the ostensible appropriateness of figuring Charles as Jove, Alice as the chaste Lady. Masque is effective insofar as the real-life masquer and the masqued role resonate with one another. Hence we might describe masque, drawing on similitudes between the historical and the dramatic, as the dramatic embodiment of the premodern signification Foucault describes as "analogical," operating in a world that "fold[s] in upon itself, duplicate[s] itself, reflect[s] itself, or form[s] a chain with itself so that things can resemble one another."[28]

Sabrina, by contrast, is masqued by a professional of whose identity we have no record.[29] What she signifies is divorced from who she is. Thus where masquers signify through similarities—analogies— between their historical and masque identities, the anonymity Sabrina's player shares with traditional antimasquers suggests the potential interchangeability of the player beneath the signified persona. In this way, Sabrina's mode of representation corresponds to Foucault's modern "signification": the "ordering of things by means of

. . . fabricated signs" for a "knowledge based upon identity and difference," not similarity.[30] Whether antimasquers in conventional masques represent a "modern" challenge to the masque semiotics of analogy is arguable. One could claim that the association between the antimasquers as signs and the blackamoors, gypsies, and other forces of "disorder" they signify is arbitrary and "fabricated," since the antimasquers are not cast with an eye to their roles resonating with particular aspects of their real-life identities. Hence, the argument would go, antimasquing constitutes modern signification, and introducing even the *possibility* of artificial/conventional rather than essential links between sign and signified (that is, masquer and persona) into the masque as a whole destabilizes the connection between person and role that aristocratic power depends on maintaining as inviolable and immutable. On the other hand, one could claim from within masque logic that antimasque and masque representation operate identically: from this perspective, the theatrical hoi polloi of antimasquers, who *have* virtually no identity by aristocratic standards, enjoy the same essential congruence between their (non-) identities and their masqued roles (figuring forth disorder and confusion) as aristocratic masquers, only at the opposite end of the scale.

But Sabrina is no antimasquer. Instead, she introduces this alternative mode of signification into the masque proper, where she becomes moreover a necessary ally in the reunification of the aristocratic family. Perhaps what we have here is an enactment in semiotic terms of the shift to modernity that will in the years after the masque's 1634 performance render virtually every other facet of aristocratic premodernity insufficient. And, I should note, the masque's engagement of this shift is ambivalent, perhaps even retracted after its initial suggestion. For one thing, Sabrina's "necessity" is not absolute: had the brothers broken Comus's wand, her participation would not have been required. Once she performs her function, furthermore, Sabrina disappears, leaving the generically familiar reunion of the aristocratic family as the final tableau. But I do wonder whether the innovative deployment of a professional masquer in the piece constitutes one reason that this is one of the last masques ever performed (masque never again being wholeheartedly embraced after the Interregnum): whether Sabrina's role contributes to deconstructing the semiotic foundations that made the genre possible.[31]

Less conjecturally, this semiotic instance of Miltonic chastity's inclusive engagement of a variety of experience, distinct from ascetic circumscription, contributes to the *Mask*'s overall distinction between true chastity and abstinent refusal. Where traditional masques invite non-aristocratic professionals onto the scene only to enact the banishment of what they represent, thereby purifying the masque community, the Ludlow masque makes this other kind of masquer— this other mode of signification—central to dispelling Comus's influence. The distinctiveness of what I am calling Sabrina's mode of signification manifests concretely within the masque as well, in the unusual irreducibility of her figure to a single allegorical or mythical quality. This is not to say that Sabrina is obliquely enigmatic, but rather that the range of significance she encodes is unexpected in a genre otherwise comprising such straightforward scenarios as *Pleasure Reconciled to Virtue, The Triumph of Peace,* or *Coelum Britannicum* (whose most descriptive transliteration might be "Heaven is British"). On this level as well, Sabrina introduces a signifying principle of undecidability; any single interpretation constitutes a potentially arbitrary selection among plausible possibilities. We know that her figure is central to the resolution . . . but we're not sure what she figures. In this way, Sabrina might be taken to figure figuration itself: not the "analogical" firmness of premodernity, but something more like undecidable, self-contradictory, modern "signification." Far from being "promiscuous," as Puritan critics of figurative rhetoric would have it, this very multiplicity and open-endedness is intrinsic to the masquer most responsible for freeing Chastity. Admitting multiple interpretive possibilities, suggesting a whole new way of signifying, Sabrina's representational plenitude constitutes the chaste alternative to the semiotic "abstinence" of fixed or single meanings.

Chastity and Charity

If chastity is not the same as abstinence for Milton, neither is it synonymous with charity. To modern ears, this distinction might seem self-evident, if not nonsensical: why *would* charity have anything to do with chastity? Indeed, to us, the former connotes giving and the latter withholding. The *Mask,* however, suggests a significant relationship between the two qualities in its pointed substitution of "chastity" for "charity" in the Lady's rehearsal of the triune Pauline virtues (faith, hope, and charity). When the Lady realizes herself to be lost, bewildered among the "thousand fantasies / . . . / Of calling shapes, and beckning shadows dire" (205ff), she banishes her apprehensions with this "champion":

> O welcom pure-ey'd faith, white-handed Hope,
> Thou flittering Angel girt with golden wings,

And thou unblemish't form of Chastity.

(213ff)

This substitution startles the listener into comparing charity and chastity, suggesting that some logic must connect them, but that the two virtues are sufficiently distinct that precision required the change.[32] To early modern Reformers, in fact, the similarity between the terms might have been more evident than the force of Milton's distinction. For charity, like chastity, entails a relation to three aspects of the world that a Reformist Christian must address: the self, other people, and God. Through charity—*caritas*—the Christian expresses the etymologically related quality of "cherishing": first for God, next for him/herself, then for the rest of society (this last is sometimes called "right use of the world"). English Reformers focus on charity as a love for God that is prior to all other obligations— political, social, personal—frequently invoking Luther's commentary on Galatians: "But here stands Paul in supreme freedom and says in clear and explicit words: 'That which makes a Christian is faith *working through love.*'"[33] Thus the heart of the Christian constitution ("that which *makes* a Christian") is "love" (*caritas*), not as an emotive relation but as the way for faith to become manifest in the world, actively "working through" experience.

As love for God expressed through the right use of his creation, charity is a broadly inclusive category. Many English Reformers follow St. Paul, however, in particularly emphasizing charity as a didactic imperative. Paul privileges the *caritas* of "edification" above holy but hermetic speech that cannot be widely understood:

> Make love your aim, and earnestly desire . . . that you may prophesy. For one who speaks in a tongue speaks not to men . . . for no one understands him. . . . On the other hand, he who prophesies speaks to men for their upbuilding and encouragement and consolation. . . . He who prophesies is greater that he who speaks in tongues, unless some one interprets, so that the church may be edified [i.e. "built up" as well as "enlightened"] . . . if you in a tongue utter speech that is not intelligible, how will any one know what is said? (1 Cor. 14)

Thus Protestant charity entails broadly disseminating knowledge rather than alms. Francis Bacon writes, "Knowledge . . . hath in it some nature of venom or malignity . . . the corrective spice, the mixture whereof maketh knowledge so sovereign, is Charity"; for Bacon, charity is the "duty" to the world that redresses "private and particular" elite intellectual interests.[34] Milton's oeuvre similarly invokes this didactic and Pauline understanding of charity. He cites "charitie, the interpreter and guide of our faith" in the *Doctrine and Discipline of Divorce* (*CP* 2.236); "the charity of patient instruction" in *Areopagitica* (*CP* 2.567); and the mind "possest . . . with the dearest charity to infuse the knowledge of [good things] into others" (*Apology, CP* 1.949). Milton's imagery for chastity and charity emphasizes their consonance: the pamphlets describe charity as "flaming" (*Of Reformation, CP* 1.591) and "unquenchable" (*Animadversions, CP* 1.715); the *Mask* depicts chastity's "Sun-clad power" (782) and "sacred rayes" (425). This close relationship between "chastity" and "charity" informs the conventional Reformist figuration of all sin as "spiritual fornication": the soul spurning her proper beloved for the seductions of Satan.[35] Charity (loving God) demands chastity (refusing all advances of improper desires).

Herein lies the cogency of the Lady's implied aggregation of chastity and charity. Hence McGuire comments, "The masque does not celebrate any specific, isolated virtue or set of virtues. It is about all the virtues . . . that are necessary to a consistent life of faith."[36] But if the formulaic Pauline context for Milton's substitution of "chastity" for "charity" suggests their congruence, it also highlights the substitution, indicating an important difference as well. So what exactly is distinctive about "chastity" to Milton? The simplest answer, of course, is that chastity presented a particularly apt occasional device for the young Alice Egerton. Beyond this, the substantial revisions made for the printed versions prepared after the masque's performance intensify the masque's thematic focus. Reassigning the work's longest declamatory defense of chastity (spoken in performance by the Attendant Spirit) to the Lady, the revisions make the figure *for* chastity articulate the potency *of* chastity. And, despite its breadth of scope, this intensely focused "chastity" is more rigorous and more delimited than "charity." Whereas the edifying principle of charity radiates knowledge as widely as it may, Milton's *Mask* fastidiously circumscribes what counts as true knowledge by demanding constant and vigilant revision of the provisional models of chastity it successively proposes, then subsequently reveals to be insufficient. This sequence begins with Comus's antimasque assertions about the proper engagement of nature—misguided, to be sure, but less obviously spurious than the arguments of most antimasques. Ensuing paradigms are not precisely wrong, but all prove lacking. The perplexed Lady trusts her "ear" as the "best guide" to the *faute-de-mieux* site where she might find someone to "inform [her] unacquainted feet" (180); unfortunately, this brings her to Comus. Thus Chastity cannot find its way based solely on instinct or attentive listening.[37] The Elder Brother attributes the Lady's absence to virtue's need for the withdrawn self-renewal of "sweet retired solitude" (376), arguing that the brothers need not urgently fear for her safety, and claims that "No goblin, or swart faery of the mine, / Has hurtfull power o're true virginity" (436f). He is, of course, only partially correct, which allegorically indicates that even a self-renewing intensification of the Lady's chastity is not, by itself, effective. The Spirit himself, although "sho[t] from Heav'n to give . . . safe convoy" (81), does not offer the direct assistance that would confirm a conventional view that chasteness invoking heavenly aid can produce true Chastity. Rather, he waits "*neerest* to the present aid / Of this occasion" (90f, emphasis added) and contributes to the Lady's cause more as a facilitator than an agent, instructing the brothers and eventually summoning Sabrina.

The Spirit, I would contend, figures *charity:* the illuminating edification that crosses the divide between heaven and earth. Although charity is instrumental in assembling the forces that enable Chastity to act freely in the world, holy guidance alone is insufficient; rather, it is the forces intrinsic to the material world that must come together to liberate fettered chastity. These worldly forces include not only the human action, human philosophy, and familial loyalty figured in the brothers, but also the qualities more perplexingly associated with Sabrina. For the similarity among virtually all the critically proposed glosses on Sabrina lies in their common basis in earthly, material experience: whether artistic, political, natural, historical, maternal, or sexual.[38] Herein lies the other crucial difference in emphasis between the largely analogous "chastity" and "charity": "right use of the world" is the primary meaning of "chastity," only one among three, as Milton articulates it, for "charity." "Right use of the world" is a particularly pertinent focus for didactically entertaining members of the wealthy Caroline aristocracy, a class with unusually ample opportunity to misuse the material world. Accordingly, the *Mask* explores the "use of the world" not only through Sabrina but also in the centerpieces of Comus's and the Lady's debate about the proper use of nature (679–779) and the brothers' dialogue contrasting active and contemplative responses to manifest evil (350–489). Scrupulously "right use of the world," in fact, can transform the worldly itself into the divine: "when a soul is found sincerely [chaste] / . . . / . . . oft convers with heav'nly habitants / Begin to cast a beam on th' outward shape / . . . / And turns it by degrees to the souls essence" (454ff).

CHASTITY AND FIGURATION

Chastity as "right use of the world" is similarly crucial to Milton's implied defense of the masque genre. For we might see masque as

a figuration of the material world itself, the density of masque spectacle distilling the sensory impressions that constitute human access
to the world. In this way, Milton's device of chastity sketches out
what it means morally to live in the world. Through its form as well
as its content, the *Mask* suggests that masque can be an ethically
viable genre for working through the complexities of living in a material world and for communicating the conclusions this analysis dis-
cerns. This is not to say that Milton sanctions other examples of the
genre; indeed, his masque of Chastity serves as a pointed contrast to
contemporary masques of beauty, pleasure, and love that, as George
Sensabaugh has detailed, offended Reformers who believed their ostensibly elevated Neoplatonic devices to occasion cheap titillation.[39]
Just as the *Apology* defends the genre of drama while condemning
distasteful plays put on by divinity students "writhing and unboning
their Clergie limmes to all the antick and dishonest gestures of Trin-
culo's, Buffons, and Bawds" (*CP* 1.887), the *Mask* constructs a defense of masque that separates the genre's epistemological potential
from the debauchery of certain court examples. Although the
masque form certainly allows superficial celebrations of illusory
chastity (particularly in the person of Queen Henrietta Maria), Milton
shows that the genre also can produce profound and interpretively
challenging tropes of chastity. Far from pandering to easy legibility
(and hence, Reformist critics contend, easy hypocrisy, easy dis-
missability), the difficulty of arriving at a conclusive gloss on, say,
Sabrina forces spectators to ponder indefinitely the relative merits of
all the various earthly supplements to divine assistance that she
might figure. In this way, masque (criticized in the seventeenth century for the ephemerality of its single performance) can extend spectators' engagement with its didactic spectacles beyond the temporal
frame of the spectacle—or subsequent reading.[40]

By masquing Chastity, clearly, Milton hopes to chasten the masque
community: proposing a "chastity" very different from Caroline court
versions, the Ludlow masque aims to produce a community equally
distinct from the courtiers of Whitehall. But this direction of influence—abstract Chastity informing a chaste community—is not one-
way. For the notion of chastity the *Mask* engenders is not precisely
a personal virtue, but rather a communal one. Although the Lady
can by herself refuse Comus's cup, she cannot liberate herself from
his chair—from the position in which the existence of evil imbricates
her—to act freely in the world without aid from the several sources
we have examined. Far from being the "stoic or self-sufficient"
(though certainly "nonconformist") virtue Christopher Kendrick describes it to be, Chastity is something that must be *made,* by multiple
figures working in concert, not merely aspired to in solitude or imi-

tated by example.[41] Hence even the best-intentioned individual is dependent on other people or other earthly forces to fully realize chastity—removing Miltonic chastity even further from ascetic withdrawal. Moreover, the masque performance itself constitutes one such instance of community enterprise. Although an individual acting alone can refuse temptation (as when the Lady declines to drink), this constitutes only the smallest part of chaste living; the communal production of chastity, by contrast, cannot come about in an isolated subject.

This community need not, furthermore, be understood only literally. In the literary autobiography Milton (known at his Cambridge college as "the Lady of Christ's") constructs in the *Apology*, he proposes chastity as a vital condition for writing. Having studied the virtuously inspiring Petrarch and Dante, he reports:

> I was confirm'd in this opinion, that he who would not be frustrate of his hope to write well hereafter in laudable things, ought him selfe to bee a true Poem, that is, a composition, and patterne of the best and honourablest things. . . . (*CP* 1.890)

Maintaining that the successful writer himself must "bee a Poem," Milton suggests that the discrete conditions of writing and being written must themselves coalesce as two of the worldly forces that can come together to produce chastity. Milton also uses this literary community, which brings together not only writer and written but also past and present poets, present and future states (the hope of "writ[ing] well hereafter"), to further refute the anti-literary strain of Puritanism that sought to censure such a range of all representational practice. Instructed by Petrarch and Dante, Milton situates himself in a community of writer-teachers devoted to the Platonic conviction that aesthetic beauty never can be divorced from moral beauty. Recounting his early years of voracious reading, Milton uses the same diction of seduction as anti-poetic critics: "I was so *allur'd* to read, that no recreation came to me better welcome" (*CP* 1.889, emphasis added). But where anti-poetic writers disavow allurement by the "father of lies" (i.e., poetry) into a specious world of falsehood, Milton accuses such castigators of "*apeirokalia*," a Platonic term that Merritt Hughes glosses as "bad taste such as produces bad conduct."[42] Instead, Milton finds it crucial that he be "allured" into the Neoplatonic circle of writers who take beauty to emanate from goodness, and harmoniously crafted artifacts to reflect the divine order of the universe. In the Ludlow masque, the Lady's diction of "even proportion" to describe the proper dispensation of "Nature's full blessing" invokes this same tradition that privileges aesthetically mediated objects as ciphers to the the harmony of nature. For "proportion"—the science of "noble numbers"—is the category that such Neoplatonists as the philosopher Campenella, the architect Palladius, and the "mage" (or geometrician) John Dee use to describe the mystical (analogical) correspondences of simple ratios between microcosm and macrocosm that are detectable in both natural and created objects: shells, leaves, right triangles, musical chords, and well-designed rooms.[43] Developing the capacity to produce properly proportioned microcosmic works (works that echo divine harmony), then, requires a faculty opposite to "apeirokalia"—the *good* taste that produces *chaste* work. Just as Milton's Lady must engage the world around her to realize her chaste potential, Milton's discussion of his literary education in chastity—as well as his decision to script a masque—suggests that developing chastity requires engaging rather than fleeing representation.

* * *

The suturing of rhetorical, representational, and sexual categories in such Puritan critiques as the Barnabe Rich passage with which we began appears shockingly illogical, misogynist, and alien. Yet, oddly, twentieth-century feminist objections to using sexual violence (or, as in the *Mask*, the unconsummated threat of rape) as a figure recapitulate this gesture. Lynn Higgins and Brenda Silver, in fact, define the purpose of their collection *Rape and Representation* as "reclaim[ing] the physical, material bodies of women from their status as 'figures.'"[44] I certainly agree that the *Mask* enacts a figuration of the female body; indeed, Kendrick has illuminated in Foucauldian terms how Milton's text institutes a move from the physical "sex" that Comus offers—one pleasure among many—to discursive "sexuality," as "the Lady's closing words turn the glass into a metaphor for sex" ("sexuality" being "*the* sin, *the* secret . . . [whose] subject . . . is the source of a new social power, [although] it is not for her to say what her power is or means").[45] But I think it unhelpfully anachronistic to assert that the process of figuration itself erases the significance of female bodily experience. Such an assumption comes about precisely because *we* live in a culture that values the figurative only as a cipher to material reality, which it encodes, sublimates, and half-reveals.

But the status of figuration itself—as well as the vulnerability encoded in the Ludlow masque's trope of menaced virginity—is distinctive in early modern culture. The still-lively tradition positing figurative rhetoric to be a uniquely privileged vehicle for truth—the tradition of Augustine, Cicero, Quintilian, and Petrarch—does not oppose the real and the figurative as nineteenth- and twentieth-century culture does, but rather considers them complementary and mutually reinforcing. As Barbara Lewalski has shown, moreover, even Reformists who criticize certain kinds of rhetorical excess believe the mode of representation they find modeled in Christ's parables to authorize the highly figurative hermeneutics of allegory, typology, and associated interpretive modes.[46] Thus a seventeenth-century figure is anything but "merely" a metaphor (as Silver et al. imply): rather, it participates in a sacred link between material reality and Ideal (Neoplatonic) and/or revealed (Christian) truth; between Scripture and history; between prophecy and fulfillment. Furthermore, the specific figure of human vulnerability functions quite differently, I think, in a Christian culture than in a secular one. Although Quilligan maintains that "the Lady's gender ma[kes] her profoundly inappropriate for figuring [Milton's] own poetic powers," the potential to be ravished is a positive good—as in Donne's Holy Sonnets—for the Christian soul yearning for possession by divine power.[47] Finally, as the communal construction I have argued it to be, the supreme virtue of chastity *demands* a certain suspension of personal boundaries. Vulnerability in the *Mask* figures not only the potential to bond with others in creating a chaste community, but also the openness to communion with God that is imaged in other sources as the marriage of Christ and his bride: the supremely significant, feminized human soul.

Lost Honor and Torn Veils: A Virgin's Rape in Music

Lydia Hamessley

Oɴᴇ of the most horrific ways that the trope of virginity surfaces in early modern texts is in conjunction with rape. Narratives that recount the involuntary loss of virginity raise many questions, particularly when these stories are written by men. For instance, a male writer may cast a violent encounter as a seduction gone wrong rather than a rape. In such a case, can the raped virgin ever tell her own story effectively, or must she remain silent? What happens to her story when her rapist tells it? Not only might her rape be reported as a thwarted seduction, but the violence might also be eroticized, oftentimes with her as the primary seducer. Are there any circumstances in which the raped virgin might reclaim her virginity? These situations and questions surface in the cantata "Accenti queruli" by the Italian composer Giovanni Felice Sances (1600–1679); the poet is unknown.[1]

Accenti queruli	Let loose your discordant voices
Spiegate all'aure,	On the breeze,
O augeletti garruli	Little chattering birds.
Com'io lamenti	Just as I
Caldi sospiri,	Sigh with searing lament.
Del cor respiri.	The deepest cry of my heart.
Vital, mando dal seno, ai venti.	I cast upon the wind
Miei sospir', miei respir,	O my sighs, my groans, and my lament!
o miei lamenti.	
Andate languidi	In languishing grief and loneliness,
Nel duol soli e ite	Go to my Lidia.
Alla mia Lidia;	Tell her I give out my last breath!
Dite ch'io spiro,	Tell her I'm dying!
Dite ch'io moro	Full of torment,
Pien di martiro,	Without reprieve from my fate.
Senza fatal ristoro.	That I am dying in suffering.
Ch'io spiro con martir, dite ch'io moro.	Tell her I am dying!

Che forse placida	Now, perhaps, relenting,
Qual pria fu rigida	While before she was insensitive
Ai pianti, a' gemiti	To my cries and groans.
Vi darà pace, vi darà vita	She will give peace, she will give life,
Nè più si audace	And no longer so bold, will say:
Dirà: Non merta aita	"He does not deserve help,
Ma all' audace in amor dò pace	But to the bold in love I give peace and life!
e vita.	
Ch'in sguardo rigido	Though with his cruel looks
Bellezze angeliche	He stole the angelic beauty
Furò dell'anima,	From my soul,
Trasse l'ardore	He drew out my desire:
Squarciò'l bel velo,	He tore at my lovely veil,
Rubò l'onore	And robbed me of my honor
Con finto zelo,	With fake passion,
O mio ardor, O mio onor,	O my desire, O my honor, my torn veil!"
squarciato velo.	
Dirà così la misera.	Thus the unhappy girl will speak.
E voi sospiri rispondete a lei:	And you my sighs answer her:
Lidia, se taci ancor, vergine	"Lidia, if you still keep silence, you are
sei;	a virgin;
Che quando sfogai teco l'ardor	For when my burning passion I released
mio,	No other was there but Lidia, Love
Altri non fù che Lidia, Amor	and I."[2]
ed io.	

The text begins with a typical pastoral setting. The narrator implores the birds around him to go to his beloved, Lidia, and tell her that he is "languishing in grief and loneliness" without her; he claims he is in fact dying due to her insensitivity. The birds, who are actually embodiments of his sighs, are then told that when they tell her of his sorrow, she will tell them her story. At that point we hear her story, told in first person, as though the narrator is quoting her. We learn that she has been "robbed of her honor with fake passion." The language she uses is clearly coded as the language of rape: her beauty has been stolen, her honor robbed, and, most significantly, her veil has been torn, an obvious reference to the breaking of the virgin's hymen. After her story, the narrator resumes his voice and instructs the birds about how they should reply to Lidia's story. They are to tell her that if she keeps silent she will still be a virgin, because when he released his burning passions, no one was there except him, Lidia, and Amor.

This text is provocative for several reasons. First, there are two levels of narrative: a primary level—the man's story, and a secondary level—the woman's story. However, these two stories are actually embedded one within the other, and both are narrated by the same speaker, the man. Even though he is ostensibly quoting the woman when "she" speaks, he is really assuming her voice, playing the ventriloquist, and the story is told from his perspective. We cannot know what she in fact would say to the birds, nor can we know if his report of her experience bears any resemblance to what really happened between them. Her version of their encounter is not only erased, but it is rewritten in such a way as to appear authentically hers. As E. Jane Burns explains in her study of Old French texts, "A man's words spoken through a woman's body, however fictive and fabricated, are not perceived or received by the reader as thoroughly male; their valence changes in accordance with the gender of the speaker articulating."[3] While Burns has shown that occasionally these "women's" words can be understood as a counterreading to the male perspective, in "Accenti queruli" Lidia's story, particularly since it clearly acknowledges the event as a rape, does not seem resisting so much as it seems like her authentic report, making the male narrator's usurpation of Lidia's voice all the more insidious. Lidia's words are actually the male ventriloquist's voice, which depends on and speaks for a *silent* woman.[4]

The structure of the poem itself enhances this effect, since the two levels of narrative are somewhat masked. Because Lidia's story begins at the end of the third stanza and does not even coincide with the beginning of a line, the two voices elide, almost melding into one. And at the end of the poem, in stanza four, where the narrative shifts back to the primary level, the male point of view is further emphasized as he quotes himself. Thus, in "Accenti queruli" the male voice remains unified while the woman's experience is given no actual separate identity and no authentic voice.

This final portion of the text leads us to another point that must be considered. Here the male narrator advises the woman to keep silent in order to retain her virginity. Paradoxically, however, he has already told her story, precluding any hymenal healing powers of silence on her part, at least insofar as we and the birds are concerned. Indeed, his invocation to her for silence not only allows him to maintain his ventriloquist stance, but also suggests further speech on his part, perhaps in the form of blackmail, if she does not maintain her silence and continue their encounters. Thus it is the male voice that claims the power to speak, especially since it speaks the story Lidia presumably would not want anyone to hear.

In his musical setting of this text Sances makes compositional choices that further enhance the power of the unified male voice.

"Accenti queruli" employs a musical device known as an ostinato—a fixed bass line usually coupled with a set harmonic progression that is repeated throughout the work. Above this ostinato the voice weaves its vocal line in what amounts to endless variations on the bass. Many of Sances's works rely on ground basses; he employed freely invented bass ostinati, as well as the set patterns of the passacaglia and the chaconne (in Italian, *ciaccona*), two ground basses that have specific musical characteristics. At this point it is necessary to outline briefly the ways these two ostinato patterns often interact with the texts they accompany in other works by Sances and his influential contemporary, Claudio Monteverdi.

The passacaglia, a four–note descending bass line usually in a minor mode, is frequently employed in laments. One of the best

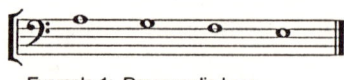

Example 1: Passacaglia bass.

known examples of this device is in the "Lament of the Nymph" by Monteverdi. Susan McClary has demonstrated the powerful effect, both structural and metaphoric, that the passacaglia has in this work.[5] The piece opens with a trio of men singing an ostinato-free chordal passage, explaining that an angry young woman has just come on the scene. After their introduction, the woman appears and sings a lament, over a passacaglia, about the betrayal by her former lover, punctuated occasionally by a word or two from the men. The men conclude the piece with an epilogue in the same style as their introduction. The nymph's florid melody attempts to escape the relentless circularity of the bass line, mirroring the nymph's own obsession with her lost beloved and her vain attempts to overcome her pain. Furthermore, the ostinato–supported melody of the nymph is framed by the trio of men singing their non–ostinato chordal prologue and epilogue. McClary argues that the men provide a rational and sane musical landscape, a musical frame, which protects the listener from contamination by the nymph's mental and musical irrationality. For our purposes, it is important to note that the two levels of narrative are marked by different musical procedures.

Sances uses a passacaglia in his monody "Usurpator tiranno,"[6] where it conveys not obsession but resignation. Although there is only one level of narrative in this piece, Sances still stops the flow of the ostinato when he interrupts the passacaglia at the final two four-line strophes with a recitative, a freely-written declamatory section. Generally, the use of recitative within these ostinato-based monodies was not unusual. They could be written to portray more graphically a text that seemed to be ill-served by the relentless bass pattern, and so recitative sections often appear for specific textual reasons. One striking example of an ostinato interrupted for textual reasons is found in another work of Monteverdi, "Zefiro torna," for two voices.[7] This piece is based on a chaconne, a ground bass in triple meter and in a major mode. Chaconnes also usually have a light playful quality due to their syncopated rhythm, and it has been suggested that vocal chaconnes "often have ironic or comic overtones."[8] The text for "Zefiro torna," by Ottavio Rinuccini, offers few complexities: there is only one narrative level, and the majority of

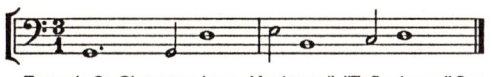

Example 2: Chaconne bass, Monteverdi, "Zefiro torna," 2vv.

the text presents a pastoral scene that is perfectly suited to a chaconne setting. The ostinato ceases only at the last stanza when the mood shifts abruptly; here the words are appropriately set to freely–composed chromatic passages. However, at the words *I sing*, the ostinato resumes. These shifts are indicated in the following: italics mark those words devoid of an ostinato.

Zefiro torna e di soavi
  accenti
L'aer fa grato e'l piè discioglie a
  l'onde,
E mormorando tra le verdi
  fronde
Fa danzar al bel suon su'l prato
  i fiori,
Inghirlandato il crin Fillide e
  Clori
Note temprando amor care e
  gioconde
E da monti e da valli ime e
  profonde
Raddopian l'armonia gli antri
  canori.
Sorge più vaga in ciel l'aurora
  e'l sole
Sparge più luci d'or, più puro
  argento
Fregia di Teti il bel ceruleo
  manto.
Sol io per selve abbandonate
  e sole

The west wind returns and with soft
  accents
makes the air gentle and releases
  swift-footed waves,
and murmuring among the green
  branches
makes the flowers dance at its lovely
  sound
and curls round the hair of Phyllis
  and Clori,
love giving rise to fond and joyful
  song,
and from mountains and valleys,
  songs resound high and low,
and the sonorous caves re–echo the
  music.
The dawn rises more lovely in the sky,
  and the sun
scatters more golden rays, and a
  purer silver
decorates Teti's beautiful sky blue
  coat.
Only I in the lonely, deserted
  forest—

L'ardor di due begli occhi e'l mio tormento.	*the fire of two bright eyes is my torment.*
Come vuol mia ventura hor piango, hor canto.	*As my fortune wills, I weep, then sing.*
Come vuol mia ventura hor piango, hor canto.	*As my fortune wills, I weep, then sing.*
Hor canto.	*I sing. [This ling sung in a free, florid passage.]*[9]

In light of these somewhat standard procedures for writing ground–bass pieces, it is revealing to examine Sances's use of the chaconne in "Accenti queruli."[10] The bass line and harmonic progression of this chaconne is very typical and is almost identical to that of Monteverdi in "Zefiro torna." The ostinato is present throughout the entire piece until the final five lines of text, which are set in a recitative, following what seems to be standard formula. One might assume that these two musical procedures would coincide with the two levels of narrative, with the recitative marking the story of the rape; however, this is not the case. The chaconne bass proceeds unchanged throughout both narrative levels of the text, and a single recitative passage appears only with the shift back to the primary level of the narrative at the end of the poem. This procedure is quite unlike that used by Monteverdi in the "Lament of the Nymph," where the two levels of narrative are clearly delineated by different musical procedures, different key areas, and different performers. It is also unlike Monteverdi's duet "Zefiro torna," which alternates ostinato sections with freely–composed music as warranted by the text. In "Accenti queruli" neither the secondary narrative level, nor those portions of text that are the most poignant or anguished are set apart musically in any way. Instead, the recitative, with its emphasis on personal expression, is reserved for the male narrator's final plea, thus privileging his point of view and further erasing the woman's identity. The irony of juxtaposing the music of a chaconne with the story of a rape is very disconcerting, yet it effectively confirms that the cantata is told from the man's point of view.

The placement of the recitative is not the only musical element that has ramifications for my reading of this piece. The chaconne itself and the distinctive way it is used throughout the piece is significant. First, it smooths the elision of voices in the text since the entrance of the secondary level of narrative does not coincide with the beginning of a statement of the chaconne. The result is that even musically we scarcely notice the narrator's usurpation of the woman's voice. Second, the chaconne inhibits the narrative flow of the piece by allowing no change of mood as the text proceeds from

ma tras-se l'ar-do- rè sqùar-ciòl' bel ve- lo rub-bò l'ho-no- re con fin-to ze-lo *con fin-to ze-lo*

o mio ar -dor o mio hon -or squar-cia- - to ve- lo o mio ar - dor o

- mio hon - or squar-cia-to ve- lo di-rà co- si la mi-se- ra e voi so-spi-ri

ri-spon-de- t'a le- i Li - dia Li - dia se ta-ci an - cor

Li-dia se ta-ci an -cor ver-gi-ne se- i che quan-do sfo-gai te-co l'ar-dor mi-

o al-tri non fù che Li - dia che Li - dia A-mor ed i- o

a light–hearted invocation to songbirds to a lament about torn veils and lost honor. By the time the account of the rape emerges, the listener is already invested in the spirited recurrent pattern of the chaconne and scarcely realizes the change not only of narrator, but of emotional content. The result of Sances's musical choice here is ironic: the gravity of the woman's story is diminished since it is relayed through the cheerful pattern of a chaconne. The reality of the rape and her loss of virginity is what is actually at stake here. Her story reads like a rape, but sounds, through the chaconne, like a harmless flirtatious encounter.

In ground-bass pieces such as "Accenti queruli," one must not ignore what the upper voice is doing; the chaconne pattern does not control the piece alone. The voice sings a constantly varying musical line above the recurrent bass and harmonic progression, and the interplay between the voice and chaconne bears examination. The first three stanzas of the poem are treated in a similar way; each is sung over a comparable number of recurrences of the chaconne: fourteen in the first stanza, and eleven in the second and third. In each of these stanzas, particular words or phrases are emphasized with long melismatic passages, and text is repeated freely for emphasis. Moreover, beginnings of lines do not necessarily coincide with the beginnings of the chaconne pattern; in fact, just the opposite usually occurs. With the poetry in this complex relationship with the ground bass, we proceed through each stanza evenly and somewhat slowly, taking in all the facets, variations, and subtleties of the narrator's pain, even dipping into a minor modality for a fleeting moment at, significantly, the word *rigida,* referring to the woman's insensitivity. Once again, Sances reveals that our sympathies are to lie with the narrator, since it is his pain at rejection that is emphasized, and done so, ironically, at the moment when he is speaking of Lidia's insensitivity. From Lidia's point of view, though, this insensitivity might be an expression of her unwillingness, perhaps her only moment of resistance however evanescent and fleeting.

Conversely, in the fourth stanza we hear Lidia's story quickly with no repetition of text, no subtlety of meaning, nor any real word emphasis until the final line. In this stanza, the text is practically recited in simple lilting rhythms over the chaconne, with every two lines of text consistently coinciding with one statement of the chaconne pattern. The buoyant, dance–like quality of this stanza is inescapable, and it proceeds rapidly; with just four statements of the chaconne we are at the end of the woman's story. At this point there is an abrupt shift from her previous declamatory singing to her florid wails and variations over *six* additional statements of the chaconne:

O mio ardor, O mio onor, squarciato velo (O my desire, O my honor, torn veil). Sances takes particular delight in the word *squarciato*, meaning torn, and writes an especially lovely melismatic passage on this word that lasts for *two* complete statements of the chaconne. After this virtuosic outcry, Sances depicts a weeping, trembling Lidia by writing the elongated pitch D over one and a half statements of the chaconne on the syllable *o*. This kind of vocal writing would have been a clear signal to the seventeenth-century singer, as it is to Julianne Baird in her recording, to embellish the pitch. This striking "pause" in the forward momentum of the section, as well as the resulting dissonance produced as the D is held over the chaconne bass, is powerful and graphic in its representation of the final moments and aftermath of the rape. At this point all energy drains away as Lidia laments her torn veil one last time.

It is crucial to note the passage of time in the entire work and particularly in this stanza. The narrator has been given much more musical time to express his feelings, and so we are invested in his predicament. Conversely, Lidia has been essentially rushed through her story until the moment of climax. Our attention is drawn not to her story, but to her outpouring of pain, suffering, and loss on the words *squarciato* and *onore*. Yet, because of the manipulation of musical time and the resulting unequal progression of the two stories over the chaconne, we seem not so much to be invited to sympathize with her pain, but rather to experience it from the distance that the male narrator established and to enjoy the spectacle of her pain with him. This moment is, in fact, the site of the most pleasure for him. All of Sances's musical choices—the placement of the recitative, the use of the chaconne, the relationship between the chaconne and the vocal line, and the manipulation of time for each character—work together to allow for a reading of this piece as a metaphoric musical representation of the male narrator's encounter with and rape of Lidia. He calls on various means of seduction in the first three verses: through a catalogue of his pain, through his sighs, and through birds—a standard trope of seduction. He is persistent, and he takes his time about it—the chaconne is a rather tenacious and patient musical form, and it cycles through his litany without fail. As his seductive maneuvers fail, his urgency finally takes over in the fourth stanza where the momentum fairly doubles as the actual rape begins, and the point of climax is quickly reached with the melisma on *squarciato velo* and the trembling on *onore*. And significantly, it is after this moment that the chaconne and the momentum of the piece finally stop completely. What follows is the recitative in which the male narrator attempts to explain away what just happened.[11]

What advice does he give Lidia in response to her beautiful cry lamenting her lost virginity? "If you keep silence, you are a virgin; / For when my burning passion I released / No other was there but Lidia, Love and I." The lines are compelling, particularly since seventeenth-century medical discourse did devise a way in which a woman could remain a virgin after losing her virginity. If she did not consent to intercourse, if she were raped, she would remain a virgin and her honor and integrity would not be compromised. Jacqens Duval followed this line of reasoning in his medical theories, which suggest that "where there was no pleasure the womb remained closed and where there was no consent the woman's moral virginity remained intact."[12] Obviously, such logic served fathers of raped daughters well—under such a system the young women were still marriageable rather than damaged goods. The narrator here, though, I imagine, is not turning to this contingency to restore her virginity. As suggested earlier, his usurpation of her voice is insidious precisely because by assuming her voice he is able to describe the rape in a way that suggests she may have encouraged him and which casts some doubt on her unwillingness. Remember, this is his story, not hers. He speaks for her in saying that her desire, or more literally, intense heat, was drawn out. In a seventeenth-century context that would mean that he had her in a position of openness, or ardor, in which she too would be aroused, if for no other reason than to be an effective incubator of the seed she was to receive. Furthermore, he suggests that Love, Amor, was present at their encounter. So it would seem that she might have a hard time reclaiming her virginity by reporting the rape using his version of the story.

Rather, it is her actual silence that will keep her virginity intact. Much like Philomela, whose rape and loss of virginity was silenced by Tereus for a year, Lidia will also remain a virgin as long as silence is maintained because, in effect, the rape will have never happened.[13] Tereus insured Philomela's silence not by killing her, but by cutting out her tongue when she threatened to reveal her story. "Accenti queruli" puts our two characters in comparable positions. Lidia still exists but has also been silenced by the male narrator who literally and musically speaks for her. The fact that the narrator tells the story at all, however, is somewhat paradoxical since he advises Lidia not to tell her story. Furthermore, why does he report their encounter like a rape at all? Since he has been in control of both his and Lidia's discourse all along, why not just tell her story unproblematically as a seduction that has gone awry, as he did when he states for Lidia that he drew out her desire? Why invoke images of lost honor and torn veils? Ironically, it is the rape itself, I would argue, that the narrator does want to remember and relive. Perhaps the Philomela story offers yet another parallel. Like Tereus, who continued to rape Philomela after she was silenced, the narrator of this piece continues to enjoy Lidia as she sings, through his words, her beautiful lament on *squarciato velo*. Her florid passages at the end of her story are more an actual reliving, from his perspective, of the delicious moment that he deflowered her than her own horror at being raped. And since the story is set to music that speaks the clearest through performance, each time the cantata is sung Lidia, with her newly–restored virginity, is raped and silenced yet again.

It is also through performance that Lidia's voice is further appropriated. "Accenti queruli" is written for a soprano voice; thus, the entire story, both the narrator's supplication and Lidia's supposed response, is intended to be sung by a high voice that is undoubtedly gendered female.[14] Sances, like the male narrator, usurps Lidia's voice, and this strategy has several effects. First, it adds another layer of authenticity to the account that Lidia sings. Indeed, Sances is now the ventriloquist who writes music for Lidia in a vocal range that we can understand to be authentically hers. When we just deal with the text, we read her words as spoken through the male narrator. But when the piece is performed musically, we hear and see Lidia sung by a female voice in a female body. But even more significantly, when this embodied Lidia sings, the rape is further eroticized. It is in this female voice that we hear Lidia's honor lost and her veil torn, not in the voice of a male narrator. Thus, Sances has taken the usurpation of Lidia's voice one step further than the narrator: the narrator reports her rape, but Sances has her perform it, embody it, presumably for the pleasure of the male listeners.[15] This is where Sances parts company with the Philomela story, which is ultimately dependent on the raped woman's silence. As Burns argues: "The gruesome rape that [Philomela] suffers establishes a crucial link between the sexual subjugation of women and female silence, positing them as necessary partners in the creation of male pleasure."[16] Lidia's literal silence is not the site of pleasure in this cantata, rather it is her performance, through the appropriation of her voice, that creates the moments of the most pleasure at the words *squarciato velo*.

I listen to "Accenti queruli" with much pleasure as well as apprehension, not so much because it tells a story no woman wants to participate in, but because it tells the story in such an appealing way.[17] The lilting quality of the chaconne and the incredibly beautiful virtuosic lines are seductive, and one is swept away by the charm of the entire cantata, especially the surges and waves of Lidia's trembling lines. But, of course, it is precisely those lines that are the problem. In her study of Robert Schumann's *Frauenliebe und -Leben,* 1840 (a song cycle ostensibly from a woman's perspective), Ruth A. Solie suggests that "the impersonation of a woman by the voices of male culture [is] a spurious autobiographical act" and that works such as *Frauenliebe* are not accurate portrayals of women's experiences. Rather, they are portrayals "of fantasy rather than of reality, of male ideology rather than of female acquiescence."[18] In such pieces, women's song is understood to be uttered by women themselves rather than the utterances of male composers who write out their fantasies to be embodied, and authenticated, by female performers. I would add "Accenti queruli" to Solie's category of spurious autobiographical acts, and not one that exists only on a textual level.[19] The music of "Accenti queruli" participates equally in the impersonation, eliding the two voices into one that sings a woman's pain and enjoys it.

Evading Rape and Embracing Empire in Margaret Cavendish's *Assaulted and Pursued Chastity*

Marina Leslie

In her fifth publication, *Nature's Pictures drawn by Fancy's Pencil to the Life* (1656), Margaret Cavendish includes an allegorical romance entitled *Assaulted and Pursued Chastity*.[1] The initially unnamed heroine of this romance suffers dramatic if generic assaults upon her virginity, and it is as unhappily predictable as it is paradoxical that the violence of the predatory assault upon her is inflamed in direct proportion to those manifest signs of her virtue—her extreme modesty and great beauty. What may, perhaps, seem less conventional about this tale is the masculine manner in which the assaulted virgin responds to these threats. This lady is no Christian martyr to virginity, nor does she wait passively for divine intervention to confirm or maintain her chastity. Instead, she takes up arms—and uses them—in defense of her virtue.

If the violence of her virginal heroine is striking, it scarcely needs pointing out that the figure of the menacing, masculine virgin was by no means Cavendish's invention. Indeed, Cavendish's deployment of the virgin-virago needed to be managed with some caution if her romance heroine were to offer a correcting, rather than an inverted, model of feminine virtue. I want to argue here that Cavendish's virginal poetics achieve their potency, in fact, by negotiating between the Scylla of the absolutist virago and the Charybdis of the monstrous usurping androgyne to arrive at a gendered allegory, featuring the martial maid as both the emblem of disordered times and the tonic to cure them.[2]

As Cavendish was well aware, the early modern virgin-virago had inherited a complex and intensely ambivalent patristic and political legacy, making her more compelling than coherent as a focus of fascination. She was variously or simultaneously represented as an object of admiration, dread, or disgust. From antiquity, Amazonian virgins, armed though they might be, were themselves prominent

179

weapons in the arsenal of misogynist literature, offering the very personification of a violently disordered domestic sphere. Despite the veritable industry of encomiastic literature celebrating the virgin queen, the cult of Elizabeth did not produce a poetics of power available for general distribution to chaste women of the Renaissance. Elizabeth's mythologized virginity was a central but not a singular strategy for representing the political body. Indeed, medieval and Renaissance political theory endowed the queen with two bodies, giving her, as Elizabeth puts it in her famous speech to the troops at Tilbury, "the body but of a weak and feeble woman; but . . . the heart and stomach of a king, and a king of England too."[3]

For Cavendish, the queenly model of chaste virtue was Charles I's French bride, Henrietta Maria, whom Cavendish served in exile as a lady-in-waiting. In the Caroline court, Henrietta Maria was the center of a Neoplatonic discourse of love adapted from French strains of courtly *préciosité* in which the ideal of *honnêteté* for women stressed the qualities of chastity, compassion, beauty, and modesty.[4] It was the chaste, companionate marriage rather than an austere, unyielding virginity that governed the themes of court masque and poetry prior to the Civil War; nonetheless, the poetics of chastity in the Caroline court were not restricted to a celebration of the monarchs' marriage or Henrietta's virtue. At his coronation, in February 1626, Charles appeared all in white rather than the customary royal purple to symbolize "that Virgin Purity with which he came to be espoused unto his Kingdom."[5] As Lois Potter points out, this symbolism was doubly reflected in his decision to be crowned on Candlemas Day, the feast of the Purification of the Virgin.[6] Commissioned by Charles to do the ceiling at Whitehall, Rubens chose to pursue these iconographical associations when he represented the apotheosis of Charles's father, James I, in a manner that D. J. Gordon argues "evolved primarily, for the assumption of the virgin."[7]

In the poetry and drama of the Caroline court, chastity was very explicitly a social metaphor used as an index of courtly favor and an instrument for the enforcement of courtly values. In their definitive study of Stuart court masque, Orgel and Strong argue that Henrietta Maria's Neoplatonic cult of chaste love, far from being a "mere courtly game," was rather, "a political assertion, exactly consonant with, and indeed implied by, the King's absolute monarchy. About the Queen revolved all passion, controlled and idealized by her platonic beauty and virtue, as about the King all intellect and will."[8]

An example of the disciplining function of the queen's chastity can be seen in Walter Montague's *The Shepherd's Paradise* (1633). This court production celebrated the queen as center of a select pastoral society, whose rules, Erica Veevers notes, are "not unlike those of a religious order. . . . Members are admitted at the discretion of the Queen, upon a vow of chastity 'which is not ever to be dispenced with', and the breach of which is punishable by death."[9]

Both Plato's *Symposium* and the cult of the Virgin informed the Catholic Henrietta Maria's Devout Humanist theology of chaste love. Combining the idealized Neoplatonic hermaphrodite with the namesake of the Heavenly Queen, Thomas Carew offered the regal amalgam, CARLOMARIA, in his masque "Coelum Britannicum" as "[t]hat great example of Matrimoniall union."[10] Carew specifically celebrates the civilizing chastity of the queen in his poem, "To the Queene" (1640), in terms alternately Amazonian and hermaphroditic:

> Thou great Commandresse, that doest move
> Thy Scepter o're the Crowne of Love,
> And through his Empire with the Awe
> Of Thy chaste beames, doest give the Law
> . . . .
> Thy sacred Lore shewes us the path
> Of Modestie and constant faith,
> Which makes the rude Male satisfied
> With one faire Female by his side
> Doth either sex to each unite
> And formes loves pure Hermophradite.[11]

These images locate in the queen a potent chastity, able to appropriate masculine prerogatives and characteristics by taming masculine violence. Cavendish's later representations of the power of chastity will similarly draw on both Amazonian and hermaphroditic models, although history would suggest the inadequacy of a court-centered poetics of chastity for Cavendish writing in the 1650s. Instead, she exploits romance conventions in *Assaulted and Pursued Chastity*, to display chastity under duress and exiled from the courtly centrality it enjoyed in Caroline masque and poetry prior to the Civil War.

Although the marriage of Charles and Henrietta Maria was, at least after the death of Buckingham, by most accounts a good one, the cohesion of that union, literal or symbolic, did not and could not represent political reality or overcome the divided state of the kingdom. The political and religious challenge to monarchical moral authority brought the symbolic chastity of the queen and the court directly under attack. The French Catholic Henrietta Maria was the ofject of tremendous Puritan suspicion, and polemical attacks on court entertainments, such as William Prynne's *Histrio-Mastix*, focused on the effeminacy of court life and the role of women as seductive influences tied to Catholic corruption. The repeated association of court and cloister in Caroline drama was utterly unredemptive for Prynne. Indeed, he complained bitterly of English gentlewomen who, like "shameless" Papish nuns, cut their hair "in token that they are now . . . freed from all subjection to men, or to their husbands."[12] Both he declared to be "adulteresses and whores" (203).

Prynne's enormous tract condemning theater appeared just as the queen and her ladies were rehearsing Montague's seven hour pastoral extravaganza, *The Shepherd's Paradise,* and his index entry "Women actors, notorious whores," was taken as a deliberate insult to Henrietta Maria. Prynne was found guilty by the Star Chamber of libel and sedition against church and state and his sentence was severe: he was stripped of his degrees, deprived of his ears, branded, and sentenced to the Tower for life.[13]

Female chastity (and its lack) can thus be seen to play a crucial role in English political discourse of the sixteenth and seventeenth centuries as a way of describing the sanctity or the pollution of the political body. The historical ambivalence toward female virginity finds its most enduring and influential articulation, however, in the early Church writings, which display the struggle to account for the oxymoron of the asexual female. The Church Fathers conferred upon the Christian virgin a privileged status that can be found throughout the patristic literature from St. Paul's encomium on the superior state of virginity for both sexes to the views on female virginity expressed by Tertullian, Cyprian, Ambrose, Jerome, Gregory of Nyssa, and Augustine. Jane Tibbetts Schulenburg observes that the highest praise was earned by those models of female virginity who had "successfully repudiated their own sexuality; they had negated their unfortunate female nature; and only in this way were they able to transcend the weaknesses and limitations of their sex. Thus as sexless beings these virgins were viewed nearly as spiritual equals."[14]

Strikingly, this elevation, based as it is on the desexing of virgins, allowed for a transsexual evaluation of their merits. Indeed, the highest praise offered by the Church Fathers is the description of these virgins as "virile" or "male."[15] However, as Jerome warns in the Letter to Eustochium, the ambitious virgin risks not only the envy of her sisters who wed but a fate far worse than theirs. The fallen virgin, he declares:

> shall sit by the waters of loneliness and lay down her pitcher; and shall open her feet to every one that passeth by and shall be polluted to the

crown of her head. Better had it been for her to have submitted to marriage with a man and to have walked on the plain, rather than to strain for the heights and fall into the depths of hell.[16]

The view that the virgin's refusal to submit to a man (in marriage) can bring about a greater fall by submitting to men (outside of marriage) belies a profound ambivalence in the patristic logic about female virginity, where the exaltation of the virginal body is linked to its unequaled potential for debasement and degradation. It is worth noting, however, that in this articulation of the virgin/whore dichotomy, the virgin is warned not only against men, but also, paradoxically, against the very ambitions she reveals in renouncing her sexuality as she "strain[s] for the heights," ambitions that may ultimately be regarded as the cause of her fall. It is not a long path from Jerome's caution to the overly ambitious virgin to Prynne's warning against aristocratic women who behave like "Papish nuns" seeking "freedom from all subjection to men," and this is a course that Cavendish travels with caution, not the less because of the ambitions she has for her virginal heroine.

Cavendish rehearses a variety of conventions concerning virgins, assaulted and armed, forcing the contradictions of these master narratives into crisis along with her virginal heroine. The very stylized nature of romance with its stock plot devices of love and loss, adventure and disguise, exile and return helps Cavendish to control the moral geography of her story, while allowing her all the latitude of the genre. Furthermore, the use of romance to disguise or promote political agendas in the mid-seventeenth century has been widely noted, and provided Cavendish with powerful generic precedent.[17] As Victoria Kahn has argued in another context, romance provided Cavendish with the perfect locus to explore "the politically charged issues of coercion and consent, force and desire."[18] In *Assaulted and Pursued Chastity*, Cavendish revises—by putting into contact—the familiar but generally opposed narratives of women's sexual victimization and female mastery. But it is only by exhausting these narrative alternatives that the formerly assaulted and pursued virgin ultimately can be established as the sign of, and, more remarkably, the agent for, political and sexual restoration.

The preface to *Assaulted and Pursued Chastity* begins with a patristic echo and its revision. Cavendish introduces a traveling virgin in the very situation Jerome warns virgins to avoid in the Letter to Eustochium. According to Jerome, even the masculine virgin cannot move among men without fear of losing both her masculine and feminine virtues. He enjoins virgins not to stray beyond the protective custody of the domestic realm governed by fathers and brothers with the following exhortation:

> Go not from home nor visit the daughters of a strange land, though you have patriarchs for brothers and rejoice in Israel as your father. Dinah went out and was seduced [corrumpitur]. I would not have you seek the Bridegroom in the public squares; I would not have you go about the corners of the city. . . . You will be wounded and stripped, you will lament and say: "The watchmen who go about the city found me: they smote me, they wounded me, they took away my veil from me." (109–11)

Cavendish's introduction to her romance seems at first a perfect endorsement of Jerome's views:

> In this following tale or discourse, my endeavor was to show young women the danger of travelling without their parents, husbands or particular friends to guard them; for though virtue is a good guard: yet it doth not always protect their persons, without human assistance; for though virtue guards, yet youth and beauty betrays, and the treachery of the one is more than the safety of the other: for ofttimes young beautiful and virtuous women, if they wander alone, find but rude entertainment from the masculine sex: as witness Jacob's daughter Dinah, which Shechem forced. (47)

If this passage contains strong echoes of Jerome, Cavendish's emphasis suggests a different moral. A woman's beauty may "betray" her, but Cavendish argues that the inability of feminine virtue *alone* to restrain the masculine sex does not demonstrate a failure of that virtue. Yet Cavendish's description does not, as one might expect, stress the evils of the "masculine sex" so much as the civil war between the woman's beauty and her virtue. This begins to suggest an interesting political allegory in which a form of self-division is paradoxically represented as a consequence of bodily integrity, a theme to which I will return later. For the present, I'd like to suggest that this passage may offer a further political dimension to Cavendish's virginal allegory in the example of Dinah whose story connects rape to empire construction.[19] Although Jerome's cautionary example of Dinah is directed at restraining the wandering virgin, Cavendish's invocation of the same biblical source may be intended to remind us of the fatal consequences of the familial protection or "human assistance" she stresses. Genesis 34 describes not only Shechem's rape of Dinah, but also the full-scale massacre that Dinah's brothers, Simeon and Levi, visit upon Shechem's people as vengeance for the deed, despite the fact that Shechem desires to marry Dinah and is circumcised for her sake.

The fear of the virgin stripped of her veil may be in part supplanted here with a veiled threat of the political consequences to those who would force virgins and hence violate the integrity of the political body.[20] Moreover, the Old Testament story might have particular resonance for Cavendish writing in exile during the Protectorate since the narrative connects loss and exile to eventual political consolidation. The massacre necessitates the flight of Israel, yet forms a crucial link in the chain of events leading to Israel's eventual foundation in the Promised Land.[21]

Although the preface of *Assaulted and Pursued Chastity* seems to subscribe to the precept that travel is an unsuitable occupation for virgins, this sentiment must immediately be adapted to the political circumstances of the story's opening, for it seems that politics has in fact forced our heroine to travel in order to *protect* her virtue when an "unjust war" and "plaguey rebellion" wrecks the peace of her native Kingdom of Riches. Those loyalists who chose to stay "sent their daughters and wives, from the fury of the inhumane multitude, choosing to venture their lives with the hazards of travels, rather than their honours and chastities by staying at home, amongst rough and rude soldiers . . ." (48).

As a transparent allegory of the Civil War that forced the royalist Cavendishes into sixteen years of exile, Cavendish's sympathies are not hard to discern, and reflect her deeply conservative views on social order and monarchical hierarchies. But Cavendish's allegory also foregrounds how the Civil War forced a redefinition or relocation of a realm safe for—or proper to—women.[22] Even though peace is restored to the Kingdom of Riches and the Lady's ambitions are, for the moment, limited to getting home, her ill-deserved fate is to be shipwrecked on the shores of the Kingdom of Sensuality, deserted by her friends, and sold to a bawd.

While the bawd awaits the return of her best customer, a subject prince of the land who was "a grand monopolizer of young virgins" (50), she prepares her prize with lengthy "lectures of Nature." These lectures pursue conventional *carpe diem* themes, urging the lady "to make best profit" of her youth and beauty. She argues: "Nature hath made nothing vainly, but to some useful end; and nothing merely for itself, but for a common benefit and general good, as earth, water, air and fire, sun, moon, stars, light, heat, cold and the like" (49).[23] The bawd goes on to warn her not to "sin against Nature," "for she is a great and powerful goddess, transforming all things out of one shape into another, and those that serve her faithfully and according as she commands, she puts them in an easy and delightful form" (49).

Such arguments, learned as they are for a bawd, only alert our heroine to her danger. Yet this metamorphic theory of nature is not entirely discredited by the source. Although the bawd enlists such arguments to corrupt her captive, the lady will later echo them in a speech that describes bodily transformations as both a function of nature and a sign of divine favor: "[T]hose that please the gods, live easy in every shape, and die quietly and peaceably; or when the gods do change their shapes or mansions, 'tis for the better, either for ease or newness" (75). The lady revises the bawd's exploitative utilitarianism to espouse a kind of liberating animist materialism. Challenging the bawd's arguments that urge the consumption of virginal bodies, the lady's pseudo-classical theology allows for the operations of a pleasurable virginal vitalism.[24] Her contention that "the soul is a kind of god in itself, to direct and guide those things that are inferior to it" (74), is not so much a Platonist assertion of the superiority of spirit to matter as it is an argument that allows Cavendish to animate virginal integrity and to make it a less inert and more dynamic instrument for enforcing as well as reflecting social order. In the end, it is the very force of the lady's virginity and not the forces enlisted against her virtue that, Cavendish suggests, will paradoxically produce and authorize the lady's remarkable physical transformations during the course of the narrative.

While she is trapped in the bawd's house, the lady is named for the first time in the story, Miseria. The etiology of her name clearly reflects the allegorical structure of this tale, but it is the *delay* in naming her that best indicates the identity-forming nature of women's circumstances, particularly where their virtue is at stake.[25] Misery defines not only our heroine's dire situation, but also the potential crisis to her virginal identity as she stands poised on the brink of total ruin.

So far Cavendish's story is utterly conventional and the reader anticipates the generic possibilities for the *raptus* narrative. Indeed, it seems clear that our virgin requires either: a) miraculous intervention, or b) the means to suicide. As for miraculous intervention, Cavendish prepares us in the preface not to anticipate such a resolution when she points out "that Heaven doth not always protect the persons of virtuous souls from rude violences" (47), thus insisting on a distinction often elided in narratives of sexual violence between the sin and the one sinned against. Her virtue will neither be protected nor defined by divine intervention. The story's nebulously classical setting might seem to clear the Christian obstacle to the alternative fate of the assaulted virgin—the "choice" of suicide. However, the implicit sympathy of the classical setting to the moral logic of the noble suicide may indeed be superfluous, since even in Christian doctrine the prohibition against self-slaying seems to be relaxed in the case of the assaulted virgin.[26] Nor were such questions regarding virtue and sin entirely academic during the Civil War, when women were often left behind to fend for themselves, or, like Cavendish, traveled abroad separated from their families.[27]

The reader is scarcely surprised when Miseria resolves to die: "for in death, said she, there is no pain; nor in a dishonourable life no content" (51). Thus, it is a considerable narrative shock when Miseria uses the pistol she cleverly (if anachronistically) smuggles into her antique chambers not on herself but on her attacker, the Prince. Brandishing her pistol she declares to the advancing Prince, who seems unable to believe she will use it: "Stay, stay, . . . I will first build me a temple of fame upon your grave, where all young virgins shall come and offer at my shrine, and in the midst of these words shot him; with that he fell to the ground" (53). Hearing the commotion within, the bawd rushes in to see the Prince "smeared in blood and the young Lady as a marble statue standing by." This tableau reverses the position of victim and victor: the prince is the one bloodied, penetrated by the discharged weapon of the Lady, who stands over him, statuesque and impassive.

This victory of Miseria over the Prince preserves her chastity, but endangers her place in the narrative. If she is not a victim, can she be considered innocent, especially when a gun replaces God as intervening moral force? While Miseria could be seen here to trigger misogynist fears of female mastery, this scene is designed rather to expose the private struggle of self-mastery to public praise or censure—a struggle in which she succeeds and the Prince fails. Demonstrating her self-sufficiency and her self-possession, Miseria draws on a long tradition of stoic humanism that, as Raymond Anselment has argued, served as a particularly powerful rhetoric for the defeated royalists.[28] Moreover, Miseria is able to transform stoic suffering into a kind of active heroism. In seizing the pistol, she refuses not only the prince, but the narratives that constrain the possible honorable— let alone heroic—responses to the threat against her. Instead of the expected scene of secret shame, she dramatizes an occasion for public honor. Promising a public testimonial to this personal assault, she declares, in effect, that if she cannot shame him in life, she will humiliate him in death. To this end, Miseria threatens him not with a martyr's shrine, but with a victor's monument, a "temple of fame."

Jean Gagin describes Cavendish's abiding interest in securing for herself lasting fame, noting that:

> Margaret Cavendish alone of all women writers of her day espoused writing as a career with the avowed intent of winning fame in accordance

with the ideals of Renaissance humanism. Paradoxically, however, her very intent was a heterodox application of these ideals, which were designed to spur gentlemen rather than ladies to heroic achievements. The only type of "fame" with which a woman was supposed to be concerned was her reputation for virtue or chastity.[29]

Assaulted and Pursued Chastity resolves the perceived contradiction of the heroic woman by making chastity an active rather than passive virtue. Cavendish's allegorical romance does not represent chastity as an immured or unworldly virtue, a jewel to be prized but hidden. Like Book Three of the *Faerie Queene, Assaulted and Pursued Chastity* displays chastity as a sacred trust, a force against enemies, and an instrument of justice, although Cavendish's heroine will differ from Spenser's Britomart in seeking personal fame rather than the fulfillment of her dynastic destiny.

The violence of the encounter between Prince and virgin ends neither the Prince's life nor Miseria's misery. The Prince recovers from his physical wounds, yet his passion for her intensifies. Cupid has pierced him, not with a dart, but with a bullet, a Petrarchan convention rendered bizarre by the literalness of the erotic violence Petrarchan conventions are designed to mask. Despite his growing passion for her, the Prince is not free to make Miseria an honorable proposal since he is already married to an old and wealthy widow. Instead, he removes her to the country, where she is held captive in the care of an ancient aunt who attends the young woman and soon grows to worship her charge.

In an act of self-naming that seems to shift the emphasis from her bad situation to her good nature, the former Miseria takes the new name Affectionata. This name makes absolutely clear that this lady is no icy Petrarchan mistress, neither condescending nor cruel. Chastity in Cavendish's story is not a virtue of negation precisely because it is not defined or delimited by masculine desire, and Affectionata is established as the owner as well as the master of her passions. She is not, however, in charge of her present circumstances, and when the Prince assaults her a second time, she swallows poison in an unsuccessful suicide attempt. Her failure to slay herself departs rather sharply from hagiographic tradition, when an effective emetic replaces the *deus ex machina* in preserving her life. However, merely surviving does not in the end prove her virtue, nor does it protect it from future assault. This will require more dramatic measures.

Affectionata has failed now to secure her freedom either by murder or by suicide. Heaven has not intervened. Even extreme methods have failed her *in extremis.* Desperation drives her and ingenuity inspires her to seek self-preservation, paradoxically enough, through the creation of a new self. She cuts off her hair, dons a page's suit of clothes and eludes her captors, making her way to the capital city where she steals aboard the first ship leaving port.

In the several adventures that follow, Miseria/Affectionata becomes the adoptive son of the benevolent captain, on whose ship she stows away, and travels through an outlandish landscape straight out of Mandeville's *Travels* (or, perhaps more aptly, an Inigo Jones's set design for an antimasque) in male disguise under the assumed name Travellia. This act of self-naming is significant in that it is the first time she chooses not only a name but something of the circumstances that determine that name. Given this, it is distinctly odd that this name seems to announce her as the traveling singular feminine personage her alias is designed to disguise. Instead, the name serves as a constant reminder that Travellia's accomplishments are not entirely attributable to, or subsumed under, a masculine imposture.[30]

Also complicating matters of gender identity is the text's persistent inconsistency in its attribution of masculine and feminine pronouns to describe or indicate Travellia. Cavendish's less charitable critics (and she has had many over the years) have pointed to such "lapses" in her work as an indication of her feeble skills in telling a coherent story, her general neglect of grammatical and orthographical conventions, or a consequence of her ambitious haste to publish. Cavendish's frequent apologies for her lack of learning are often used as material evidence against her. But the humility topos should not be taken any more literally for women writers than for their male contemporaries; and indeed, such modest protestations need to be all the more carefully scrutinized in view of the considerable social stigma risked by women seeking publication in a cultural context where chastity was equated with silence. While I would argue for a deliberately experimental Cavendish, these pronominal inconsistencies, whether unintended or measured, point in any case to the considerable fluidity in her representation of gendered identities. For even if one accepted that such inversions were accidental rather than intended, the questions they raise do not go away, but rather multiply to raise questions about the psychological or cultural forces that drive such substitutions.

I would argue, moreover, that the confusion for the reader does not derive from the alternation of pronouns per se. The reader always knows who Travellia is, and her identity is never in doubt even when her gender is. The source of confusion derives rather from Cavendish's refusal to establish or maintain any distinction between a private female essence, and an assumed public, masculine role. In this sense, Travellia breaks with the decorum generally maintained by Shakespeare's cross-dressed heroines, or Spenser's cross-dressed knight of Chastity, Britomart, where internally experienced and externally observed events register on separate and gendered scales. This disjunction between "real" and perceived genders is precisely what drives the double-entendres and much of the bawdy humor in Shakespeare's comedies as well as the quest (for Britomart's true identity and destined mate) in Spenser's *Faerie Queene*. In these texts the reader is relied upon to make the gendered "correction" that seeing through disguise enables, a correction which, even when delayed, or infused with homoerotic tension, confers upon characters coherent identities (no matter how fictional) and gives them recognizable motives.[31]

Like Cavendish's Travellia, Shakespeare's cross-dressed heroines are generally *forced* by extreme circumstances to assume male garb; unlike Travellia, however, they express discomfort with or distance from the imposture. Julia, dressed as a page in *Two Gentlemen of Verona* to escape "the loose encounters of lascivious men," wonders about the damage she might do to the very reputation she is endeavoring to preserve: "how will the world repute me / For undertaking so unstaid a journey / I fear it will make me scandalized" (2.7.59–61). Rosalind in *As You Like It* rejects the notion that her male garb changes her in any way: "Dost thou think though I am caparisoned like a man, I have a doublet and hose in my disposition?" (3.2.204–6). With these representations of female cross-dressing in Shakespeare in mind, Linda Woodbridge has argued that "transvestite disguise does not blur the distinction between the sexes but heightens it."[32]

Cavendish, by contrast, neither inverts nor corrects gender roles through transvestism. Rather than disguising or disclosing gender by turns, her use of cross-dressing generally works to destabilize and challenge gender as a natural marker of identity and difference. It is interesting to note in this regard that when Cavendish praises Shakespeare, she does not choose to admire his heroines' masculine accomplishments or their feminine virtues; rather, she attributes to the Bard the ability to metamorphose himself into a woman.[33]

In *Gender Trouble*, Judith Butler elaborates her theory about the "performativity of gender" as follows:

> That gender reality is created through sustained social performances means that the very notions of an essential sex and a true or abiding masculinity or femininity are also constituted as part of the strategy that conceals gender's performative character and the performative possibili-

ties for proliferating gender configurations outside the restrictive frames of masculinist domination and compulsory heterosexuality.

Genders can be neither true nor false, neither real nor apparent, neither original nor derived. As credible bearers of those attributes, however, genders can also be rendered thoroughly and radically *incredible*.[34]

Butler is careful to emphasize that if gender is performative, it is not like a garment one has the power to select and don for the day and put away in the evening. The subject is already gendered or "decided by gender" from the start.[35] Nonetheless, it is just this idea of gender rendered "incredible" that is most suggestive for a textual analysis of *Assaulted and Pursued Chastity*, and cross-dressing is only one of the vehicles for producing this effect. The imaginary cross-cultural transactions are at least as important in the textual play of gendered norms.

One such cross-cultural encounter occurs when Travellia is seized along with "his" "father," the captain, by a purple-skinned and white-haired people. In this episode, Travellia faints dead away at the prospect of being stripped naked before their orange-skinned, black-haired king:

> but Travellia was so affrighted, that he fell down in a swound[.] Those that touched him started back when they saw him dead; but the old man [i.e., the captain] bending him forward, brought him to life again: whereupon they straight thought that their touching him killed him, and that the old man had power to restore life, which made them afraid to touch them anymore, for that disease of sounding was not known to them. . . . (68)

Described from the perspective of the purple citizens who look on, this inexplicable behavior appears to be a miraculous death and reanimation since swooning is a "disease" unknown among them. Layering the native astonishment with a Christian allegory of resurrection, the text doubly reconfigures what might in other contexts be taken as feminine weakness. This is, of course, no celebration of multiculturalism—indeed, the credulity of their captors is later brutally exploited by Travellia and the captain—but the episode does suggest the imaginative possibilities for early modern feminism in the discovery (or the invention) of other cultural models. Moreover, it is worth noting that Cavendish does not offer a single corrected European perspective of this event, since the outcome allows the captain to continue in the mistaken belief that Travellia is a boy. At this point in the narrative Travellia's adoptive father would no more have understood the fainting of Travellia as a manifestation of (or reversion to) female nature than would the purple men who looked on. The captain would have almost certainly taken this delicacy in the young European as a sign of "his" manifest (and yet disguised) noble nature.

The insistence on the masculine pronoun in this incident renders gender incredible as sufficient—let alone universal—explanation of human behavior. Far from marking Travellia as weak, the fainting spell reveals her to her captors as powerful and mysterious, an outcome that exemplifies the text's persistent refusal to embody weakness as feminine, strength as masculine. Rather than simply invert these associations (and thus reproduce familiar negative images of the effeminate male and the aggressive, manly female), Cavendish displays the very vulnerability of the chaste virgin as a source of hidden strength, drawn from his/her hermaphroditic nature. Travellia represents not an inversion of "proper" gender roles so much as a hermaphroditic combination of female and male, defensive and aggressive, vulnerable and powerful.

This is especially evident when Travellia secures their release armed with two pistols and dressed in a grass skirt, with "a garland of flowers on his head" and "his hair which was grown in that time" untied and "spread upon his back" (70). This dress, regarded as utterly exotic by their captors, constitutes a kind of double or even treble cross-dressing that defies categorization as either theatrical or natural. The display is at once martial and pastoral, masculine and feminine, and yet neither recognizably European nor native. Through violence and eloquence, Travellia brings the colorful natives to frightened submission. And, after fatally shooting their chief priest, Travellia instructs them (without a shred of the ironic deference with which Montaigne treats his cannibals) how to become "a civilized people" (75).

This narrative seizes and revalues the ambiguous sexual geographies evident in the dominant discourses of early modern England where, as Peter Stallybrass has described it, "woman's body could be both symbolic map of the 'civilized' and the dangerous terrain that had to be colonized."[36] In Cavendish's romance, Travellia's body is represented as civilizing rather than civilized, colonizer rather than colonized. She is at once a feminine figure for the vulnerability produced by exile and the masculine agent of conquest and conversion.

Travellia's ultimate challenge, however, will be going home, as the final episode shifts the site of conflict away from the exotic to focus on domestic struggles. The stage for this "return" is not Travellia's homeland, but the Kingdom of Amity, where she seeks refuge from the renewed pursuit of the Prince. The sexualized geography of the allegory is explicit when Travellia becomes the Queen of Amity's principal advisor and general in her war with the King of Amour.[37] The chief cause of this war, we are told, was that the Queen was "averse and deaf to his suit" (89), a proposal of marriage that is quite explicitly attributed to the twin motives of love and empire expansion. It is of course an allegorical imperative rather than coincidence that causes the Prince to turn up as the opposing general in the service of the King of Amour.

The ensuing war enlarges and politicizes the struggle between the Prince and Travellia, as the military engagement between Amour and Amity lays out the allegorical grounds for working out the relationship between sexual conflict and political strife. The presumed correlation between domestic and political spheres, a staple of political theory, is revisited in Cavendish's romance, but not without some striking revisions. Rather than naturalize politics through the synecdoche of the familial unit, Cavendish politicizes the erotic crisis of this episode; and yet the slippage of gender markers makes this military engagement something more than a routine battle of the sexes.

When Travellia learns that her Queen has been taken hostage, she is described as:

> high enraged, which choler begot a masculine and courageous spirit in her, for though she could not have those affections in her for the Queen as a man, yet she admired her heroic virtues, and loved her as a kind and gracious princess to her, which obligations made her impatient of revenge. (95)

The battle that follows pits the valor, the military strategy, as well as the rhetorical ability of Travellia and the Prince on an even playing field. The two eventually meet head to head in a duel, the consequences of which divide absolutely between the physical and the political body. Travellia is wounded due to her inexperience and her physical disadvantage, but her troops, inspired by her eloquence, win the day, and it is the Prince who is taken hostage. Travellia's lack of brute force in no way diminishes her military talents or her real powers, which are not limited to her body. Here the bleeding Travellia has been penetrated by the Prince's weapon, but she has neither been violated nor vanquished. Her personal defeat is figured as part of her larger political victory, a powerful allegory for the vanquished royalist cause during the Interregnum.

The ensuing exchange of hostages uncovers the identity of Travellia to the Prince and the King, but not to the Queen, who remains heartsick for her general with whom she has fallen desperately in love. Cavendish goes so far as to show the King and Prince bickering over the King's jealousy of Travellia, even though at this point they both know her to be a woman. By delaying and enacting only in stages the discovery of her identity, Cavendish is clearly allowing a greater range of emotion 'twixt amity and amour, showing that these terms are neither defined nor delimited by gender. When the Queen finally learns from the Prince Travellia's true nature (Travellia never willingly puts aside her masculine guise), Cavendish describes her state: "her color came and went, moved by her mixed passions, anger and love; angry that she was deceived, yet still did love, as wishing she had been a man" (112). The line "wishing she had been a man" leaves ambiguous which of them she would have be the man, but leaves absolutely unambiguous her continuing love, as she directs her anger at the deception rather than the beloved. Even later, when the Queen is under no delusion as to Travellia's gender and has recovered from her initial shock, she playfully says of a visit to Travellia that she is "a-courting her hard-hearted lover" (113). When the Queen plays, in Petrarchan terms, the male suitor to Travellia's virtuous mistress, she simply assumes the masculine role previously played by Travellia rather than "correcting" their gendered positions. Cavendish seems determined to make these women the subject, rather than the object, of both civility and passion.

In the end, the Queen learns to pity the King *because* of the love she has suffered for Travellia, a love that is described by favorable comparisons rather than distinctions and is found to be enabling rather than distracting. The connection between Travellia and the Queen of Amity is not depicted as an immature relation to be contained by or redirected toward heterosexual bonding, and their alliance is not put aside even when news arrives that the Prince's wife has conveniently died, and all the physical obstacles to a double wedding are removed. Although Travellia does not object to the now honorable possibility of union with the Prince, the Queen immediately puts conditions on the match:

> I have promised your mistress to protect her against your outrageous assaults; but since your suit is just, and your treaty civil, I will yield her to you, upon that condition you carry her not out of my kingdom; for since I cannot marry her, and so make her my husband, I will keep her if I can, and so make her my friend. (114)

The civilizing force of the Queen's now chaste love, augmented by the love of the people, determines that the Prince will be Viceroy of Amity, but that Travellia will rule.

Sarah Heller Mendelson has observed that in Cavendish's fiction "the focus is not on love per se but on a woman's 'will to power.'"[38] Certainly the denouement of this narrative is dependent on understanding this, as we see so little of Travellia's amorous feelings for the Prince. But what is interesting to note is how Cavendish defines and realigns female power. The initially powerless Travellia gains a power more effective than firearms by assuming a masculine identity, but, in the end, power is not located in her external masculine armor—through which she can be and is wounded—but in her unassailable chastity in which her rhetorical, military, and political strengths reside.

Travellia's eventual re-feminization does not require her to renounce her "masculine" achievements, nor does it make her in marriage an abject subject to the Prince. But if Cavendish embraces the possibility of female power, she distances herself from the topsy-turvy carnival world of the woman-on-top.[39] Cavendish's royalist politics and her contempt for the unruly hordes never changed; hers is not a popular or populist feminist vision. In *Assaulted and Pursued Chastity,* Cavendish embodies a royalist diaspora in the virginal Travellia, a figure whose vulnerability and strength are similarly attributed to her great virtue. Travellia is not an Amazonian virago who challenges "rightful" male authority. Neither does she seek to usurp masculine prerogatives to become the monstrous man-woman. She is rather forced to become the compensatory hermaphrodite whose masculine virtues are brought on or provoked by the lack of virtuous male authority or masculine self-constraint.

Moving beyond the narrow range of female power authorized by Henrietta Maria's court-based chastity cult, Cavendish constructs out of her exile a far-ranging chastity whose very victimization authorizes great acts of valor on a world stage. Thus, Cavendish attempts to reconcile in her allegory what may have seemed to her contemporaries two incompatible narratives: one featuring political restoration, the other female emancipation. The assaulted virgin represents allegorically the violently displaced and disinherited political body, a body that remains intact through exile and a series of adversities. But at the same time, the narrative of *Assaulted and Pursued Chastity* constitutes a reproach to failed aristocratic virtues. This virgin is, after all, not assaulted by "rough and rude soldiers," but by a Prince who eventually becomes her mate. The violation of the political body is thus figured as a function of an aristocratic intemperance and lack of self-governance.[40] The ultimate restoration of a proper order is, in fact, a new order under which female chastity is something more than a reservoir of feminine value for masculine use. Instead, chastity is offered as a powerful symbolic source of just governance and at the same time the justification of female power and self-governance.

Four years after the publication of *Assaulted and Pursued Chastity,* the monarchy was restored and the Cavendishes returned to England where Margaret Cavendish's voluminous writing and her extraordinary costumes (often involving breeches) equally contributed to earning her the nickname "Mad Madge." Dorothy Osborne quipped that "there are many soberer people in Bedlam."[41] Samuel Pepys, who concluded that she was a "mad, conceited, ridiculous woman," nonetheless recorded in minute detail the extraordinary lengths to which he would go in order to catch the merest glimpse of her passing.[42] Margaret Cavendish persuaded her husband to a quiet life away from court at Welbeck, and her appearances in London were the more celebrated for being rare.

One such appearance, chronicled by Pepys, was Cavendish's famous visit to the Royal Society. Her unusual costume was described in a ballad composed by the diarist John Evelyn in which appears the following stanza:

> But, Jo! her head-gear was so pretty,
> I ne'er saw anything so witty;
> Though I was half afeared,
> God bless us! when I first did see her:
> She looked so like a Cavalier,
> But that she had no beard.[43]

Despite the fact that Cavendish had nothing but praise for the virtuosi, she was a double unsettling presence, both as a female philosopher and as a masculine woman. Her hermaphroditic costume was not just a double but a paradoxical construction, for it subverted even as it dramatized her status in this scientific society as a *persona non grata.* Whether she embraced the guise as an evasion of, or an affront to, the social standards which denied her participation as an intellectual equal, the spectacle she embodied effectively challenged by destablizing the very "nature" of her position in the company of the Fellows of the Royal Society, even as they revealed nature's secrets in various scientific demonstrations performed for her personal edification.

In the end, however, I would suggest that it was neither the Duchess's literary and philosophical ambitions nor her taste for crossdressing per se that fully account for Cavendish's reputation for madness, for in neither of these was she entirely singular. It was, rather, the peculiar combination of these masculine habits and her feminine virtues that made her so utterly incomprehensible to her contemporaries. In her youth, she was by her own report so shy and awkward in her service of Henrietta Maria that she was taken for "a Natural Fool" by the more polished and worldly attendants of the court. But, she adds, "I rather chose to be accounted a Fool, than to be thought rude or wanton. . . ."[44] However, Cavendish's experiments in cross-dress were not entirely culturally reconcilable to this self-representation. By assuming male dress, the masculine woman was most often and most passionately condemned for revealing a lustful and lascivious nature.[45] In the Restoration, wearing breeches was a custom shared by actresses and prostitutes, professions that enthusiasts of Restoration theater conflated no less than the anti-theatrical William Prynne.[46] Thus it is that the entry on Cavendish in the *Dictionary of National Biography* concludes that "Her occasional appearances in theatrical costume, and her reputation for purity of life . . . contributed to gain her a reputation for madness."[47]

Throughout her oeuvre, Cavendish makes frequent protestations of her personal and intellectual chastity. In her biography, *A True Relation of My Birth, Breeding and Life,* which appears in the same volume as *Assaulted and Pursued Chastity,* she declares "I am Chast, both by Nature and Education, insomuch as I do abhorre an unchast thought."[48] Nonetheless, as a female author, Cavendish was already a hybrid, an androgyne, a monster, every time she picked up her pen. The learned woman was, in Patricia Labalme's phrase, "an intellectual transvestite."[49] Despite the presumed opposition of female authorship and chastity, Cavendish would seem to exploit their semiotic proximity in the cultural construction of the *virilis femina.* Cavendish's actual practice of cross dressing was—in its very superfluity—designed to focus attention on her masculine art and draw it away from her female "nature." But some cultural narratives are more powerful than others, and we should not be entirely surprised if, in the end, Cavendish was found not only textually but personally illegible. John Stainsby, in his epitaph for Margaret Cavendish, Duchess of Newcastle, would remember her simply as "Welbeck's illustrious whore."[50]

Notes

Foreword (Margaret W. Ferguson)

1. See the editors' introduction for a useful discussion of the range of meanings associated with "virginity" and "chastity."

2. We need more research on how and when discourses about virginity correlate with—or ignore—discourses on same-sex erotic practices in the Middle Ages and the early modern era. Those latter discourses, as Natalie Zemon Davis and Arlette Farge have noted, generally showed the "double standard" to work *against* men; at the very least, the discourses imply gender-asymmetries different from but linked to those that obtain in the virginity debates. For some early Christian commentators, for instance, sex between women, however, "unnatural," seemed less sinful than sex between men because the former appeared "to lack the penetration that constituted the central evil of sodomy" (Davis and Farge, in *A History of Women: Renaissance and Enlightenment Paradoxes,* ed. Davis and Farge [Cambridge: Harvard University Press, 1993], p. 440). Implicitly defining virginity as a specifically female attribute, John Boswell argued that the (relative) tolerance for male same-sex practices in early medieval monasteries and church schools depended in part on a view that if "vows of chastity" were broken by erotic relations between men, it was "less sinful, some claimed, than bringing wives to adultery or deflowering virgins" (Davis and LaFarge, *History of Women,* p. 440, referring to Boswell's *Christianity, Social Tolerance, and Homosexuality: Gay People in Western Europe from the Beginning of the Christian Era to the Fourteenth Century* [Chicago: University of Chicago Press]). See also Valerie Traub, "The (In)Significance of "Lesbian" Desire in Early Modern England," in *Queering the Renaissance,* ed. Jonathan Goldberg (Durham, N.C.: Duke University Press, 1994), 62–83.

3. Richard Halpern, "Puritanism and Maenadism in 'A Mask,'" in *Rewriting the Renaissance,* ed. M. Ferguson, M. Quilligan, and N. Vickers (Chicago: University of Chicago Press, 1986), p. 94.

4. Cited in the editors' introduction, from Hastrup, "The Semantics of Biology: Virginity," in *Defining Females: The Nature of Women in Society,* ed. Shirley Ardener (New York: Croom Helm, 1978), p. 63.

5. John Bugge, *Virginitas: An Essay in the History of a Medieval Ideal,* International Archives of the History of Ideas, Series Minor, 17 (The Hague: Martinus Nijhoff, 1975), p. 1.

6. Leslie here cites Jane Tibbetts Schulenberg, "The Heroics of Virginity: Brides of Christ and Sacrificial Multilation," in *Women in the Middle Ages and Renaissance,* ed. Mary Beth Rose (Syracuse, NY: Syracuse University Press, 1986), p. 32.

7. Cited from *John Milton: Complete Poems and Major Prose,* ed. Merritt Hughes (Indianapolis: The Odyssey Press, 1957), p. 695.

8. Some critics have begun to explore this dimension of Milton's thought: see Gregory Bredbeck, *Sodomy and Interpretation: Marlowe to Milton* (Ithaca: Cornell University Press, 1991). For more general treatments of the distinct but related phenomena of "homoeroticism" and what Eve Kosofsky Sedgwick defines as "homosocial relations" in *Between Men: English Literature and Male Homosocial Desire* (New York: Columbia University Press, 1985), and for various perspectives on the terminological problems raised by studying modalities of love and friendship between men in the early modern period, see Jonathan Goldberg, *Sodometries: Renaissance Texts, Modern Sexualities* (Stanford, CA: Stanford University Press, 1992); Goldberg's edited collection *Queering the Renaissance* (cited above, n. 2); Bruce R. Smith, *Homosocial Desire in Shakespeare's England: A Cultural Poetics* (Chicago: University of Chicago Press, 1991).

9. Jacques Derrida, *Dissemination*, trans. Barbara Johnson (Chicago: University of Chicago Press, 1981), p. 7.

10. For one discussion of this tradition, see Stephanie Jed, *Chaste Thinking: The Rape of Lucrece and the Birth of Humanism* (Bloomington and Indianapolis: Indiana University Press, 1989).

Introduction: The Epistemology of Virginity (Kathleen Coyne Kelly and Marina Leslie)

1. Simone de Beauvoir, *The Second Sex*, trans. and ed. H. M. Parshley (1952: New York: Random House/Vintage Books, 1989), p. 152.

2. *Virginal Sexuality and Textuality in Victorian Literature* (Albany: State University of New York Press, 1993), a collection of essays edited by Lloyd Davis, attempts to do the same for the construction of virginity in the late nineteenth century. Davis offers a Foucauldian analysis of virginity, locating it within a variety of discourses that construct not only sexuality, but "nature, patriarchy, the family, economics, morality, religion, metaphysics, psychology, medicine, literature, even politics and royalty" (p. 4).

3. Early patristic writers usually identified three distinct states of female chastity: virginity, widowhood, and marriage. However, later writers sometimes formulated their own models. Aldhelm (late seventh century), for example, replaces this tripartite scheme with another: *virginitas* (spontaneous desire for celibacy), *castitas* (continent marriage), and *iugalitas* (accession to the necessity of procreation) in *De virginitate* XIX (*PL* 89.116–17). Aldhelm compares the three states in an elaborate set of metaphors: "virginity is the sun, chastity a lamp, conjugality darkness . . . virginity is a queen, chastity a lady, conjugality a servant . . . virginity is the royal purple, chastity the re-dyed fabric, conjugality the undyed wool." *Aldhelm: Prose Works*, trans. Michael Lapidge and Michael Herren (Cambridge: D. S. Brewer; Totowa, NJ: Rowman & Littlefield, 1979), p. 75.

4. Thomas Aquinas's disquisitions on temperance, abstinence, chastity, and virginity in the *Summa Theologiae* illustrate some of the difficulties in defining these terms. He says that *castitas*, for example, "has a proper and a metaphorical meaning" ("Dicendum quod nomen castitatis dupliciter accipitur," p. 160). Aquinas also speaks of *spiritualis castitas* (which is "refrain[ing] from enjoying things against [God's] design") and its opposite, *spiritualis fornicatio* (which is "delighting in things against God's order," p. 160–61). *Summa Theologiae*, ed. and trans. Thomas Gilby (Blackfriars and New York: McGraw Hill; London: Eyre and Spottiswoode, 1968).

5. However, *virginitas*, says Aquinas (citing Augustine), dwells in the soul: "non consistit in carne," pp. 168–69.

6. Kirsten Hastrup, "The Semantics of Biology: Virginity," *Defining Females: The Nature of Women in Society*, ed. Shirley Ardener (New York: Croom Helm, 1978), 49–65, p. 63.

7. John Bugge's *Virginitas: An Essay in the History of a Medieval Ideal* (The Hague: Martinus Nijhoff, 1975) remains an important starting point for an understanding of virginity in Western Europe. Vern L. Bullough and James Brundage's collection of essays, *Sexual Practices and the Medieval Church* (Buffalo, NY: Prometheus Books, 1982), Peter Brown's *The Body and Society: Men, Women, and Sexual Renunciation in Early Christianity* (New York: Columbia University Press, 1988), and Pierre J. Payer's *The Bridling of Desire: Views of Sex in the Later Middle Ages* (Toronto and Buffalo: University of Toronto Press, 1993) provide valuable insights into the psychology of sexuality. Jane Tibbets Schulenberg's "The Heroics of Virginity: Brides of Christ and Sacrificial Mutilation" (*Women in the Middle Ages and Renaissance: Literary and Historical Perspectives*, ed. Mary Beth Rose [Syracuse, NY: University of Syracuse Press, 1986], pp. 29–72), is an excellent short study of the virgin in the text.

8. Recent studies that focus on Elizabeth as the Virgin Queen include Philippa Berry, *Of Chastity and Power* (London and New York: Routledge, 1989) and Helen Hackett, *Virgin Mother/Maiden Queen: Elizabeth I and the Cult of the Virgin Mary* (Basingstoke, England: Macmillan Press, 1995).

9. See Jonathan Goldberg, *James I and the Politics of Literature* (Baltimore: Johns Hopkins University Press, 1983; Stanford, CA: Stanford University Press, 1989).

10. *The Progresses, Processions and Magnificent Festivities of James I*, 4 vols., ed. John Nichols (New York: AMS Press, 1968), 1:337ff.

11. See Lawrence Stone, *The Family, Sex and Marriage in England 1500–1800* (New York: Harper and Row, 1977), pp. 192–202. The question famously raised by Joan Kelly-Gadol's essay "Did Women Have a Renaissance?" is still provoking debate among feminist Renaissance scholars. The essay is in *Becoming Visible: Women in European History*, ed. Renate Bridenthal and Claudia Koonz (Boston: Houghton Mifflin, 1977), pp. 137–64; rpt. in *Women, History, and Theory: The Essays of Joan Kelly* (Chicago: University of Chicago Press), pp. 19–50. See also Joan Kelly[-Gadol], "Notes on Women in the Renaissance and Renaissance Historiography," in *Conceptual Frameworks for Studying Women's History* (Bronxville, NY: Sarah Lawrence Publications, 1976). An important collection of essays on the representation of women in the Renaissance is *Rewriting the Renaissance: The Discourses of Sexual Difference in Early Modern Europe*, ed. Margaret W. Ferguson, Maureen Quilligan, and Nancy J. Vickers (Chicago: University of Chicago Press, 1986).

12. John Rogers, "The Enclosure of Virginity: The Poetics of Sexual Abstinence in the English Revolution," *Enclosure Acts: Sexuality, Property, and Culture in Early Modern England*, ed. Richard Burt and John Michael Archer (Ithaca and London: Cornell University Press 1994), 229–50, p. 237.

13. *English Lyrics of the 13th Century*, ed. Carleton Brown (Oxford: Clarendon Press, 1932), pp. 68–74, ll. 71–72.

14.

> Mayde, al so ich þe tolde,
> Þe ymston of þi bur
> He is betere an hundred folde

Þan alle þeos in heore culur;
He is i-don in heouene golde
and is ful of fyn amur.

(177–82)

A Vernon MS poem, "Of Clene Maydenhod" ("Off a trewe loue clene & derne") also promotes the general idea that earthly treasures cannot compare to virginity. In *Minor Poems of the Vernon MS* II, ed. F. J. Furnivall (E.E.T.S. O.S. 117, London, 1892), pp. 464–68.

15. *Hali Meiðhad,* ed. Bella Millett, E.E.T.S O.S. 284 (London: 1982), p. 4.

16. *Hali Meiðhad,* pp. 18–19.

17. For an overview of the patristic texts (along with a compelling argument on the role of virginity as an alternative both inside and outside patriarchy), see Elizabeth Castelli, "Virginity and Its Meaning for Women's Sexuality in Early Christianity" (*Journal of Feminist Studies in Religion* 2 [1986]: 61–86). For a fuller discussion of patristic writings on virginity, see Joyce Salisbury, *Church Fathers, Independent Virgins* (London and New York: Verso, 1991), chapter 1, "The Early Fathers on Sexuality: The Carnal World."

18. In *Kissing the Rod: An Anthology of Seventeenth-Century Women's Verse,* ed. Germaine Greer, Susan Hastings, Jeslyn Medoff, and Melinda Sansone (London: Virago Press, 1988), pp. 188–89. Also see "A Virgin Life" by Jane Barker in the same volume, pp. 360–61.

19. In the electronic archive of the Women Writers Project (M17C.4:VIRGINS.WWPPRT02 [subfile VIRGINS]), ll. 23–24. Line numbers henceforth quoted in the text.

20. A. D. Harvey, "Virginity and Honour in *Measure for Measure* and Davenant's *The Law against Lovers*" (*English Studies* 75, no. 2 [1994]: 123–32), p. 123, n. 1. After the Reformation, the medieval exaltation of married chastity (as abstinence) is replaced by the notion of connubial moderation.

21. Although convents did offer women unusual opportunities for learning, it is important not to romanticize the motives or exaggerate the autonomy of women who took vows of celibacy. Margaret L. King's observations are instructive: "I would suggest that when learned women (or men, for that matter) themselves chose a celibate life, they did so at least in part because they sought psychic freedom; when, on the other hand, men urged chastity upon learned women, they did so in part to constrain them." "Book-Lined Cells: Women and Humanism in the Early Italian Renaissance," *Beyond Their Sex: Learned Women of the European Past,* ed. Patricia LaBalme (New York: New York University Press, 1980), p. 78.

22. See Heather Dubrow, *A Happier Eden: The Politics of Marriage in the Stuart Epithalamium* (Ithaca and London: Cornell University Press 1990), for a study of the evolution of the conduct-book in the Renaissance.

23. Juan Luis Vives, *A very fruitful and pleasant book called the Instruction of a Christen Woman,* trans. Richard Hyrde (London, 1528?), p. xvii.

24. Paradox XII, "That Virginity is a Vertue," in *Paradoxes and Problems,* ed. Helen Peters (Oxford: Clarendon Press, 1980), pp. 56–57.

"Blæju þöll—Young Fir of the Bed-Clothes": Skaldic Seduction (William Sayers)

1. *Eyrbyggja saga,* ed. Einar Ól. Sveinsson and Matthías Þórðarson, Íslenzk fornrit 4 (Reykjavík: Hið íslenzka fornritafélag, 1935), ch. 28, st. 21. Verse that figures in

the family sagas is transcribed from the Íslenzk fornrit series and cited by chapter and stanza. Other skaldic verse (only the corpus up to about the year 1200 is reviewed in this study) is taken from *Den norske-islandske skjaldedigtning*, ed. Finnur Jónsson, 4 vols. (Copenhagen: Villadsen and Christensen, 1912–15), and follows Jónsson's normalization of the texts (for typographical convenience, the Old Norse/Icelandic "hooked o" has been replaced with "ö"). The source of these poems is abbreviated *Skj.* 1B in references, followed by page and stanza number. These editions also provide versions of the Old Norse original in which syntax is regularized in order to make explicit the interpretative strategy, since at times several sequences of the nominal elements are theoretically valid. Citations in such "decrypted" sequence are marked with an * on the analogy of reconstructed forms in historical linguistics. In the English translations, all tentative, the complex periphrastic imagery is rendered literally and is then equated in parentheses to its more prosaic referents. As with the image in the title of this paper, *blæju þöll* "young fir of the bed clothes," this can lead to unforeseen stylistic effects which are, ironically, not disconsonant with the multi-bottomed nature of skaldic imagery, although the shift in register toward the comic is undesirable. Freer translation, in this case with "spruce in the sheets," has a pleasure of its own, although the consideration of underlying ideology is doubtless best advanced by an attempt at a literal rendering.

2. *Eyrbyggja saga*, ch. 28, st. 22.

3. Snorri Sturluson, *Skáldskaparmál*, in *Edda Snorra Sturlusonar*, ed. Finnur Jónsson (Copenhagen: Gyldendal, 1931), ch. 58; trans. Anthony Faulkes as *Snorri Sturluson: Edda* (London and Melbourne: Dent, 1987).

4. Interpretation of the scene is still at issue; discussion in Bjarne Fidjestøl, *Det norrønne fyrstediktet* (Øvre Ervik: Alvheim and Eide, 1982) and "The Contribution of Scaldic Studies," in *Viking Revaluations*, ed. Anthony Faulkes and Richard Perkins (London: The Viking Society for Northern Research, 1993), pp. 100–120; Ludovica Koch, "Le Bouclier et la corne à bière. Étude sur la conception de la poésie et du poète chez Bragi Boddason et Egill Skalla-Grímsson," *Studi Nederlandesi-Studi Nordici* 22 (1979): 125–63; Helga Kress, "Vad en kvinna kväder: kultur och kön på Island i fornnordisk medeltid," *Nordisk kvinnolitteraturhistoria*, ed. Elisabeth Møller Jensen *et al.*, vol. 1, *I Guds namn, 1000–1800* (Höganäs: Wicken, 1993), 22–81; Lars Lönnroth, "Skaldemjödet i berget," *Bonniers Litterära Magasin* 1 (1994): 30–40; Lotte Motz, *The Beauty and the Hag: Female Figures in Germanic Faith and Myth*, Philologica Germanica 15 (Vienna: Fassbaender, 1993); Birgit Sawyer and Peter Sawyer, *Medieval Scandinavia: From Conversion to Reformation, circa 800–1500*, The Nordic Series 17 (Minneapolis and London: University of Minnesota Press, 1993).

5. Jenny Jochens has advanced a stimulating thesis on the developmental history of erotic poetry under the title "From Libel to Lament: Male Manifestations of Love in Old Norse," in *From Sagas to Society: Comparative Approaches to Early Iceland*, ed. Gísli Pálsson (Enfield Lock, Middlesex: Hisarlik Press, 1992), pp. 247–64. In her view, amorous verse, which went under the name of *mansöngvar*, was originally directed by male poets towards the female slaves of another man's household. As a collective, ON *man* certainly covered female slaves, but more generally meant "household, house-folk." I would propose that *mansöngr* referred to "amorous verse directed at *dependent* females," not only slaves and bondwomen, but unmarried daughters, sisters, and nieces who were members of a household.

6. *Grágás, Islændernes Lovbog I Fristatens Tid, udgivet efter det Kongelige Bibliotheks Haandskrift*, ed. Vilhjálmur Finsen, 2 vols. (Copenhagen: Gyldendal, 1852–83, repr. Odense: Odense University Press, 1974), 1b:184, 2:392–93. The Icelandic law code seems elaborated on a Norwegian original, but in none of the extant

redactions of law tracts from Norway is erotic verse named in this context. One may compare the gnomological injunction of the *Edda* poem *Sigrdrífomál* that men not lure women to love or tempt girls with promises of pleasure (*Edda: Die Lieder des Codex Regius*, ed. Gustav Neckel, 4th rev., ed. Hans Kuhn (Heidelberg: Carl Winter—Universitätsverlag, 1962), sts. 28, 32.

7. On *seiðr* see Motz, *The Beauty and the Hag;* Gísli Pálsson, "The Name of the Witch: Sagas, Sorcery, and Social Context," in *Social Approaches to Viking Studies,* ed. Ross Samson (Glasgow: Cruithne Press, 1991), pp. 157–68; and Dag Strömbäck, *Sejd: Textstudier i nordisk religionshistoria,* Nordiska texter och undersökningar 5 (Stockholm: Hugo Geber, and Copenhagen: Levin og Munskgaard, 1935). For a debatable historical alternation in the gender of practitioners, see Jenny Jochens, "Old Norse Magic and Gender: Þáttr Þorvalds ens víðförla," *Scandinavian Studies* 63 (1991): 305–17. Skaldic poetry is said to have originated with Óðinn's priests, "song smiths" (*Ynglinga saga,* ch. 6, in Snorri's *Heimskringla,* ed. Bjarni Aðalbjarnarson, Íslenzk fornrit 26–28 [Reykjavík: Hið íslenzka fornritafélag, 1941–51]). This same section of the work refers to Óðinn's ability to transform men in battle, both to weaken enemies and strengthen those he favored as berserks. The immediately following chapter deals with the god's acquisition of sorcery (*seiðr*) from the love goddess, Freyja.

8. Significant studies are Carol Clover, "Maiden Warriors and Other Sons," *The Journal of English and Germanic Philology* 85 (1986): 35–49; "The Politics of Scarcity: Notes on the Sex Ratio in Early Scandinavia," *Scandinavian Studies* 60 (1988): 147–88, "Regardless of Sex: Men, Women and Power in Early Northern Europe," *Speculum* 68 (1993): 363–87; Roberta Frank, "Marriage in Twelfth- and Thirteenth-Century Iceland," *Viator* 73 (1973): 473–84; Anne Heinrichs, "*Annat er várt eðli:* The Type of the Prepatriarchal Woman in Old Norse Literature," in *Structure and Meaning: New Approaches to Old Norse/Icelandic Studies,* ed. John Lindow, Lars Lönnroth, and Gerd Wolfgang Weber (Odense: Odense University Press, 1988), pp. 110–40; Judith Jesch, *Women in the Viking Age* (Woodbridge: Boydell and Brewer, 1991); Jenny Jochens, "The Church and Sexuality in Medieval Iceland," *Journal of Medieval History* 6 (1980): 377–92, "Consent in Marriage: Old Norse Law, Life and Literature," *Scandinavian Studies* 58 (1986): 142–76, "The Medieval Icelandic Heroine: Fact or Fiction?" *Viator* 17 (1986): 35–50, "Before the Male Gaze: The Absence of the Female Body in Old Norse," in *Sex in the Middle Ages: A Book of Essays,* ed. Joyce E. Salisbury (Hamden, CT: Garland, 1991), pp. 3–29, *Old Norse Images of Women* (Philadelphia: University of Pennsylvania Press, 1996), *Women in Old Norse Society* (Ithaca: Cornell University Press, 1996); Helga Kress, "Mandom og misogyni: noen refleksjoner omkring kvinnesynet i *Njáls saga*," *Gardar* 10 (1979): 35–51; Lars Lönnröth, "*Skírnismál* och den fornisländska äktenskapsnormen," in *Opuscula septentrionalia: Festskrift til Ole Widding, 10.10.1977,* ed. Bent Chr. Jacobsen, et al. (Copenhagen: Reitzel, 1977), pp. 154–78. For an overview of the divorce question, see Jakob Benediktsson, "Skilsmisse: Island," in *Kulturhistoriskt lexikon för nordisk medeltid,* 22 vols. (Malmö: Allhem, 1956–78), vol. 15 (1970), cols. 508f.

9. Cathy Jorgensen Itnyre, "A Smorgasbord of Sexual Practices," in *Sex in the Middle Ages: A Book of Essays,* ed. Joyce E. Salisbury (New York and London: Garland), pp. 146–56; Grethe Jacobsen, "Sexual Irregularities in Medieval Scandinavia," in *Sexual Practices and the Medieval Church,* ed. Vern L. Bullough and James Brundage (Buffalo, NY: Prometheus Books), pp. 72–88.

10. Freyja, on the other hand, is a constant feature of the mythological scene. She is predictably a keen connoisseur of *mansöngvar* (*Gylfaginning,* par. 23). As Freyja's intervention was sought by those whose unions were otherwise denied

(*Gylfaginning*, par. 35), she is allied with the seductive love poet in working against family interests. Moreover, as Freyja taught sorcery to the gods, love poetry and magic were associated in the mythic sphere as they were in the legal.

11. Perhaps too dismissively, Birgit and Peter Sawyer write: "Virgins are rare in the profane literature of thirteenth-century Scandinavia. Their absence may have been in part because of the great importance of marriage and marriage alliances in Scandinavia, especially in Iceland, where, in the absence of a superior authority, social stability largely depended on the links so formed between families," *Medieval Scandinavia*, 201. Relatively infrequent is a remark like Gyða's in *Haralds saga hárfagra*, ch. 3, in *Heimskringla*, that she would not waste her maidenhood on a husband who ruled only a petty kingdom.

12. Kormákr puns on *Steingerðr* (*Kormáks saga*, in *Vatnsdœla saga*, ed. Einar Ól. Sveinsson, Íslenzk fornrit 7 [Reykjavík: Hið íslenzka fornritafélag, 1939], ch. 3, st. 8) (discussion in Roberta Frank, "Onomastic Play in Kormákr's Verses," *Mediaeval Scandinavia* 3 [1970]: 7–34); Egill on *Ásgerðr* (*Egils saga Skallagrímssonar*, ed. Sigurður Nordal, Íslenzk fornrit 2 (Reykjavík: Hið íslenzka fornritafélag, 1933), ch. 56, st. 23; Óláfr Haraldsson, later Norwegian king and saint, on *Ingibjörg*, *Skj.* 1B 221: 8. Naturally, compounds like *Ásdís* increased the opportunities for witty lexical manipulation. The convention seems to have been to confine the name clues to a single *helming* and to pun on the nominal elements of two or more kennings, although the parts of the periphrastic expression might ostensibly belong to different "syntactic strands." In Halli's stanza, *hirðiDÍS* provides a clue that onomastic punning is likely. *Vangr* "field" had a near-homonym *vangi* "upper part of the cheek" or the part of the face contoured by the cheekbone. In addition to "(heathen) god," *áss* could mean "thick pole; main beam; yard of a sail" and also "rocky ridge" (the image selected by Egill in his stanza). Halli appears to have hidden Ásdís's name in the initial words of lines one and two of his second *helming*, with *vangs* intended to recall *vangi* as the "ridge (*ás*) of the cheek." Leiknir's verse invites similar dissection.

13. Óláfr Haraldsson, *Skj.* 1B 211: 8.

14. *Eyrbyggja saga*, ch. 19, st. 16.

15. *Skj.* 1B 135.

16. *Skj.* 1B 210: 4.

17. *Gunnlaugs saga ormstunga*, in *Vatnsdœla saga*, ch. 11, st. 14. Snorri Sturluson's suggested bynames for women, from passages dealing with different kinds of periphrastic and metonymical denomination, are explained with a taxonomical rigor that appears quite modern (*Skáldskaparmál*, chs. 31, 47, 68).

18. *Skj.* 1B 212: 10.

19. This comment draws on the phrasing of Kathryn Gravdal, *Ravishing Maidens: Writing Rape in Medieval French Literature and Law* (Philadelphia: University of Pennsylvania Press, 1991), p. 104. Somewhat more active female figures in non-erotic verse are the fetches (*fylgjur*), tutelary spirits attached to a family or individual, who may appear to announce their withdrawal and thus the incumbent's imminent death, e.g., *Víga-Glúms saga*. Judith Jesch ("Women Poets in the Viking Age: An Exploration," *New Comparison: A Journal of Comparative and General Literary Studies* 4 [1987]: 2–15) investigates the question of female skalds, but the preserved stanzas, from a half-dozen poets, are fully conventional and on well known "male" themes. The male-female debate is not entirely lacking in Old Norse literature, however, but often takes the form of the mutual interrogation of hero and giantess or witch; see Kress, "Mandom og misogyni"; Motz, *The Beauty and the Hag*; Pálsson, "The Name of the Witch"; Karen Swenson, *Heroes and Monsters in Verbal Combat:*

Genre Definition in Old Norse Literature, Studies in Scandinavian Literature and Culture 3 (Columbia, S.C.: Camden House, 1991).

20. Óláfr Haraldsson, *Skj.* 1B 212: 11.

21. Since the standards of the genre move the subjects towards ideal status, and many of the stylistic techniques involve displacement, referred meaning, and wordplay, one must address the question of irony or perceived irony, that is, the impression that the young woman is being praised beyond her merits. This is largely dependent on the genre's and public's acceptance of hyperbole. Only in those instances in which we judge the poet to have been malicious, i.e, motivated by a desire to harm the reputation of the girl's kin rather than simply win her favor, need we speak of an ironic disparity between subject and style, but this irony is not intrinsic to the poem. These considerations raise, however indirectly, the question of emotions in Old Norse literature and the degree to which the relatively closed surface of the sagas and skaldic verse can be plumbed for sentiments that may be thought consonant with those of a modern sensibility or may, on the other hand, be *sui generis;* see the provocative discussion in William Ian Miller, "Emotions and the Sagas," in *From Sagas to Society,* pp. 89–109.

22. *Skj.* 1B 134: 5.

23. *Skj.* 1B 134: 5.

24. *Skj.* 1B 6: 2.

25. *Skj.* 1B 146: 2; cf. Kormákr's set of verses on this motif, ch. 19, sts. 55–59.

26. *Skj.* 1B 93.

27. *Gunnlaugs saga ormstungu,* in *Borgfirðinga sögur,* ed. Sigurður Nordal and Guðni Jónsson, Íslenzk fornrit 6 (Reykjavík: Hið íslenzka fornritafélag, 1943), ch. 11, st. 18.

28. *Hallfreðar saga,* in *Vatnsdœla saga,* ch. 5, st. 4.

29. *Hallfreðar saga,* ch. 10, st. 28.

30. E.g., Hallar-Steinn in *Skáldskaparmál,* par. 47. Skaldic poets often turn to artisanal metaphors to describe their composition and, among these, examples of woodworking are prominent. This perspective also appears to underlie many of the terms used to characterize the names of the various poetic meters. On this analogy, one might liken the skaldic stanza to an old-fashioned wooden puzzle, whose pieces must be correctly positioned for it to form a compact and regular whole.

31. *Skj.* 1B 286: 2.

32. *Hallfreðar saga,* ch. 9, st. 22; cf. Kormákr, ch. 27, sts. 84–85.

33. Jochens, "Before the Male Gaze."

34. Ch. 3, sts. 1–10.

35. *Hallfreðar saga,* ch. 9, st. 24.

36. *Bjarnar saga Hítdælakappa,* in *Borgfirðinga sögur,* ch. 2, st. 10.

37. *Skj.* 1B 6: 2; Kormákr on missed meetings, ch. 5, st. 16, ch. 9, st. 26.

38. *Bjarnar saga hítdælakappa,* ch. 12, st. 3.

39. *Eyrbyggja saga,* ch. 29, st. 24.

40. *Skj.* 1B 285.

41. Ch. 10, st. 26; cf. Kormákr, ch. 8, sts 23, 25.

42. *Gunnlaugs saga,* ch. 10, st. 11.

43. *Bjarnar saga hítdælakappa,* ch. 5, st. 2.

44. *Skj.* 1B 351: 20.

45. Þórmóðr, *Fóstbrœðra saga,* in *Vestfirðinga sögur,* ed. Björn K. Þórólfsson, Íslenzk fornrit 6 (Reykjavík: Hið íslenzka fornritafélag, 1943), ch. 11, st. 9.

46. Jeffrey Jerome Cohen, rev. of *Feminist Approaches to the Body in Medieval Literature,* ed. Linda Lomperis and Sarah Stanbury (Philadelphia: University of Penn-

sylvania Press, 1993), *Bryn Mawr Medieval Review* 94.4.6 [No. 6, April 1994] (BMR-L@cc.brynmawr.edu).

47. *Gunnlaugr*, ch. 11, st. 19.

48. W. Emmerich, *Untersuchungen zur Rolle von Intriganten und Bösewichten in einigen Íslendingasögur* (Leipzig, 1955).

49. Ch. 28, st. 23.

50. Ch. 28.

51. *Skj.* 1B, 385: 4; cited in Snorri's *Skáldskaparmál*, par. 47.

52. This phrasing is adapted from Faulkes's translation of Snorri's *Edda* (115ff), where he writes "I have fixed the likeness. . . ."

Rhetoric, Power, and Integrity in the Passion of the Virgin Martyr (Maud Burnett McInerney)

I am deeply endebted to R. Howard Bloch, who provoked me to write this paper in the first place, and who read an early draft with characteristic attention and generosity.

1. On the context and audience of *Seinte Margarete* (and the other texts in the Katherine Group), see the introduction to *Medieval English Prose for Women: Selections from the Katherine Group and Ancrene Wisse*, ed. Bella Millett and Jocelyn Wogan-Browne (Oxford: Clarendon, 1990). All citations from *Seinte Margarete* are from this edition, and will be noted parenthetically by page and line number. Translations are mine, although influenced by Millett and Wogan-Browne.

2. Studies on the *Canterbury Tales* as a whole tend to overlook or underestimate the Second Nun's Tale; but see Jerome Mandel, *Geoffrey Chaucer: Building the Fragments of the Canterbury Tales* (Madison, N.J.: Fairleigh Dickinson University Press, 1992), pp. 71–91; Paul A. Olson, *The Canterbury Tales and the Good Society* (Princeton: Princeton University Press, 1986), pp. 127–59; C. David Benson, *Chaucer's Drama of Style: Poetic Variety and Contrast in the Canterbury Tales* (Chapel Hill: University of North Carolina Press, 1986), pp. 131–146.

3. "The male martyr is portrayed as a man of action; the description of the female martyr can bring a more emotive tone to the narrative, if the heroine is portrayed as a persecuted woman. The pathetic elements are closely associated with feebleness, rousing the spectators' sympathies and their potential predisposition for sadism and masochism." Phyllis Johnson and Brigitte Cazelles, *Le Vain Siècle Guerpir: A Literary Approach to Sainthood through Old French Hagiography of the Twelfth Century* (Chapel Hill: University of North Carolina Press, 1979), pp. 130–31.

4. Elizabeth Alvilda Petroff notes the same identity between virginity and faith in "Transforming the World: The Serpent Dragon and the Virgin Saint," *Body and Soul: Essays on Medieval Woman and Mysticism* (New York: Oxford University Press, 1994), p. 99.

5. Aquinas, *Summa Contra Gentiles* III:2:ci–cx, trans. English Dominican Fathers (London: Burnes, Oates and Washbourne, 1928).

6. Gerhild Scholz Williams, *Defining Dominion: The Discourses of Magic and Witchcraft in Early Modern France and Germany* (Ann Arbor: University of Michigan Press, 1995), p. 46.

7. Ovid, *Metamorphoses*, ed. W. S. Anderson (Leipzig: Teubner, 1977), 7, ll. 192–200. References are to this edition and all translations from the Latin are mine.

8. For a comprehensive treatment of Roman magic, see Anne-Marie Tupet, *La Magie dans la Poesie Latine* (Paris: Les Belles Lettres, 1976).

9. The association of magical women with serpents is, of course, ancient and ubiquitous. To the figures of Eve and Medea, one might add those of the Minoan snake-goddess, Cleopatra with her asps, and Mélusine, who was half serpent and half woman. Most of these women were possessed of persuasive if not actually magical speech.

10. This point is borne out by the thirteenth-century chronicle of Ralph of Coggeshall, who tells the story of a young woman who, as a result of her vow of virginity, is arrested by the authorities, along with her mentor (an older woman), interrogated, imprisoned, and eventually executed. The girl is a heretic and her mentor a witch, who escapes by flying away with a magic ball of string. According to Ralph, the girl's death "caused a great deal of astonishment to many, for she emitted no sigh, not a tear, no groan, but endured all the agony of the conflagration steadfastly and eagerly, like a martyr of Christ." Quoted in Edward Peters, *The Magician, the Witch and the Law* (Philadelphia: University of Pennsylvania Press, 1978), p. 36.

11. Petroff notes the way that her occupation as a shepherdess installs her in the tradition of folk and fairy tales; it also sentimentalizes her to a large degree. "Transforming the World," p. 99.

12. Jacques de Voragine, *La Legende Dorée*, ed. Teodor de Wyzewa, 2 vols. (Paris: Perrin, 1960). This is a modern French translation. Further references are indicated parenthetically as *LA*.

13. These figures do not, of course, include the eleven thousand virgins martyred with St. Ursula, who are enough to confound statistical analysis and are in any case probably a typographical error.

14. St. Catherine of Alexandria alone converts fifty pagan philosophers, the emperor's wife, and his prime minister. Given the remarkable rate of conversion achieved by the virgin martyrs, I find Cazelles's argument that the "stake of hagiographic romance is a locus where the heroine becomes both highly visible and deprived of any verbal or active power" unconvincing. See *The Lady as Saint: A Collection of French Hagiographic Romances of the Thirteenth Century* (Philadelphia: University of Pennsylvania Press, 1991), p. 54.

15. Augustine, *City of God against the Pagans* 18.23, Loeb Library, trans. George E. McCracken (Cambridge: Harvard University Press, 1957); Jerome, *Adversus Jovinianum* 2.13, in *A Select Library of the Nicene and Post-Nicene Fathers*, ed. Philip Schaff and Henry Wace, vol. 6 (Grand Rapids, MI: Eerdmans, 1952); Peter Abelard, *De Ordine Sanctimonialium*, in *La vie et les Epistres Pierre Abaelart et Heloys sa Fame*, ed. Eric Hicks (Paris: Champion, 1991), p. 139. For the female body as paradigm for the virgin body, see Jocelyn Wogan-Browne, "Chaste bodies: frames and experiences" in *Framing Medieval Bodies*, ed. Sarah Kay and Miri Rubin (Manchester: Manchester University Press, 1994), pp. 24–25.

16. Text and translation from Peter Dronke, *Hermes and the Sibyls: Continuations and Creations* (Cambridge: Cambridge University Press, 1990), p. 11. The bracketed line is Dronke's conjecture.

17. Peter Brown, *The Body and Society: Men, Women and Sexual Renunciation in Early Christianity* (New York: Columbia University Press, 1988), p. 271.

18. *Acts of John* 113, in *New Testament Apocrypha*, ed. E. Hennecke, quoted in Brown, *Body*, p. 192.

19. Jean Gerson wrote a tract on the subject called *On Pollution;* Constantine the African and Thomas Aquinas both dealt with the issue. See Joan Cadden, *Meanings*

of Sex Difference in the Middle Ages: Medicine, Science and Culture (Cambridge: Cambridge University Press, 1993), p. 141 ff.

20. Brown, *The Body and Society*, pp. 52–53.

21. *Acts of Paul and Thecla* 4, in Brown, *The Body and Society*, p. 156.

22. Brown, *The Body and Society*, p. 170.

23. Euripides' *Hippolytos* is an absolute anomaly, a young man whose insistence on preserving his virginity makes him almost monstrous in his peculiarity. For a discussion of the representation of virgin bodies in the classical period, see Giulia Sissa, *Greek Virginity*, trans. Arthur Goldhammer, (Cambridge: Harvard University Press, 1990). Sissa argues that the hymen, that "material token of female intactness, which makes it possible to conceive of a woman's first act of sexual intercourse as a definite, recognizable wound" (p. 2) is a product of the post-Classical imagination, in which the patristic writers had a particular interest precisely because of its vulnerability.

24. Michel Foucault, quoting Achilles Tatius, in *The Care of the Self: The History of Sexuality*, vol. 3, trans. Robert Hurley (New York: Random House, 1986), p. 231. Italics mine. One wonders whether it was a deliberate irony on Foucault's part to include the only discussion of female virginity under the general heading of "Boys."

25. I do not have the space to review here the history of misogyny in the early centuries of the Christian era, and the degree to which the feminine becomes associated with temptation and sin. See Elaine Pagels, *Adam, Eve, and the Serpent* (New York: Vintage, 1988), esp. pp. 78–97; R. Howard Bloch, *Medieval Misogyny and the Invention of Western Romantic Love* (Chicago: University of Chicago Press, 1991), esp. pp. 37–91.

26. Bloch, *Medieval Misogyny*, p. 100. Bloch's interest, however, is on the way that the patristic writers construct virginity as a rhetorical impossibility. Mine is in the effect of their rhetoric upon the virgin bodies that lie behind it.

27. Tertullian, "On the Veiling of Virgins," in *The Ante-Nicene Fathers*, vol. 4, ed. Alexander Roberts and James Donaldson (Grand Rapids, MI: Eerdmans, 1979), p. 29.

28. Tertullian, "On the Veiling of Virgins," p. 34.

29. *The Passion of St. Perpetua*, in Elizabeth Petroff, *Medieval Women's Visionary Literature* (New York: Oxford University Press, 1986), p. 76.

30. On Thecla's historicity, see Dennis MacDonald, *The Legend and the Apostle: The Battle for Paul in Story and Canon* (Philadelphia: Westminster, 1983), pp. 90–96. See also the discussion of Thecla in Pagels, *Adam, Eve, and the Serpent*.

31. 1 Timothy 2.11–15; this letter may be pseudo-Pauline. New Revised Bible.

32. See Amy Richlin, *The Garden of Priapus* (Princeton: Princeton University Press, 1983) for an extended discussion of the Roman concept of *os impurum* (foul mouth) as a contaminating influence on language. The poet Juvenal claimed to find the woman who talked too much about literature more offensive than a violent or murderous one (*Satire* VI). See also Bloch on "Woman as Riot," *Medieval Misogyny*, p. 17ff.

33. Pagels, *Adam, Eve, and the Serpent*, p. 20.

34. Encratis is a special case in several ways: she is the only woman named in a poem to the "Eighteen Holy Martyrs of Caesaraugusta," and she survived her martyrdom for some time, a fact that fascinates Prudentius, who describes her torture (one breast was cut off and she seems to have died of gangrene sometime after she was mutilated) with stomach-turning vividness. He gives no details of her life or behavior before her passion, but describes her as *violenta virgo* ("mighty virgin"); the adjective presumably refers to verbal rather than physical forcefulness.

35. Prudentius, *Peristephanon,* Loeb Classics, trans. H. J. Thomson (Cambridge: Harvard University Press, 1953), pp. 142–57. References are to this edition and line numbers are indicated parenthetically; translations are mine.

36. Ambrose, *Exhortatio ad virgines* in Brown, *Body,* p. 354.

37. For a different assessment of Cecelia's speech, see Gail Berkeley Sherman, "Saints, Nuns and Speech in the *Canterbury Tales,*" in *Images of Sainthood in Medieval Europe,* ed. Renate Blumenfeld-Kosinski and Timea Szell (Ithaca and London: Cornell University Press, 1991). Sherman argues that the Second Nun's speech cannot be efficacious because it is not really addressed to the public and does not involve any true exchange. It seems to me that the Second Nun is here imitating her subject. In the hagiographical narrative generally speech is private in that, while it may be addressed to the pagan interrogator, he will always refuse to hear it. The virgin's speech is really intended for God alone. This does not make the martyr's words powerless; rather, it is precisely this potent and unanswerable speech which produces conversions during the interrogation scenes.

38. All references are to the *Riverside Chaucer,* ed. Larry Benson (Boston: Houghton Mifflin, 1987).

39. Sherry L. Reames, "The Cecilia Legend as Chaucer Inherited it and Retold It: The Disappearance of an Augustinian Ideal" *Speculum* 55 (1980): p. 53.

40. Paul Beichner, "Confrontation, Contempt of Court, and Chaucer's Cecelia," *Chaucer Review* 8 (1973–74): 204.

41. Reames, "The Cecilia Legend," p. 57.

42. Robert Boenig, *Chaucer and the Mystics: The Canterbury Tales and the Genre of Devotional Prose* (Lewisburg, PA: Bucknell University Press, 1995).

43. For a nuanced discussion of this issue, see Wogan-Browne, "Saints' Lives and the Female Reader," *FMLS* 27 (1991); esp. pp. 315–16.

King by Day, Queen by Night: The Virgin Camille in the *Roman d'Eneas* (Wendy Chapman Peek)

1. Isidore of Seville, *Etymologiae sive Originum,* ed. W. M. Lindsey (1911; rpt., Oxford: Clarendon Press, 1962), bk. XI, ch. ii, p. 21.

2. More recently, Aimé Petit has pointed out that Camille is the perfect woman (because beautiful and chaste) as defined by Proverbs 31.10 ("La Reine Camille dans *Le Roman d'Eneas,*" *Les Lettres Romanes* 36, no. 1 [1982]: 37). For an extended discussion of Amazons as noble savages, see John Block Friedman, *The Monstrous Races in Medieval Art and Thought* (Cambridge: Harvard University Press, 1981), esp. pp. 163–77.

3. On this point, see Giovanna Angeli's influential argument that these antique romances were produced in an atelier assembled under Henry's patronage (*L'"Enéas" e i primi romanzi volgari* [Milan: Riccardo Ricciardi, 1971]).

4. R. Howard Bloch, *Medieval French Literature and Law* (Berkeley: University of California Press, 1977) and *Etymologies and Genealogies: A Literary Anthropology of the French Middle Ages* (Chicago: University of Chicago Press, 1983).

5. To minimize Camille would in fact be more consistent with the medieval poet's pattern of deleting large amounts of Virgilian material.

6. All citations from the *Aeneid* refer to the edition of R. A. B. Mynors (*P. Vergili Maronis Opera* [Oxford: Clarendon Press], 1969). All citations from the *Roman d'Eneas* refer to the edition of J.-J. Salverda de Grave (Paris: Classiques Français du Moyen Age, 1983, 1985). All translations of the *Eneas,* unless noted otherwise, are

by John A. Yunck, *Eneas: A Twelfth-Century French Romance* (New York: Columbia University Press, 1974).

7. Daniel Poirion emphasizes Camille's incongruity with the romance heroine by stating that she appears "as the psychological antithesis of Lavine, just as Dido is the moral antithesis," ("De l'"Énéide' à l'"Eneas': mythologie et moralisation," *Cahiers de civilisation médiévale x*ᵉ*—xii*ᵉ *siècles* 19, no. 3 [July-September 1976]: 228); my translation.

8. Julia Kristeva, *Powers of Horror: An Essay on Abjection,* trans. Leon S. Roudiez (New York: Columbia University Press, 1982), pp. 2, 4.

9. In his analysis of Kristeva's work, John Lechte points out that because her theory of the abject is grounded in culture, it can be a tool for "reflection in moral and social philosophy, not to mention politics" (*Julia Kristeva* [London: Routledge, 1990], p. 160).

10. There is no question, however, that Lavine is still the object of exchange between men. The development of her character only masks the reality of marriage as a political tool in the twelfth century. For a recent argument on the *Eneas'* decidedly masculinist focus, see Christopher Baswell, "Men in the *Roman d'Eneas:* The Construction of Empire," in *Medieval Masculinities: Regarding Men in the Middle Ages,* ed. Clare A. Lees, Medieval Cultures 7 (Minneapolis: University of Minnesota Press, 1994), pp. 149–68. An important article that focuses on the construction of both femininity and masculinity within romance is Simon Gaunt, "From Epic to Romance: Gender and Sexuality in the *Roman d'Eneas,*" *Romanic Review* 83, no. 1 (1992): 1–27.

11. As Simon Gaunt writes, "It is as if Enéas is an epic hero, defined in relation to other men, up to and including the end of the second part of the text; he then emerges as a romance hero, defined . . . through his relationship with a woman" ("Epic to Romance," p. 1).

12. This observation comes from Christiane Marchello-Nizia ("De l'*Énéide* à l'*Eneas:* Les Attributs du Fondateur," in *Lectures médiévales de Virgile: Actes du Colloque organisé par l'École française de Rome [Rome, 25–28 octobre 1982]*, Collection de l'École française de Rome 80 [Rome: École française, 1985], p. 251–66). To emphasize the increased centrality of Lavine in the battle between Eneas and Turnus, the medieval poet twice invokes the idea, once voiced by Lavine and again by Eneas, that her love for Eneas will inspire him in battle, the suggestion being that without such inspiration he might not have defeated Turnus (ll. 8756–62; 9051–64).

13. Marchello-Nizia, "De l'*Énéide* à l'*Eneas,*" p. 262; my translation.

14. See Marchello-Nizia's detailed analysis of the "*fame: regne*" rhyme in the *Eneas,* ("De l'*Énéide* à l'*Eneas,*" pp. 252–54).

15. I say "his" land, because although Eneas appears to Turnus (and, often, the reader) as an invader, he claims that Italy is his as a descendant of Dardanus (ll. 9347–66).

16. Yunck, *Eneas,* pp. 235–36; Salverda de Grave, *Roman d'Eneas,* ll. 9038–47.

17. Baswell, "Men in the *Roman d'Eneas,*" p. 159.

18. Bloch, *Medieval French Law and Literature,* p. 9.

19. Ibid., p. 124.

20. *Dictionary of the Middle Ages,* s.v. "Henry II."

21. In "The Amazons and the End of the World," Vincent DiMarco provides a summary of medieval works that represented Amazons as threats to established order (including their susceptibility to conversion to the Antichrist), in *Discovering*

New Worlds: Essays on Medieval Exploration and Imagination, ed. Scott D. Westrem (New York: Garland Press, 1991), pp. 69–90.

22. Yunck, *Eneas*, pp. 134–35; Salverda de Grave, *Roman d'Eneas*, ll. 3962–81.

23. The most famous of the critical comments is J. Crosland's: "We would gladly have dispensed with the conventional description of Camilla and her ridiculous horse" ("*Eneas* and the *Aeneid*," *Modern Language Review* 29 [1934]: 285).

24. Yunck, *Eneas*, p. 192; Salverda de Grave, *Roman d'Eneas*, ll. 6907–08, 6928–32, 6978–83.

25. Jean-Charles Huchet, *Le Roman Médiévale* (Paris: Presses Universitaire de France, 1984), p. 65.

26. Yunck, *Eneas*, pp. 194–95; Salverda de Grave, *Roman d'Eneas*, ll. 7082–95. Huchet (*Le Roman Médiévale*) gives a more detailed discussion of this scene on p. 76.

27. Huchet, *Le Roman Médiévale*, p. 67; my translation.

28. Kristeva, *Powers of Horror*, p. 35. Emphases in text.

29. Ibid. Emphases in text. See Cynthia Chase's helpful discussion of the abject in her review of *Powers of Horror, Desire in Language*, and "L'Abjet d'amour" in *Criticism* 26, no. 2 (Spring 1984): 193–200.

30. Julia Kristeva, "L'abjet d'amour," *Tel Quel* 91 (Spring 1982): 17–32.

31. Jacques Lacan, *Écrits*, trans. Alan Sheridan (New York: Norton, 1977).

32. Kristeva, *Powers of Horror*, p. 161.

33. It must be noted, however, that for Kristeva abjection occurs prior to the oedipal stage, when the child does not yet conceive of itself as a subject, nor of the abject as an object.

34. Kristeva, *Powers of Horror*, p. 2.

35. By way of example, Kristeva tells of the Enga of New Guinea, where over-population is seen as a threat. Consequently, strong pollution taboos concerning women's bodies are in place, which have the effect of restricting population growth (*Powers of Horror*, p. 78).

36. Walter Map, *De Nugis Curialium*, trans. Montague R. James, Cymmrodorion Record Series 9 (London: The Honourable Society of Cymmrodorion, 1923), p. 260.

37. Amy Kelly, *Eleanor of Aquitaine and the Four Kings* (Cambridge: Harvard University Press, 1950; rpt., New York: Vintage Press, 1957), p. 121.

38. W. L. Warren, *Henry* II (Berkeley: University of California Press, 1973), p. 242.

39. On this point, see Lee Patterson, *Negotiating the Past* (Madison: University of Wisconsin Press, 1987), esp. pp. 157–83; Christopher Baswell, "Men in the *Roman d'Eneas*"; Raymond J. Cormier, *One Heart One Mind: the Rebirth of Virgil's Hero in Medieval French Romance* (University, MS: Romances Monographs 3, 1973); and Huchet, *Le Roman Médiévale*, p. 12.

40. John A. Yunck, in the introduction to his translation of the *Eneas*, suggests that the description of the tomb may be based on lore of Byzantine automata (p. 207, n. 129).

41. Yunck, *Eneas*, p. 206; Salverda de Grave, *Roman d'Eneas*, ll. 7669–7718. David J. Shirt points out that the death of Camille suggests also the death of Lavine's resistance to marriage: "Both women are anxious to retain their virginity; Camilla because of her amazonic feminism which she expresses in word and deed.... Lavine does not wish to get involved with a man because she has been terrified out of her wits by her mother's gruesome analysis of love. . . . However, in the case of both women the cause of *virginitas* is doomed" ("Metaphor as a structuring device in the 'Roman d'Eneas'," Reading Medieval Studies 10 [1984]: 98). Winthrop Weth-erbee reads Camille's stasis as an emblem for "the contingency of the characteristic

optimism of [romance's] themes" in "Romance and Epic in Chaucer's *Knight's Tale*," *Exemplaria* 2, no. 1 (March 1990): 304.

42. Parallels between the tombs (and characters) of Camille and Pallas are numerous. For more on Pallas as threat to romance ideology, see Christopher Baswell, "Eneas's Tent and the Fabric of Empire in the *Roman d'Eneas*," *Romance Languages Annual* 2 (1990); 43–48; Simon Gaunt, "From Epic to Romance"; and William Burgwinkle, "Knighting the Classical Hero: homo/hetero Affectivity in *Eneas*," *Exemplaria* 5, no. 1 (Spring 1993): 1–44.

43. Aeneas does linger over the image of his past carved on Juno's temple, an act that Virgil gently criticizes by writing (1.464–65) "atque animum pictura pascit inani / multa gemens . . ." [With many tears and sighs he feeds his soul on what is nothing but a picture] (*The Aeneid of Virgil*, trans. Allen Mandelbaum [Berkeley: University of California Press, 1971], p. 17). For a valuable analysis of this scene, see Lee Patterson's "'Rapt with Plesaunce': Vision and Narration in the Epic," *English Literary History* 48 (1981): 455–75.

44. Arguing along similar lines, Poirion sees Camille (and Pallas) as "two victims sacrificed to the god of desire, aggressive, possessive and virile" ("De l'Énéide' à l' 'Eneas,'" p. 229); my translation.

45. See Kristeva, *Powers of Horror*, p. 109 on purification rites and the abject.

DIANA'S "BOWE YBROKE": IMPOTENCE, DESIRE, AND VIRGINITY IN CHAUCER'S *PARLIAMENT OF FOWLS* (KATHRYN L. LYNCH)

1. In the order listed, Robert W. Uphaus, "Chaucer's *Parlement of Foules:* Aesthetic Order and Individual Experience," *Texas Studies in Literature and Language* 10 (1968): 349–58; Michael R. Kelley, "Antithesis as the Principle of Design in the *Parlement of Foules*," *The Chaucer Review* 14 (1979): 61–73; D. S. Brewer, "The Genre of the 'Parlement of Foules,'" *The Modern Language Review* 53 (1958): 321–26; Dorothy Bethurum, "The Center of the *Parlement of Foules*," in *Essays in Honor of Walter Clyde Curry* (Nashville, TN: Vanderbilt University Press, 1954), pp. 39–50; Robert W. Frank, Jr., "Structure and Meaning in the *Parlement of Foules*," *PMLA* 71 (1956): 530–39; James Dean, "Artistic Conclusiveness in Chaucer's *Parliament of Fowls*," *The Chaucer Review* 21 (1986): 16–25; R. M. Lumiansky, "Chaucer's *Parlement of Foules:* A Philosophical Interpretation," *Review of English Studies* 24 (1948): 81–89; and John P. McCall, "The Harmony of Chaucer's *Parlement*," *The Chaucer Review* 5 (1970): 22–31. I am not suggesting that the unitary principles discovered by these critics are spurious ones. As many have argued, the poem does, I believe, make a Boethian argument about the continuity of human and divine love, even as I still believe that it participates in a philosophical dialogue about the role of the will in making choices about that love; see my essay "The *Parliament of Fowls* and Late Medieval Voluntarism, Parts I and II," *The Chaucer Review* 25 (1990): 1–16, 85–95. But none of these unitary principles can account for the poem's lack of proportion, its uncertainties, and for its failure to reach signficant closure.

2. H. M. Leicester, "The Harmony of Chaucer's Parlement: A Dissonant Voice," *The Chaucer Review* 9 (1974): 15–34; Robert M. Jordan, "The Question of Unity and the *Parlement of Foules*," *English Studies in Canada* 3 (1977): 373–85.

3. David Lorenzo Boyd, "Compilation as Commentary: Controlling Chaucer's *Parliament of Fowls*," *South Atlantic Quarterly* 91 (1992): 945–64.

4. All citations of Chaucer are from Larry D. Benson, gen. ed., *The Riverside Chaucer*, 3rd ed. (Boston: Houghton Mifflin, 1987).

5. Jordan, "The Question of Unity," p. 385.

6. Russell Peck, "Love, Politics, and Plot in the *Parlement of Foules*," *The Chaucer Review* 24 (1990): 290–305; "In effect Chaucer has dramatized the formation of political states in response to erotic compulsions" (301).

7. My interpretation is probably, then, most similar to that of Elaine Tuttle Hansen, in *Chaucer and the Fictions of Gender* (Berkeley and Los Angeles: University of California Press, 1992), pp. 108–40, except that I will be assigning the female more explicit psychological power and will, therefore, be seeing the ending of the poem as less conclusive and authoritative than Hansen does.

8. John M. Fyler, however, sees the conflict in the garden as taking place, to some extent, between Venus and Diana; see *Chaucer and Ovid* (New Haven: Yale University Press, 1979), pp. 93–94. See also Hansen, *Chaucer and the Fictions of Gender,* pp. 127–28.

9. The phrase is Jane Tibbetts Schulenburg's, in "The Heroics of Virginity: Brides of Christ and Sacrificial Mutilation," in *Women in the Middle Ages: Literary and Historical Perspectives,* ed. Mary Beth Rose (Syracuse, NY: Syracuse University Press, 1986), pp. 29–72.

10. Hansen, *Chaucer and the Fictions of Gender,* p. 128.

11. Ibid., pp. 23–28.

12. *The Riverside Chaucer* mentions only this version in its explanatory note to lines 232–59 (p. 998); and Emerson Brown, Jr., in an important and otherwise thorough essay on the connotations of Priapus, mentions the second telling only briefly and in a footnote, devoting his main discussion to the version in *Fasti* I; see "Priapus and the *Parlement of Foulys*," *Studies in Philology* 72 (1975): 260.

13. Ovid, *Fasti,* trans. Sir James George Frazer, 2nd ed., rev. G. P. Goold, Loeb Classical Library (Cambridge: Harvard University Press, 1989), i.393–440, vi.319–48, pp. 28–33, 342–45.

14. Giovanni Boccaccio, *The Book of Theseus,* trans. Bernadette Marie McCoy (New York: Medieval Text Association, 1974), 7.60, p. 178; *Teseida,* ed. Salvatore Battaglia (Florence: Sansoni, 1938), p. 208: "Vesta, che 'n calere / non poco gli era e 'nver di cui cotale / andava."

15. See Sigmund Freud's classic study, "The Taboo of Virginity," in *Papers on Metapsychology, Papers on Applied Psychoanalysis,* vol. 4 of *Collected Papers,* trans. Joan Riviere (1925; rpt. London: Hogarth Press, 1948), pp. 217–35. Freud, however, attributes the taboo to male wariness of immature female rejection of the man who replaces her father, rather than, as Simone de Beauvoir does, to a general fear of the power of female sexuality (see below, note 16). For a rationale for studying Freud's theories of psychosexual development in connection with medieval texts, see below, note 42.

16. Simone de Beauvoir, *The Second Sex,* trans. H. M. Parshley (New York: Knopf, 1952), p. 141.

17. See Schulenburg, "The Heroics of Virginity," *Women in the Middle Ages;* also, John Bugge, *Virginitas: An Essay in the History of a Medieval Ideal* (The Hague: Martinus Nijhoff, 1975).

18. Ambrose, *On Virginity,* trans. Daniel Callam (1980; rpt. Saskatoon, Saskatchewan: Peregrina, 1987), 7.36, p. 22; Ambrose was forced into maintaining the illogical proposition that "the population is the highest where a commitment to virginity is strongest."

19. The debate over whether or not the Wife plotted with her fifth husband to kill number four suggests the strength of the association of female sexuality with life-threatening violence. Even if we dismiss the idea that the Wife was implicated in

an actual murder, her fifth husband tells numerous stories that link wives with murder of their husbands or lovers (lines 721–71), and her behavior has aroused the suspicions of numerous modern critics; see Susan Crane's summary of the case for and against the murder, "Alison of Bath Accused of Murder: Case Dismissed," *Enqlish Language Notes* 25 (1988): 10–15.

20. Bugge, *Virginitas*, p. 20.

21. Shakespeare, *Measure for Measure*, ed. J. W. Lever (London and New York: Methuen, 1965), p. 50.

22. Bugge, *Virginitas*, pp. 142–43.

23. Michael R. Allen, *The Cult of the Kumari: Virgin Worship in Nepal*, 2nd ed. (Kathmandu: Madhab Lal Maharjan, 1983), pp. 9–10.

24. de Beauvoir, *The Second Sex*, p. 141.

25. Jacquart and Thomasset, *Sexuality and Medicine in the Middle Ages*, trans. Matthew Adamson (Princeton: Princeton University Press, 1988), pp. 75, 191–92.

26. N. M. Penzer, "Poison-Damsels," *Poison-Damsels and Other Essays in Folklore and Anthropology* (London: Sawyer, 1952), p. 25.

27. *The Early English Versions of the Gesta Romanorum*, ed. Sidney J. H. Herrtage, E.E.T.S. E.S. 33 (London: Trubner, 1879), pp. 340–41.

28. *Secretum Secretorum: Nine English Versions*, ed. M. A. Manzalaoui, E.E.T.S. O.S.276 (Oxford: Oxford University Press, 1977), 1:47; see also pp. 142, 329. Also, Commentary B, in *Women's Secrets: A Translation of Pseudo-Albertus Magnus's De Secretis Mulierum with Commentaries*, trans. Helen Rodnite Lemay (Albany: State University of New York Press, 1992), p. 131; for a wider survey, see Penzer, "Poison-Damsels," pp. 17–29.

29. St. Augustine, *The City of God against the Pagans*, trans. William M. Green, 7 vols. (Cambridge: Harvard University Press, 1963), vol. 2: 6.9, 7.24, pp. 344, 345, 464, 465.

30. *The Travels of Marco Polo*, trans. Ronald Latham (New York: Penguin, 1958), p. 172.

31. Ibid., p. 173.

32. *The Bodley Version of Mandeville's Travels*, ed. M. C. Seymour, E.E.T.S. 253 (London: Oxford University Press, 1963), p. 109.

33. de Beauvoir, *Second Sex*, p. 142.

34. Tom Moore, "The Virgin and the Unicorn," in *Images of the Untouched: Virginity in Psyche, Myth and Community*, ed. Jeanne Stroud and Gail Thomas (Dallas, TX: Spring, 1982), p. 51.

35. In *The Apocrypha and Pseudepigrapha of the Old Testament in English*, ed. R. H. Charles, trans. D. C. Simpson, 2 vols. (Oxford: Clarendon Press, 1913), vol. 1: pp. 216–25.

36. Penzer, "Poison-Damsels," p. 41.

37. *Mandeville's Travels*, p. 109. Such fear of the power of the woman's sexual organ may not be unrelated to medieval cases of vaginism or penis captivus; see J. D. Rolleston, "Penis Captivus: An Historical Note," *Janus* 39 (1936): 196–201, rpt. in *Sex in the Middle Ages: A Book of Essays*, ed. Joyce E. Salisbury (New York: Garland, 1991), pp. 232–37, and C. Grant Loomis, "Three Cases of Vaginism," in *Sex in the Middle Ages*, pp. 237–38.

38. Freud, "On the Universal Tendency to Debasement in the Sphere of Love," in *On Sexuality: Three Essays on the Theory of Sexuality and Other Works*, trans. James Strachey, ed. Angela Richard (New York: Penguin, 1977), p. 251.

39. Russell Peck, "Love, Politics, and Plot," p. 298.

40. Ibid.

41. Ibid.

42. I would defend the use of Freud specifically and of psychoanalytic theory generally on historical grounds. Freud's theories were elaborated from a late nineteenth-century patriarchal society whose childrearing practices were, in the most important ways, not that different from medieval ones. As Dorothy Dinnerstein has argued, the female monopoly on early child care, certainly no less the norm in the Middle Ages than today, is essentially responsible for Freudian outcomes, for later male rivalry for and female ambivalence about the mother (see *The Mermaid and the Minotaur: Sexual Arrangements and Human Malaise* [New York: HarperCollins, 1976]). If anything, early childhood in the Middle Ages, among the propertied classes, was even more similar to the typical childhood in Freud's time and in his social class than in the typical middle class childhood of today. The widespread use of wet nurses, for example, with whom medieval babies frequently lived their first two years, reminds one of the "complication of desire" introduced into Freud's childhood by his Catholic Czech nurse; see Shulamith Shahar, *Childhood in the Middle Ages* (New York and London: Routledge, 1990); cp. John Brenkman, *Straight, Male, Modern: A Cultural Critique of Psychoanalyis* (New York: Routledge, 1993), p. 137.

43. Freud, "The Sexual Life of Man," in *A General Introduction to Psychoanalysis,* trans. Joan Riviere (New York: Liveright, 1935), p. 268.

44. A. C. Spearing, *The Medieval Poet as Voyeur: Looking and Listening in Medieval Love-Narratives* (Cambridge: Cambridge University Press, 1993), p. 216.

45. Jane Flax, *Thinking Fragments: Psychoanalysis, Feminism, and Postmodernism in the Contemporary West* (Berkeley and Los Angeles: University of California Press, 1990), p. 18; Flax's critique of Freud applies as well to Lacan, although the consequences of the repression of the pre-oedipal differ in the two theorists: "For Lacan the self cannot 'really' exist precisely because it comes into being in and through the desire of the m/other. Thus Lacan merely inverts Freud's theory of primary narcissism. In Lacan's theory there are only others, never a self; even the self is an other to itself. Analysis can go no further than confronting the patient with this ontological estrangement" (p. 18).

46. In recent years feminist critics of the classical psychoanalytic approach have offered major revisions to Freudian and Lacanian theory that replace the emphasis from the oedipal to the pre-oedipal period when the young child experiences a blissful, but also threatening, oneness (the feeling Freud called "oceanic") with the mother on whom he or she is dependent for satisfaction of the most basic human physical and emotional needs. Studies that have been important to me here, in addition to Flax, include Dorothy Dinnerstein (cited above); Nancy Chodorow, *The Reproduction of Mothering: Psychoanalysis and the Sociology of Gender* (Berkeley and Los Angeles: University of California Press, 1978); Chris Weedon, *Feminist Practice and Poststructuralist Theory* (Oxford and New York: Basil Blackwell, 1987), pp. 43–73; and Patricia Waugh, *Feminine Fictions: Revisiting the Postmodern* (London and New York: Routledge, 1989), pp. 34–87.

47. Flax, *Thinking Fragments,* p. 90.

48. See Hansen, *Chaucer and the Fictions of Gender,* pp. 114–15.

49. Brenkman, *Straight, Male, Modern,* p. 237. Most of the feminist revisions of psychoanalysis that foreground pre-oedipal experience (see above, note 46) focus on the mother/daughter relationship. Brenkman is especially useful for the critic discussing a male writer, like Chaucer, because his modifications of Freud specifically call into question the timing of the male negotiation of the oedipal experience, which he sees as something that happens not simply once but again at different

points of maturation as the young man seeks to reach new understandings of his early childhood: "The son's desire is Oedipalized not in infancy, during the so-called Oedipal phase, but retroactively from experiences during latency and adolescence. . . . And the connotations of possession are acquired through the social instruction and cultural modeling the son receives from the father or, more precisely, from his identifications with him" (pp. 25–26).

50. Ibid., pp. 182, 183.

51. Ibid., p. 170.

52. The verse of which this is the final line is clearly a translation of Macrobius's description of the origins of the *insomnium* in his *Commentary on the Dream of Scipio*, trans. William Harris Stahl (New York: Columbia University Press, 1952), pp. 88–89.

53. R. Howard Bloch, "Chaucer's Maiden's Head: *The Physician's Tale* and the Poetics of Virginity," *Qui Parle* 2 (1988): 35; see also his *Medieval Misogyny and the Invention of Western Romantic Love* (Chicago: University of Chicago Press, 1991), p. 111.

54. Robert L. Entzminger, "The Pattern of Time in *The Parlement of Foules*," *Journal of Medieval and Renaissance Studies* 5 (1975): 11. Versions of this argument are also made by Bernard F. Huppé and D. W. Robertson, Jr., in *Fruyt and Chaf: Studies in Chaucer's Allegories* (Princeton: Princeton University Press, 1963), pp. 101–48; Paul A. Olson, "*The Parlement of Foules:* Aristotle's *Politics* and the Foundations of Human Society," *Studies in the Age of Chaucer* 2 (1980): 53–69; in a recent analysis, Kathleen Hewitt restates this argument as an opposition of literary sources, in which the disequilibrium of Cicero's *Somnium* is brought back into balance by the poet's affirming use of the *De planctu naturae* of Alain de Lille; "'Ther It Was First': Dream Poetics in the *Parliament of Fowls*," *The Chaucer Review* 24 (1989): 20–28.

55. See, for example, J. A. W. Bennett, *The Parlement of Foules: An Interpretation* (Oxford: Clarendon Press, 1957); Uphaus, cited above, note 1; George D. Economou, *The Goddess Natura in Medieval Literature* (Cambridge: Harvard University Press, 1972), pp. 125–50; Victoria Rothschild, "*The Parliament of Fowls:* Chaucer's Mirror Up to Nature," *Review of English Studies* 35 (1984): 164–84; Robert B. Burlin, in *Chaucerian Fiction* (Princeton: Princeton University Press, 1977), pp. 83–94.

56. Charles O. McDonald, "An Interpretation of Chaucer's *Parlement of Foules*," *Speculum* 30 (1955): 444.

57. Rhoda Hurwitt Selvin, "Shades of Love in the *Parlement of Foules*," *Studia Neophilologica* 37 (1965): 146–60; Jack B. Oruch, "Nature's Limitations and the *Demande d'Amour* of Chaucer's *Parlement*," *The Chaucer Review* 18 (1983): 23–37; Hugh White, "Chaucer Compromising Nature," *Review of English Studies* 40 (1989): 157–78; even David Aers's much-cited "The *Parlement of Fowls:* Authority, the Knower and the Known," *The Chaucer Review* 16 (1981): 1–17, which problematizes the political virtue of Africanus, still focuses on the way that Nature's role mediates between Cicero and Venus by undermining claims to a "transcendental viewpoint" (esp. pp. 9–14).

58. Huppé and Robertson, *Fruyt and Chaff*, p. 143.

59. Fyler, *Chaucer and Ovid*, p. 90.

60. Hansen, *Chaucer and the Fictions of Gender*, p. 140.

Menaced Masculinity and Imperiled Virginity in Malory's *Morte Darthur* (Kathleen Coyne Kelly)

1. Thomas Laqueur, *Making Sex: Body and Gender from the Greeks to Freud* (Cambridge: Harvard University Press, 1990), p. 22.

2. A number of patristic and medieval authors who discuss virginity make it very clear that their subject is *female* virginity; see Cyprian, *De Habitu Virginum;* Tertullian, *De Velandis Virginibus* and *Ad Uxorem;* Jerome, *Ad Eustochium;* Ambrose, *De Virginibus ad Marcellinam* (which includes a catalog of female virgins), *De Virginitate,* and *De Institutione Virginis;* Augustine, *De Sancta Virginitate.* (Exceptions: John Chrysostom intended *De Virginitate* for women, but he also addresses men, albeit in an abstract way. Tertullian's *Exhortatione Castitatas* is addressed to a friend who has recently lost his wife.) Aldhelm explicitly addresses his *De Virginitate* (late seventh century) to the nuns at Barking, though he could have easily included men in his audience, since Barking was one of the monasteries in England that housed both men and women. Along with a list of female virgins—and without precedent—Aldhelm also includes a catalogue of male virgins. Did he mean to address the monks after all, or did he use examples of male virgins as a way to suggest that the maintenance of male virginity is a burden that women (second Eves all) must help to shoulder along with the responsibility for their own integrity?

3. Tertullian, *De Virginibus Velandis, PL* 2.951. See Joan Cadden, *Meanings of Sex Difference in the Middle Ages: Medicine, Science, and Culture* (Cambridge, England: Cambridge University Press, 1993), pp. 260–61, for a brief discussion of the word *virgo* and its eventual use as a masculine form by patristic writers.

4. Monique Wittig, "The Mark of Gender," *Feminist Issues* 5.2 (Fall 1985): 3–12.

5. Laqueur, *Making Sex,* p. 22. Carol Clover draws on Laqueur's arguments in "Regardless of Sex: Men, Women, and Power in Early Northern Europe" (*Speculum* 68.2 [April 1993], 363–87). She describes "a world in which a physical woman could become a social man, a physical man could . . . become a social woman," p. 387.

6. Quoted in Kirstin Hastrup, "The Semantics of Biology: Virginity," *Defining Females: The Nature of Women in Society,* ed. Shirley Ardener (New York: Croom Helm, 1978), 49–65, p. 64, n. 10.

7. See also my "Malory's Body Chivalric" (*Arthuriana* 6.4 [Winter 1996]: 52–71), which focuses on subjectivity, masculinity, and violence in the *Morte Darthur.*

8. I do not attempt to distinguish between those instances in the *Morte Darthur* when the homosocial is "merely" an act of bonding and those instances when it may have a homoerotic valence. In *Between Men: English Literature and Male Homosocial Desire* (New York: Columbia University Press, 1985), Eve Kosofsky Sedgwick argues that "desire" is "a structure . . . the affective or social force, the glue . . . that shapes an important relationship. How far this force is properly sexual (what, historically, it means for something to be 'sexual') [is] an active question" (p. 2). She also argues that "the place of drawing the boundary between the sexual and the not-sexual . . . *is* variable but is *not* arbitrary" (p. 22). Thus, the homosocial as male-male desire is not necessarily fixed at any one point in a narrative. It is a "modern supposition," says Jonathan Goldberg, "that a line can be drawn between homosocial and homosexual relations." *Sodometries: Renaissance Texts, Modern Sexualities,* (Stanford, CA: Stanford University Press, 1992), p. 163. One reason that such a buffer can be so easily inserted is that in current criticism, the homoerotic has been strongly coded as male. That is, the term *homoerotic* is almost invariably used to describe male-male desire. I would go so far as to say that the term is in danger of losing its generic meaning, and is becoming gender-specific. Recently, however, this trend in criticism has been challenged by scholars who are exploring what I call the "lesboerotic." For a general discussion that privileges female-female desire, see Bonnie Zimmerman, "Perverse Reading: The Lesbian Appropriation of Literature," *Sexual Practice, Textual Theory: Lesbian Cultural Criticism,* ed. Susan J. Wolfe and Julia Penelope (Cambridge, MA and Cambridge, England: Blackwell, 1993), pp. 135–49. In medieval studies, Carolyn Dinshaw takes Geraldine Heng's

essay, "Feminine Knots and the Other *Sir Gawain and the Green Knight*" (106, no. 3 [1991]: 500–514) to its lesboerotic conclusion in her 1994 MLA paper, "When the Goods Get Together: *Sir Gawain and the Green Knight.*" Also see Dinshaw, "A Kiss is Just a Kiss: Heterosexuality and its Consolations in *Sir Gawain and the Green Knight,*" in *Diacritics* 24, no. 2–3 (Summer-Fall 1994): 205–26, p. 209, n. 8.

9. *The Works of Sir Thomas Malory*, 3rd. ed., ed. Eugène Vinaver, rev. P. J. C. Field (Oxford: Clarendon Press, 1990), p. 314. Hereafter, all quotations from the *Morte Darthur* will be cited in the body of the text by page number.

10. Larry Benson, *Malory's* Morte Darthur (Cambridge, Harvard University Press, 1976), p. 88. Joan Cadden cites Bernard of Gordon, who "placed chastity tenth on a list of things a tutor should teach a young man and first on the list of traits to be encouraged in young women." *Meanings of Sex Difference*, pp. 262–63.

11. For example, Malory says of Launcelot and Elayne: "Now we leve them kyssynge and clyppynge, as was a kyndely thynge" (p. 804).

12. In the episode in which Gareth and Lyones attempt to become lovers, Lyonett directs our attention to the matter of Lyones' honor and integrity, not Gareth's— though it is Gareth who is wounded in the thigh as punishment (p. 333ff.).

13. Jerome, "Neque enim aureum vas et argenteum tam carum Deo fuit, quam templum corporis virginalis." Letter XXII, to Eustochium, in *Select Letters of St. Jerome*, ed. T. E. Page, E. Capps, and W. H. D. Rouse, trans. F. A. Wright (Cambridge: Harvard University Press/Loeb Classical Library, 1933), pp. 104–5.

14. Ambrose, *De Virginibus* II, *PL* 16.225.

15. Peter Brown, *The Body and Society: Men, Women, and Sexual Renunciation in Early Christianity* (New York: Columbia University Press, 1988), p. 356.

16. In *The Body and Society*, Brown says that, in the early church, "perpetual virginity . . . never acquired the unambiguous association with specifically female chastity that it achieved in other ages, both in the pagan world and in later forms of Catholic Christianity" (p. xv).

17. See Brown, *The Body and Society*, pp. 60–61, 66–72.

18. John Bugge, *Virginitas: An Essay in the History of a Medieval Ideal* (The Hague: Martinus Nijhoff, 1975), p. 135.

19. Aquinas makes an interesting point about bodily integrity that can be applied equally to men and women: "corruptio carnis maxime in seminis resolutione consistit; quæ potest fieri sine concubitu, vel in dormiendo vel etiam vigilando. Sed sine concubitu non videtur perdi virginitas" ("our fleshy vessel is broken with the pouring out of seed, which may happen without intercourse when asleep or awake. Yet apparently virginity is not lost without intercourse"). In the Galenic system, both men and women were thought to emit seed during intercourse. *Summa Theologiae*, vol. 43, ed. and trans. Thomas Gilby (Blackfriars and New York: McGraw Hill; and London: Eyre and Spottiswoode, 1968), pp. 168–69. Aquinas also says "ergo virginitas dicitur per remotionem prædictæ corruptionis, consequens est quod integritas membri corporalis per accidens se habet ad virginitatem" ("since virginity is defined in terms of moral integrity, the unbroken hymen is incidental to it"), pp. 170–71.

20. See Giulia Sissa, *Greek Virginity*, trans. Arthur Goldhammer (Cambridge: Harvard University Press, 1990) for an overview of classical medical, gynecological, and literary representations of virginity and the symbol of the hymen.

21. Soranus (second century A.D.) states: "it is a mistake to assume that a thin membrane [ὑμένα, "hymen"] grows across the vagina, dividing it, and that this membrane . . . bursts in defloration." *Soranus' Gynecology*, trans. Owsei Temkin (Baltimore: John Hopkins University Press, 1956), p. 15. For the Greek text on which this translation is based, see *Sorani Gynaeciorum Libri IV, De Signis Fracturarum,*

De Fasciis, Vita Hippocratis Secundum Soranum, ed. Johannes Ilberg, *Corpus Medicorum Graecorum IV* (Liepzig and Berlin: B. G. Teubner, 1927), pp. 11–12. Though Soranus acknowledges that women often bleed at first intercourse (and describes the sensitive tissue that is the source of the blood—what modern medicine identifies as the hymen), he is mainly interested in refuting the notion that a "hymen" *seals* the female genitalia. The Greek word *hymen* denoted any sort of membranous tissue in the body.

22. Albertus Magnus, *Women's Secrets: A Translation of Pseudo-Albertus Magnus' De Secretis Mulierum with Commentaries,* trans. Helen Rodnite Lemay (Albany: State University of New York Press, 1992), p. 128. For an overview of medieval medical ideas on virginity, see Esther Lastique and Helen Rodnite Lemay, "A Medieval Physician's Guide to Virginity," in *Medieval Sexuality: Essays,* ed. Joyce Salisbury (New York: Garland, 1991), pp. 56–79.

23. William of Saliceto, *Summa conservationis,* fol. i3ra, trans. by Helen Rodnite Lemay, in "William of Saliceto on Human Sexuality" (*Viator* 12 [1981]: 165–81), pp. 175, 176.

24. *La Tavola Ritonda,* 2 vols., ed. F. L. Polidori (Bologna, 1864–65), p. 159.

25. Mark Lambert argues that Launcelot's "prominent values are shame and honor. . . . Lancelot does not feel tainted or stained by lust . . . rather, he is indignant that his sacrifice of worship is not being properly valued." *Malory: Style and Vision in Le Morte Darthur* (New Haven, CT: Yale University Press, 1975), p. 204, n. 98.

26. Beverly Kennedy argues most vigorously for constructing a chronology of Launcelot's sexual experience in *Knighthood in the* Morte Darthur (Cambridge, England: D. S. Brewer, 1985). R. M. Lumiansky constructs a chronology of his own in "'The Tale of Launcelot': Prelude to Adultery," *Malory's Originality* (Baltimore: Johns Hopkins University Press, 1964), pp. 91–98.

27. Malory/the narrator is reluctant to commit himself on the issue of Launcelot's virginity. When Launcelot is trapped in Gwenyver's bedchamber, Malory says in a famous passage, "whether they were abed other at other maner of disportis, me lyste nat thereof make no mencion" (p. 1165). See Kevin T. Grimm, "The Reception of Malory's *Morte Darthur* Medieval and Modern," (*Quondam et Futuris* 2, no. 3 [1992]: 1–14), for an appreciation of the ambiguities in the Launcelot and Gwenyver relationship. Stephen C. B. Atkinson argues that Malory leaves the question of adultery "stubbornly unanswerable" in "Malory's Lancelot and the Quest of the Holy Grail," *Studies in Malory,* ed. James W. Spisak (Kalamazoo, MI: Western Michigan University, Medieval Institute Publications, 1985), 129–52, p. 130.

28. Lambert (*Malory: Style and Vision in Le Morte Darthur*) reads this episode as "the measurability of knightliness," and as a moving celebration of knightliness (p. 57). He argues for humility as the chief lesson to be learned, along with the idea that the demands of the body chivalric take precedence over those of the individual: "for Malory knightliness is one soul in one hundred and forty bodies" (p. 59). The famous catalog of knights, Lambert argues, emphasizes fellowship (p. 62). Robert L. Kelly takes up the ambiguities of the Urré episode in "Wounds, Healing, and Knighthood in Malory's Tale of Lancelot and Guenevere," *Studies in Malory,* ed. James W. Spisak (Kalamazoo, MI: Western Michigan University, Medieval Institute Publications, 1985), pp. 173–97.

29. In "Malory's Ideal of Fellowship" (*Review of English Studies* n.s. 43.171 [1992]: 311–28), Elizabeth Archibald observes that the word *fellowship* functions in a "double sense" as "the bond between members of the Round Table as well as the friendship between individual knights" (p. 317). The term, she argues, takes on an importance and resonance that are not found in Malory's sources. Jill Mann, though

her interest is not the homosocial per se, suggests that the words *hole, body,* and *togidir,* among others, are particularly crucial to our understanding of the poem; see her remarks on the knightly body as a "testing ground of . . . validity . . . a repository of truths" in "Malory: Knightly Combat in *Le Morte D'arthur,*" *Medieval Literature: Chaucer and the Alliterative Tradition,* Part One of the New Pelican Guide to English Literature, ed. Boris Ford (Harmondsworth, England: Penguin, 1984, rpt. 1991), pp. 331–39, p. 338. Also see Lambert, *Malory,* pp. 63–65.

30. A few examples: when Launcelot is with Elayne ("they lay togydir," p. 795; they are "in bedde togydyrs," p. 804); when Launcelot is with Gwenyver ("For, as the Freynshhe booke seyth, the quene and sir Launcelot were togydirs," p. 1165).

31. See Anne Clark Bartlett, "Cracking the Penile Code: Reading Gender and Conquest in the Alliterative Morte Arthure" (*Arthuriana* 8.2 [Summer 1998]: 56–76), for a homosocial reading of the battle between Gawain and Priamus in the *Alliterative Morte Arthure.*

32. In *Gender and Romance in Chaucer's* Canterbury Tales (Princeton: Princeton University Press, 1994), Susan Crane explores the "analogies that connect . . . the demands of courtship and male friendship." She argues that "the heterosexual relation imitates the chivalric one, expanding and complicating knightly identity" and "heterosexual interaction patterns itself on male relations" (pp. 47, 52 n. 29). How one conducts oneself on the battlefield is translated to courtship behavior, and this reifies both masculine and feminine roles. However, according to Crane, the influence flows in only one direction (pp. 21, 23). By norming behavior according to a heterosexual blueprint, Crane's argument suppresses what I see as a two-way, sometimes homoerotic flow. I would not argue for a cause-effect relation so much as for a parallel development.

33. The Tristram-Mark-Isode triangle is also supplemented, first by Palomydes, and then by Keyhydns, brother to Isode le Blaunche Maynys.

34. Gary Ferguson, "Symbolic Sexual Inversion and the Construction of Courtly Manhood in Two French Romances," *Arthurian Yearbook III* (1993): 203–13. Ferguson is reading Chrétien de Troyes's *Chevalier de la Charrete* and Béroul's *Roman de Tristan.*

35. Both R. M. Lumiansky and Lambert point to Arthur's silence—he never asks whose blood it is. Launcelot, Arthur, and Gwenyver, says Lambert, are "concerned with the Queen's shame rather than her guilt"; he sees the episode as a "loose end" (p. 188). The knights are also ashamed because Mellyagaunce has Gwenyver at his mercy, and not because of any evidence of adultery (p. 189, n. 79). Lumiansky, *Malory's Originality* (Baltimore: Johns Hopkins University Press, 1964), pp. 227ff., and Lambert, *Malory,* pp. 187ff.

36. Cadden, *Meanings of Sex Difference,* p. 205.

37. Malory's version of this scene in the *Queste de Saint Graal* is actually much less lurid than that in the original. In the standard edition that we have now, Percivale's remorse and suffering are more drawn out. See Vinaver's notes on this passage, pp. 1543, 1556.

38. Brown, *Body and Society,* p. 169.

39. See Jerome Mandel, "The Idea of Coherence and the Feminization of Knights in Malory's 'Alexander the Orphan'" (*Arthurian Yearbook III* [1993]: 91–105), in which he argues that Alexander regularly feminizes the knights he defeats.

40. Thaïs E. Morgan, in a published conversation with Robert Con Davis, in *Men Writing the Feminine: Literature, Theory, and the Question of Genders* (Albany: State University of New York Press, 1994), p. 193.

41. Morgan, *Men Writing the Feminine,* p. 193.

42. Jacques Derrida, "The Double Session," *Dissemination,* trans. Barbara Johnson (Chicago: University of Chicago Press, 1981), 173–285, pp. 208, 209. The "hymen is the structure of *and/or,* between *and* and *or,*" p. 261.

43. Galahad's analogue is the Virgin Mary. She is also both an opening and a cover, embodying as she does the contradiction of the maternal virgin. In "Stabat Mater," Julia Kristeva asks, "what is it about the representation of the Maternal in general, and about the Christian or virginal representation in particular, that enables it . . . to calm social anxiety and supply what the male lacks?" *The Female Body in Western Culture: Contemporary Perspectives,* ed. Susan Rubin Suleiman (Cambridge: Harvard University Press, 1986), pp. 100–118, pp. 101, 102.

Il Trionfo della Pudicizia: Menacing Virgins in Italian Renaissance Domestic Painting (Cristelle L. Baskins)

1. See Margaret L. King, *Women of the Renaissance* (Chicago: University of Chicago Press, 1991); Constance Jordan, *Renaissance Feminism: Literary Texts and Political Models* (Ithaca: Cornell University Press, 1990); and Christiane Klapisch-Zuber, *Women, Family and Ritual in Renaissance Italy,* trans. Lydia Cochrane (Chicago: University of Chicago Press, 1985).

2. Paolo da Certaldo, *Libro di buoni costumi,* trans. Alfredo Schifiani (Florence, 1945), p. 73.

3. Francesco da Barbaro, "On Wifely Duties," in *The Earthly Republic,* ed. Benjamin Kohl (Philadelphia: University of Pennsylvania Press, 1978), p. 211.

4. Leon Battista Alberti, *The Family in Renaissance Florence,* trans. Renée Neu Watkins (Columbia, SC: University of South Carolina Press, 1969), p. 213. See also Guido Ruggiero, "Più che la vita caro: Onore, matrimonio e reputazione femminile nel tardo rinascimento," *Quaderni storici* 66 (1987): 753–75.

5. Baldassare Castiglione, *The Courtier,* trans. Charles Singleton (New York: Doubleday, 1959), p. 241. See also Pamela J. Benson, *The Invention of the Renaissance Woman* (University Park: Pennsylvania State University Press, 1992), pp. 73–90.

6. Stephanie H. Jed, *Chaste Thinking: The Rape of Lucretia and the Birth of Humanism* (Bloomington: Indiana University Press, 1989).

7. Alberti, *Family,* p. 211.

8. Elizabeth S. Cohen, "No Longer Virgins: Self-Presentation by Young Women in Late Renaissance Rome," in *Refiguring Woman: Perspectives on Gender and the Italian Renaissance,* ed. Marilyn Migiel and Juliana Schiesari (Ithaca: Cornell University Press, 1991), pp. 169–91.

9. See my *Cassone Painting, Humanism and Gender in Early Modern Italy.* (Cambridge: Cambridge University Press, 1998); Anne B. Barriault, *Spalliera Paintings of Renaissance Tuscany: Fables of Poets for Patrician Homes* (University Park: Pennsylvania State University Press, 1994); and Paul Schubring, *Cassoni: Truhen und Truhenbilder der italienischen Frührenaissance* (Leipzig, 1923).

10. See John K. Lydecker, *The Domestic Setting of the Arts in Renaissance Florence* (Ph.D. dissertation, Johns Hopkins University, 1988); Lydecker, "Il patriziato fiorentino e la committenza artistica per la casa," in *I ceti dirigenti nella Toscana del Quattrocento* (Florence: Francesco Papafava, 1987), pp. 209–21. For conspicuous consumption in fifteenth-century Florence see Richard Goldthwaite, "The Empire of Things: Consumer Demand in Renaissance Italy," in *Patronage, Art and Society in Renaissance Italy,* ed. Francis W. Kent and Patricia Simons (Oxford: Clarendon Press, 1987), pp. 153–75.

11. See Mary Fitzgerald, *Deschi da Parto: Birth Trays of the Florentine Quattro-cento* (Ph.D. dissertation, Syracuse University, 1986). See also Sir John Pope-Hennessy and Keith Christiansen, *Secular Painting in 15th-Century Tuscany: Birth Trays, Cassone Panels, and Portraits* (New York: Metropolitan Museum of Art, 1980).

12. See Ellen Callmann, *Apollonio di Giovanni* (Oxford: Clarendon Press, 1975), for such a shop specializing in domestic pictures. Callmann, "Apollonio di Giovanni and Painting for the Early Renaissance Room," *Antichità viva* 27 (1988): 5–18.

13. For patrician marriage ideology and practice see Anthony Molho, *Marriage Alliance in Late Medieval Florence* (Cambridge: Harvard University Press, 1994); and Gene Brucker, *Giovanni and Lusanna: Love and Marriage in Renaissance Florence* (Berkeley: University of California Press, 1986).

14. See Cristelle L. Baskins, *Lunga pittura: Narrative Conventions in Tuscan Cas-sone Painting ca. 1450–1500* (Ph.D. dissertation, UC–Berkeley, 1988), ch. 2; *Pe-trarch's Triumphs: Allegory and Spectacle*, ed. Konrad Eisenbichler and Amilcare Ianucci (Ottawa: Dovehouse, 1990); Jean Seznec, "Petrarch and Renaissance Art," in *Francesco Petrarca, Citizen of the World*, ed. Aldo S. Bernardo (Albany: State University of New York Press, 1980), pp. 133–50; Lutz S. Malke, "Contributo alle figurazioni dei *Trionfi* e del *Canzoniere* del Petrarca," *Commentari* 28 (1977): 236–61; Giovanni Carandente, *Trionfi nel Rinascimento* (Rome, 1963); and Werner Weis-bach, *Trionfi* (Berlin: Grote, 1919).

15. See Francesco Petrarca, *I Trionfi*, ed. Guido Bezzola (Milan: Rizzoli, 1984) ll. 19–30; my citations are taken from *The Triumphs of Petrarch*, trans. Ernest H. Wil-kins (Chicago: University of Chicago Press, 1962). Henceforth, all line numbers will be given in the body of the text. Interpretive studies of the poem are numerous: see Aldo S. Bernardo, *Petrarch, Laura and the Triumphs* (Binghamton, NY: MRTS, 1974); and Marguerite Waller, *Petrarch's Poetics and Literary History* (Amherst: University of Massachusetts Press, 1980).

16. Brucia Witthoft, "Marriage Rituals and Marriage Chests in Quattrocento Flor-ence," *Artibus et Historiae* 5 (1982): 43–59.

17. Ibid. Anne J. Schutte, "Il Trionfo delle donne: Tematiche di rovesciamento dei ruoli nella Firenze rinascimentale", *Quaderni storici* 44 (1980): 474–496; and Klapisch-Quber, *Women, Family and Ritual*, 178–212.

18. Klapisch-Zuber, *Women, Family and Ritual*, pp. 225–28.

19. For a discussion of virginity viewed as a health problem in early modern Europe, see Laurinda S. Dixon, *Perilous Chastity: Women and Illness in Pre-Enlightenment Art and Medicine* (Ithaca: Cornell University Press, 1995).

20. Federico Zeri, "I frammenti di un celebre Trionfo della Castità," in *Quaderni di Emblema* I (Bergamo, 1971), pp. 59–65. For the central combat see Martin Davies, *The National Gallery: The Earlier Italian Schools* (London, 1951), pp. 143–44.

21. Erwin Panofsky, "Blind Cupid," in *Studies in Iconography* (New York: Harper and Row, 1972), pp. 95–128.

22. David Summers, "Figure come fratelli: A Transformation of Symmetry in Re-naissance Painting," *Art Quarterly* 1 (1977): 59–88; Summers, "Contrapposto: Style and Meaning in Renaissance Art," *Art Bulletin* 59 (1977): 336–61.

23. Patricia Simons, "Women in Frames: the Eye, the Gaze, the Profile in Renais-sance Portraiture," *History Workshop* 25 (1988): 4–30.

24. See the discussion of the blazon as a shield/mirror in Nancy Vickers, "The Blazon of Sweet Beauty's Best: Shakespeare's *Lucrece*," in *Shakespeare and the Question of Theory*, ed. Patricia Parker and Geoffrey Hartman (New York: Methuen, 1985), pp. 95–115; and Vickers, "This Heraldry in Lucrece's Face," in *The Female Body in Western Culture*, ed. Susan Suleiman (Cambridge: Harvard University Press, 1986), pp. 209–22.

25. Diane Owen Hughes, "Regulating Women's Fashion," in *A History of Women: Silences of the Middle Ages,* ed. Christiane Klapisch-Zuber (Cambridge: Harvard University Press, 1992), pp. 136–58; Hughes, "La moda proibita: La legislazione suntuaria nell'Italia rinascimentale," *Memoria* 11–12 (1984): 82–105; and Hughes, "Sumptuary Laws and Human Relations in Renaissance Italy," *Disputes and Settlements: Law and Human Relations in the West,* ed. John Bossy (Cambridge: Cambridge University Press, 1983), pp. 69–99.

26. Patricia Emison, "The Word Made Naked in Pollaiuolo's *Battle of the Nudes,*" *Art History* 13 (1990): 261–75.

27. Sharon Fermor, "Movement and Gender in Sixteenth-Century Italian Painting," in *The Body Imaged: The Human Form and Visual Culture Since the Renaissance,* ed. Marcia Pointon (Cambridge: Cambridge University Press, 1993), pp. 129–45.

28. For an introduction to the social control of women see Samuel K. Cohn, "Donne in piazza e donne in tribunale a Firenze nel rinascimento," *Studi storici* 22 (1981): 515–33; Camille Naish, *Death Comes to the Maiden: Sex and Execution, 1431–1933* (New York and London: Routledge, 1991); and Samuel Y. Edgerton, Jr., *Pictures and Punishment: Art and Criminal Prosecution During the Florentine Renaissance* (Ithaca: Cornell University Press, 1985).

29. See Sherrill Cohen, *The Evolution of Women's Asylums since 1500* (New York: Oxford University Press, 1992).

30. See Nancy Vickers on Petrarca's poetic practice: "Diana Described: Scattered Woman and Scattered Rhyme," in *Writing and Sexual Difference,* ed. Elizabeth Abel (Chicago: University of Chicago Press, 1982), pp. 95–109. For double messages and misogynistic contradiction see also Susan L. Smith, *The Power of Women: A Topos in Medieval Art and Literature* (Philadelphia: University of Pennsylvania Press, 1995).

31. Barriault, *Spalliera Paintings,* pp. 146–47.

32. Charles Seymour, Jr., *Early Italian Paintings in the Yale University Art Gallery* (New Haven: Yale University Press, 1970), pp. 194–95. Fitzgerald, *Deschi da Parto,* pp. 279–81; the *desco* displays family arms of the Griselli and Piccolomini.

33. See Vilmos Tatrai, "Gli affreschi del Palazzo Petrucci a Siena," *Acta Historiae Artium* 24 (1978): 177–83; Davies, *Earlier Italian Schools,* pp. 367–72; Jill Dunkelton et. al., *From Giotto to Durer: Early Renaissance Painting in the National Gallery* (New Haven: Yale University Press, 1991), pp. 86–88.

34. For this picture see Burton B. Fredericksen, *The Cassone Paintings of Francesco di Giorgio* (Los Angeles: Anderson, Ritchie and Simon, 1969), pp. 17–22. A similar panel in a private collection, attributed to Neroccio de' Landi, is illustrated in Ellen Callmann, *Beyond Nobility: Art for the Private Citizen in the Early Renaissance* (Allentown, PA: Allentown Art Museum, 1980), pp. 9–10.

35. Compare this temple with a humanist's imaginary construction in Margaret L. King, "Goddess and Captive: Antonio Loschi's Epistolary Tribute to Maddalena Scrovegni (1389)," *Medievalia et Humanistica* 10 (1981): 103–27.

36. See Donald K. Hedrick, "The Ideology of Ornament: Alberti and the Erotics of Renaissance Urban Design," *Word and Image* 3 (1987): 111–37; and Patricia Simons, "Renaissance Palaces, Sex and Gender: The 'Public' and 'Private' Spaces of an Urban Oligarchy" (unpublished manuscript).

37. Davies, *Earlier Italian Schools,* p. 144. The original text appears in Prince V. M. d'Essling and E. Muntz, *Pétrarque* (Paris, 1902), p. 142.

METAPHOR AND THE MYSTIFICATION OF CHASTITY IN VIVES'S *INSTRUCTION OF A CHRISTEN WOMAN* (NANCY WEITZ MILLER)

The epigraphs are: Robert Greene, *Penelope's Web* (London 1601), sig. E4; Robert Aylett, *Peace with her Foure Garders, viz. Five Morall Meditations* (London, 1622),

p. 18; Sigmund Freud, "Femininity," in *New Introductory Lectures on Psychoanalysis,* ed. James Strachey (New York: W.W. Norton, 1965), p. 131.

1. Erasmus, *De Civilitate Morum Puerilium,* trans. Robert Whitington (London, 1532), sigs. B1ᵛ, C1ᵛ, D1. I have modernized spelling. *De Civilitate* appeared first around 1526. The English translation, in catechism form and used as a schoolbook, was introduced in 1532. In all, there were more than 130 editions of Erasmus's book in Latin and translation by the eighteenth century. For a discussion of *De Civilitate,* see Norbert Elias, *The Civilizing Process: The History of Manners* (New York: Urizen Books, 1978), pp. 53–84, passim.

2. There are of course a few notable exceptions—More's daughters (particularly Margaret Roper), Jane Grey, and Elizabeth I were taught logic, rhetoric, and languages. They, however, were not typical.

3. Joan Larsen Klein, introduction to selections from *Instruction of a Christian Woman,* in *Daughters, Wives, & Widows: Writings by Men about Women and Marriage in England, 1500–1640,* ed. Joan Larsen Klein, (Urbana and Chicago: University of Illinois Press, 1992), pp. 97–98. Valerie Wayne also discusses *Instruction's* publication history in "'Some Sad Sentence': Vives' *Instruction of a Christen Woman,*" in *Silent But for the Word,* ed. Margaret P. Hannay (Kent, OH: Kent State University, 1985), pp. 15–29; The *Revised Short-Title Catalogue* lists eight English editions: 1529?, 1540?, 1541, 1547, 1557 (two editions), 1585, and 1592.

4. The following is a selection of studies that focus on Vives, the humanists, and women's education: Foster Watson, *Vives and the Renascence Education of Women* (New York: Longmans, Green & Co., 1912); Pearl Hogrefe, *The Thomas More Circle: A Program of Ideas and Their Impact on Secular Drama* (Urbana: University of Illinois Press, 1959); Diane Valerie Bayne, "*The Instruction of a Christian Woman:* Richard Hyrde and the Thomas More Circle," *Moreana* 45 (1975): 5–15; Elizabeth Patton, "Second Thoughts of a Renaissance Humanist on the Education of Women: Juan Luis Vives Revises His *De institutione feminae Christianae,*" *ANQ* n.s. 5 (1992): 111–14; Gloria Kaufman, "Juan Luis Vives on the Education of Women" *Signs* 3 (1978): 891–96; Constance Jordan, *Renaissance Feminism: Literary Texts and Political Models* (Ithaca and London: Cornell University Press, 1990); Pamela Joseph Benson, *The Invention of Renaissance Woman* (University Park: Pennsylvania State University Press, 1992), pp. 171–81; and Janis Butler Holm, "Struggling with the Letter: Vives's Preface to *The Instruction of a Christen Woman,*" in *Contending Kingdoms: Historical, Psychological, and Feminist Approaches to the Literature of Sixteenth-Century England and France,* ed. Marie-Rose Logan and Peter L. Rudnytsky (Detroit: Wayne State University Press, 1991), pp. 265–97. Although most earlier studies of *Instruction* acknowledge that, for Vives, the goal of education is to protect chastity, they focus almost exclusively upon Vives's approach to formal education for girls (that is, formal studies of arts and languages). In fact, Vives devotes very little attention to formal studies in his plan for the education of women. Like most conduct books, *Instruction* does delineate which books are allowable for young women to read; these are, predictably, moral authors. Vives also mentions that women should practice writing by copying wise sentiments into their commonplace books. See Valerie Wayne, "'Some Sad Sentence.'"

5. I see Vives struggling with a similar problem for a female audience that Philippa Berry describes in her study of the male-centered courtly literature:

The Renaissance discourses of love certainly attempted to deny the materiality of the chaste woman they idealized: to exclude the female body, and feminine sexuality, from their idea of a chaste woman as exclusively spiritual (and as thereby inspiring a conviction in their own godlike powers). But the mysterious bodily presence of woman haunts these systems, insisting upon a paradoxical conjunction of nature and spirit under the sign of woman. (3–4)

See Philippa Berry, *Of Chastity and Power: Elizabethan Literature and the Unmarried Queen* (London and New York: Routledge, 1989).

6. Juan Luis Vives, *A very fruitful and pleasant book called the Instruction of a Christen Woman*, translated by Richard Hyrde (London, 1529?). All quotations are from this edition and signature numbers are cited in the text. I have modernized spelling and minimally edited punctuation.

7. Holm, "Struggling with the Letter," p. 283. Holm suggests that the disjunction between Vives's apology for brevity and the actual length and *copia* of the work signals a larger disruption of the text: "Vives's text, the purpose of which is to articulate definite limits for feminine experience and identity, defies its own professed boundaries, represents itself in such a way as to prevent itself from identifying with itself; its reason and rhetoric are at odds" (p. 272). For convenience and to avoid confusion, I, like Holm, refer to the text as Vives's despite Hyrde's mediation as translator, since I am interested in the version that English women read. The disjunctions that Holm perceptively notes here are, I believe, diffused in the contemporary culture and exist beyond this single text.

8. Carlos G. Noreña speculates upon the possible sources for Vives's position on love, including Stoic, Platonic, patristic (particularly Augustine), and Neoplatonic (Bruni and Ficino). See his *Juan Luis Vives and the Emotions*, (Carbondale and Edwardsville: Southern Illinois University Press, 1989), pp. 178–79. See also his recent English translation of Juan Luis Vives, *The Passions of the Soul: The Third Book of De Anima et Vita*, trans. Carlos G. Noreña, (Lewiston, New York: Edwin Mellen Press, 1990), chapters 2–4.

9. Noreña, *Vives and the Emotions*, p. 45.

10. Metaphor, as one of the primary rhetorical (and some would argue, cognitive) tropes, is a frequent object of analysis. The following are studies that I have found particularly useful for approaching early modern texts: William Empson, *The Structure of Complex Words* (Cambridge: Harvard University Press, 1989) and Patricia Parker, *Literary Fat Ladies: Rhetoric, Gender, Property* (London and New York: Methuen, 1988), chapter 3.

11. On cultural relationships between sin, sexuality, and pollution, see Mary Douglas, *Purity and Danger: An Analysis of the Concepts of Pollution and Taboo*, 2nd ed. (London: Routledge, 1978).

12. Noreña, *Vives and the Emotions*, p. 43. See also Margaret L. King, *Women of the Renaissance* (Chicago: University of Chicago Press, 1991), pp. 41–42; and Ian MacLean, *The Renaissance Notion of Woman* (Cambridge: Cambridge University Press, 1980), chapter 4. In his 1620 defense of women, Christopher Newstead argues that women are "the weaker vessels: and weaknesse alwayes is the most subject to gape after pleasures, and in their bodies." See *An Apology for Women: or, Womens Defence* (London, 1620), p. 11.

13. Many English Renaissance and Restoration comedies take as a theme the tyrannous custom of keeping women imprisoned at home until forced to marry a man of their fathers' choice. See, for example, Shakespeare's *Taming of the Shrew* and Aphra Behn's *The Rover*. Compare Milton's view of arranged marriages: "As for the custom that some parents and guardians have of forcing marriages, it will be better to say nothing of such a savage inhumanity." See Milton, *Doctrine and Discipline of Divorce*, ed. J. Max Patrick and Arthur M. Axelrad, in *The Prose of John Milton*, ed. J. Max Patrick, (Garden City, NY: Anchor Books, 1967), pp. 143–201, p. 161.

14. Laura Mulvey's landmark essay on cinema helped to develop a theory of "the gaze." Patricia Parker has recently noted how applicable this theory is to early modern literature. See Mulvey, "Visual Pleasure and Narrative Cinema," *Screen* 16 (1978): 6–18; and Parker, *Literary Fat Ladies*, p. 64.

15. This formula is Galenic in origin. See MacLean, *Renaissance Notion of Women*, chapter 3, for a discussion of Renaissance physiology.

16. Julia Kristeva posits the category of the "abject" as the boundary between subject and object, which Lynda Nead discusses in her study of the female nude in art:

> Subjectivity is organized around an awareness of the distinction and the sense of the body as a unified whole, defining the form and limits of corporeal identity. . . . It is the individual's recognition of the impossibility of a permanently fixed and stable identity that provokes the experience of abjection . . . The abject, then, is the space between subject and object; the site of both desire and danger. (32)

See Lynda Nead, *The Female Nude: Art, Obscenity, and Sexuality* (London and New York: Routledge, 1992).

17. As Constance Jordan points out, Vives would not condone women actually wearing armor, as this would be an unnatural appropriation of masculinity. See her *Renaissance Feminism*, p. 118. The fear of women wearing men's clothing and donning weapons is one aspect of the more general early modern fear of female disorder and rebellion. The legendary Amazons, for example, were considered so frightening and dangerous because their government was in direct opposition to traditional patriarchal authority, whereas female Christian warriors fight to uphold the patriarchy. See Simon Shepherd, *Amazons and Warrior Women* (Brighton: Harvester Press, 1981).

18. John Bugge, *Virginitas: An Essay in the History of a Medieval Ideal* (The Hague: Martinus Nijhoff, 1975), pp. 49–52.

19. See *OED* entries for "rape" and "ravishment." See also the material on rape in T.E., *The Law's Resolutions of Women's Rights*, in *Daughters, Wives, & Widows*, pp. 55–61; and J. B. Post, "Ravishment of Women and the Statutes of Westminster," in *Legal Records and the Historian*, ed. J.H. Baker (London: Royal Historical Society, 1978), pp. 150–64.

20. See Sherry B. Ortner, "The Virgin and the State," *Feminist Studies* 4 (1978): 19–35.

21. Vives, *The Passions of the Soul*, pp. 12–13.

22. In a seventeenth-century funeral sermon, preacher Stephen Geree makes such distinctions between true and false beauty:

> Next to birth that which commends a woman is Beauty, wherewith men are much taken, and even bewitched as it were, sometimes to the losse of their wits and lives also, if they cannot obtaine. Now there is no beauty to the beauty of holinesse, which is the blessed Image of God, Ephes. 4.24, and makes us like our Lord and Saviour, who is altogether lovelie, Cant. 5.16. All other beauty is but blacknesse to this, which is the true beauty of every gracious woman fearing God, and which she most of all prizeth and seekes after. (15–16)

Stephen Geree, *The Ornament of Women, Or, A Description of the true excellency of Women. Delivered in a sermon at the funerall of M. Elizabeth Machell* (London, 1639).

23. Noreña, *Vives and the Emotions*, p. 10.

24. Vives as translated by Noreña, *Vives and the Emotions*, p. 45.

FIGURING CHASTITY: MILTON'S LUDLOW MASQUE

The epigraphs are: John Milton, *The Complete Poetry of John Milton*, ed. John T. Shawcross, rev. ed. (New York: Doubleday, 1971), 780ff (hereafter cited parenthetically); and Barnabe Rich, *My Ladies Looking Glasse* (London, 1616), 44.

1. See Peter Stallybrass, "Patriarchal Territories: The Body Enclosed," in *Rewriting the Renaissance: The Discourses of Sexual Difference in Early Modern Europe*, ed. Margaret W. Ferguson, Maureen Quilligan, and Nancy J. Vickers (Chicago: University of Chicago Press, 1986); Catherine Belsey, *The Subject of Tragedy: Identity and Difference in Renaissance Drama* (London: Methuen, 1985); Suzanne W. Hull, *Chaste, Silent, and Obedient: English Books for Women 1475–1640* (San Marino, CA: The Huntington Library, 1982).

2. The Ranters advocated radical freedom of speech and behavior for women as well as men, claiming, in a representative argument by Laurence Clarkson, "There is no such act as drunkenness, adultery and theft in God. . . . What act soever is done by thee in light and love, is light and lovely, though it be that act called adultery" (quoted in Christopher Hill, *The World Turned Upside Down: Radical Ideas During the English Revolution* [New York: Viking, 1972], p. 172).

3. Furthermore, the presumed performance version of the masque (extant in manuscript) allows the Lady fewer lines than the printed ones. The 1645 Bridgewater MS (generally taken to be the performance version) also assigns the longest declamatory defense of chastity to the Attendant Spirit, rather than to the Lady (who speaks it in the print versions of 1637 and following).

4. Lucy Hutchinson, *Memoirs of the Life of Colonel Hutchinson*, ed. Julius Hutchinson, rev. ed. C. H. Firth (London: George Routledge and Sons, 1906), p. 64.

5. On the copious scope of anti-theatrical arguments, see Jonas Barish, *The Antitheatrical Prejudice* (Berkeley and Los Angeles: University of California Press, 1981).

6. Quoted in Virginia Gildersleeve, *Government Regulation of the Elizabethan Drama*, Columbia University Studies in English, series 2, vol. 4, no. 1 (New York: Columbia University Press, 1908), p. 164.

7. William Prynne, *Histrio-mastix, The Players Scourge* (London, 1633), sigs. **8v-***.

8. John Rainolds, *Th'Overthrow of Stage Playes* (London, 1599), quoted in Barish, *Antitheatrical Prejudice*, p. 91.

9. Patricia Parker, *Literary Fat Ladies: Rhetoric, Gender, Property* (London: Methuen, 1987).

10. Dudley Fenner, *The Artes of Logicke and Rhetoricke* (1584), rpt. in *Four Tudor Books on Education*, ed. Robert D. Pepper (Gainesville, FL: Scholars' Facsimiles and Reprints, 1966), p. 168. On rhetoric as "harlot," see also Brian Vickers, *Classical Rhetoric in English Poetry* (London: Macmillan, 1970).

11. Maryann Cale McGuire, *Milton's Puritan Masque* (Athens: University of Georgia Press, 1983), p. 1.

12. Several critics have discussed the formal consequences of scripting a Reformed masque, although in rather different terms than mine. Georgia Christopher argues in "The Virginity of Faith: *Comus* as a Reformation Conceit" (*English Literary*

History 43 [1976]: 479–98) that the Ludlow masque expresses Calvinist/Lutheran doctrine through a generically conventional device; on the other hand, McGuire and to a lesser extent Cedric Brown contend that the *Mask*'s Reformist aims reshape its form (see McGuire, *Milton's Puritan Masque;* Brown, *John Milton's Aristocratic Entertainments* [Cambridge: Cambridge University Press, 1985]). Brown believes that Milton's aristocratic entertainments manifest their "ardently, idealistically re-formist spirit" thematically, within their genre; however, in Brown's view, Milton replaces the constitutive masque ethos of aristocratic self-celebration with one of examination, such that "through festivity, nobility itself is seriously evaluated, its education under particular scrutiny" (p. 2). McGuire, by contrast, maintains that Milton's re-evaluations of truth and virtue violate masque convention significantly enough to alter such formal parameters as the relationships between antimasque and masque, visual and verbal. Angus Fletcher's *The Transcendental Masque: An Essay on Milton's "Comus"* (Ithaca: Cornell University Press, 1971) contends that the Ludlow masque expands the possibilities of the masque form, subsuming reli-gious and social issues as well as the aesthetic and literary ones that form the principal basis of his argument.

13. Douglas Bush, of course, disagrees, describing the *Mask*'s chastity as an "all-embracing vision of perfection." (*Mythology and the Renaissance Tradition in English Poetry,* rev. ed. [New York: Norton, 1963], p. 279). Among the readers taking the opposite position—that specifying just what chastity is constitutes a major prob-lematic of this masque—McGuire's argument is most similar to mine in her conclu-sion that Milton not only raises hermeneutic questions but also suggests answers. Stanley Fish draws attention to the *Mask*'s pointed embroilment of spectator/readers in interpretive difficulties, but believes that "No one of the questions raised by the masque is to be answered unequivocally" ("Problem Solving in *Comus,*" in *Illustri-ous Evidence: Approaches to English Literature of the Earlier Seventeenth Century,* ed. Earl Miner [Berkeley and Los Angeles: University of California Press, 1975], p. 126). In a related argument, Maureen Quilligan discusses how Milton's *Mask* engages Spenser's model of Guyon and the Palmer, who "in negotiating the linguis-tically dense landscape of fallen language in *The Faerie Queene,* reveal reading to be a process of making intepretive discriminations . . . that simultaneously are also ethical and political choices" (*Milton's Spenser* [Ithaca: Cornell University Press, 1983], p. 14). In another analysis taking the position that the *Mask* critiques conven-tional knowledge, Joseph Loewenstein addresses the *Mask*'s insistence on looking beyond conventional sources of illumination when he takes Echo's failure to re-spond to the Lady as a figure for the limitations of "pastoral voices, of the simple volubilities of nature" (*Responsive Readings: Versions of Echo in Pastoral, Epic, and the Jonsonian Masque* [New Haven: Yale University Press, 1984], p. 6).

14. Michel Foucault, *The Order of Things: An Archaeology of the Human Sciences* (1966; New York: Vintage Books, 1973).

15. Leah Marcus suggests this last aspect in discussing the *Mask* as an admoni-tory reference to a rape case pending appeal before Bridgewater. See "Justice for Margery Evans: A 'Local' Reading of *Comus,*" in *Milton and the Idea of Woman,* ed. Julia M. Walker (Urbana: University of Illinois Press, 1988.)

16. John Milton, *Complete Prose Works of John Milton,* gen. ed. Don M. Wolfe, 7 vols. (New Haven: Yale University Press, 1953–1966), 3:347; 365. Hereafter *CP.*

17. *Ben Jonson,* ed. C. H. Herford and Percy and Evelyn Simpson, 11 vols. (Oxford: Clarendon Press, 1925–52), 7:209.

18. Marcus, *The Politics of Mirth: Jonson, Herrick, Milton, Marvell, and the De-fense of Old Holiday Pastimes* (Chicago: University of Chicago Press), p. 171.

19. Herford and Simpson, *Ben Jonson,* 7:182.

20. Comus's rhetoric moreover associates him specifically with the courtly culture that constitutes the milieu of conventional masques but of Ludlow's antimasque. On Comus's courtliness, see Bush's description of Comus as "cavalier" in *English Literature in the Earlier Seventeenth Century, 1600–1660* (Oxford: Clarendon Press; New York: Oxford University Press, 1945), 365.

21. In a recent essay, John Rogers argues that the version of the masque printed in 1637 in fact argues *for* virginal sexual abstinence, suggesting that the 1637 revisions shift the Lady's emphasis from the potentially conjugal "chastity" of the performance version to an apocalyptically potent state of virginity. As Rogers notes, however, the "radical" 1637 praise of virginity hardly melds seamlessly with the "liberal" version performed in 1634; hence the Lady's *assertion* of autonomous radical virginity constitutes a separate topic from my discussion of the performance's 1634 *demonstrations* of the limitations of virginity. See "The Enclosure of Virginity: The Poetics of Sexual Abstinence in the English Revolution," in *Enclosure Acts: Sexuality, Property, and Culture in Early Modern England,* ed. Richard Burt and John Michael Archer (Ithaca: Cornell University Press, 1994). Richard Halpern, by contrast, argues that the performance version itself is ambivalent about the relationship between radical virginity and marriageable chastity, claiming the "mythical contradictions" more implied than represented in the masque cause the text to "wander from its official ideological stance" ("Puritanism and Maenadism in *A Mask,*" in *Rewriting the Renaissance,* 88–105; ed. Ferguson et al. p. 89).

22. For a helpful discussion of the "middle way" of married love that English Platonists celebrate, in contrast to the continental Neoplatonist dualism between carnal wantonness on the one hand and utter rejection of physical love on the other, see Mark Rose, *Heroic Love: Studies in Sidney and Spenser* (Cambridge: Harvard University Press, 1968).

23. John Calvin, *Institutes of the Christian Religion,* trans. Henry Beveridge (Edinburgh, 1863).

24. See especially William Kerrigan, *The Sacred Complex: On the Psychogenesis of "Paradise Lost"* (Cambridge: Harvard University Press, 1983); A. S. P. Woodhouse, *The Heavenly Muse: A Preface to Milton* (Toronto: University of Toronto Press, 1972); Fletcher, *Transcendental Masque;* D. C. Allen, *The Harmonious Vision: Studies in Milton's Poetry* (Baltimore: Johns Hopkins University Press, 1954); and McGuire, *Milton's Puritan Masque.*

25. Brown, *Milton's Aristocratic Entertainments.*

26. Glosses on Sabrina include John Guillory's reading of the nymph as figuring secular poetry (*Poetic Authority: Spenser, Milton, and Literary History* [New York: Columbia University Press, 1983]); Helen Cooper on the "regenerating, mythic powers of the earth in the territories for which the Earl bears responsibility" ("Location and Meaning in Masque, Morality, and Royal Entertainment," in *The Court Masque,* ed. David Lindley [Manchester: Manchester University Press, 1984], p. 147); Loewenstein on Sabrina as grace (*Responsive Readings*). Marcus's "Justice for Margery Evans" and Barbara Breasted's "*Comus* and the Castlehaven Scandal" (*Milton Studies* 3 [1971]: 201–24) link Sabrina with victims of sexual violence: Marcus with a Welsh girl whose complaint Bridgewater may review in his new office, Breasted more generally with the Castlehaven rape and sodomy scandal tainting Lady Bridgewater's family; C. L. Barber discusses Sabrina's aiding the Lady in terms of "innocent cherishing of femininity by femininity" ("*A Mask Performed at Ludlow Castle:* The Masque as a Masque," in *A Maske at Ludlow: Essays on Milton's "Comus,"* ed. John Diekhoff [Cleveland: Press of Case Western Reserve University,

1968], p. 206); Christopher Kendrick discusses her as "a virginal but *motherly* echo of the Lady" in "Milton and Sexuality: A Symptomatic Reading of *Comus*," in *Remembering Milton: Essays on the Texts and Traditions*, ed. Mary Nyquist and Margaret W. Ferguson [New York: Methuen, 1987], p. 51). Fletcher interprets Sabrina as the "embodiment of an 'intertwining' of the self and the world around the self" (*Transcendental Masque*, p. 206).

27. Rosemond Tuve, *Images and Themes in Five Poems by Milton* (Cambridge: Harvard University Press, 1957), p. 132n.

28. Foucault, *Order of Things*, pp. 25–26.

29. There are Miltonists who believe Sabrina was performed by an aristocrat. The *Variorum Milton* remarks only that Sabrina and also Comus were "perhaps paid professionals" (A. S. P. Woodhouse and Douglas Bush, eds., *A Variorum Commentary on the Poems of John Milton* [New York: Columbia University Press, p. 1972], vol. 2, part 3, 735). Diekhoff reports that both David Masson and Marjorie Nicolson assumed that an Egerton relative played the nymph. I find Diekhoff's counterargument fully pursuasive, however: "I doubt it. The chief *parts* included Comus and Thyrsis, but obviously the chief *persons* were the Earl's children. If others of the family had played the other parts, they would be listed in the manuscript" (Diekhoff, *A Maske at Ludlow*, p. 5).

30. Foucault, *Order of Things*, pp. 59; 63.

31. There are isolated examples of post-Caroline masque: Marvell scripted a wedding masque for Cromwell's daughter; Dryden presented a "Secular Masque" to celebrate the turn of the eighteenth century; but masque never again became a central practice.

32. Malcolm Mackenzie Ross conveys the appropriate amazement: "Faith, Hope, and Chastity. And the greatest of these is chastity!" *Poetry and Dogma: The Transfiguration of Eucharistic Symbols in Seventeenth-Century English Poetry* (New Brunswick, NJ: Rutgers University Press, 1954), p. 196.

33. Martin Luther, *Luther's Works*, ed. Jaroslav Pelikan, 55 vols. (St. Louis: Concordia, 1955–86), 27:31, emphasis added.

34. Bacon, *Francis Bacon*, ed. Brian Vickers (Oxford and New York: Oxford University Press, 1996), p. 124.

35. Jason P. Rosenblatt has describes how the sexualized figures for sin in *Paradise Lost* express this common Reformist view. See "Audacious Neighborhood: Idolatry in *Paradise Lost*, Book I," *Philological Quarterly* 54, no. 3 (Summer 1975): 553–68; see also McGuire, *Milton's Puritan Masque*.

36. McGuire, *Milton's Puritan Masque*, p. 149.

37. In *The Untuning of the Sky: Ideas of Music in English Poetry 1500–1700* (Princeton: Princeton University Press, 1961), John Hollander connects the Lady's belief to Renaissance privileging of the aural faculty; as noted above, Loewenstein believes that Echo's failure to respond to the Lady critiques the latter's belief in self-sufficiency (*Responsive Readings*). On the Lady's song to Echo, see also Louis L. Martz, *Poet of Exile: A Study of Milton's Poetry* (New Haven: Yale University Press, 1980).

38. Loewenstein's association of Sabrina with grace might seem an exception, but I think that even grace constitutes an worldly category insofar as Milton stresses grace (in *Paradise Lost*, for example) as the aspect of divinity that enacts the incarnation, making earthly experience meaningful and redeemable.

39. George Sensabaugh, "Platonic Love and the Puritan Rebellion," *Studies in Philology* 37, no. 3 (July 1940): 457–81.

40. Both critics and defenders of masque discuss its ephemerality. On the first side, Hutchinson and other pragmatic Puritan detractors are horrified by the expense of the one-time event. On the second, Jonson's distinction between the preservable text of a masque and the evanescent "carcass" of its set, dismantled (apparently by plebian revelers) immediately after the performance, constitutes an important part of his famous quarrel with Inigo Jones about the merits of the pen (poetry) versus the pencil (visual art). See D. J. Gordon, "Poet and Architect: The Intellectual Setting of the Quarrel between Ben Jonson and Inigo Jones," in *The Renaissance Imagination: Essays and Lectures by D. J. Gordon,* collected and ed. Stephen Orgel (Berkeley: University of California Press, 1975).

41. Kendrick, "Milton and Sexuality," p. 47.

42. Quoted in *CP* I: 888, n. 14.

43. H. James Jensen comments that the well-crafted artwork reflects "in its own order and harmony the harmony God created in the universe. In this way, a work of art, the microcosmic reflection of the macrocosm, expresses and appeals to the most rational part of the mind, as well as to the highest emotions" (*The Muses' Concord: Literature, Music, and the Visual Arts in the Baroque Age* [Bloomington: Indiana University Press, 1976], p. 3). For a discussion of the "united theory of the imagination which joins the philosopher . . . and the poet," see Joseph A. Mazzeo, "Universal Analogy and the Culture of the Renaissance," *Journal of the History of Ideas* 15 (1954): esp. p. 304.

44. Lynn A. Higgins and Brenda R. Silver, "Introduction: Rereading Rape," *Rape and Representation* (New York: Columbia University Press, 1991), p. 4. This objection is common: to cite two more examples, Kathryn Gravdal discusses how the "troping of rape leads the audience to ignore the physicality of rape and its literal consequences" (*Ravishing Maidens: Writing Rape in Medieval French Literature and Law* [Philadelphia: University of Pennsylvania Press, 1991], p. 43); Leo C. Curran criticizes Ovid scholarship that "glosses over . . . [the] reality [of rape] and prefers eumphemism [*sic*]" ("Rape and Rape Victims in the Metamorphoses," *Arethusa* 11, nos. 1 and 2 [Spring/Fall 1978], 213–41: 214). I would like to clarify that I am not making any political or ethical claims *for* the appropriateness of figuring rape, but rather comparing the relationship between the categories of rhetoric and sexual violence in a variety of writers.

45. Kendrick, "Milton and Sexuality," pp. 53–54. Kendrick's suggestion is all the more intriguing when we further contextualize the relationship between Reformist chastity and gender, for it is possible to argue that the specificity of *feminine* chastity Kendrick assumes in fact emerges, rather anomalously, in the passage he cites from the *Mask.* For in most cases where Milton genders chastity, he focuses far more on masculine chastity, as in *Of Education*'s interest in fostering a "chastely masculine" nation and particularly in the *Apology*'s claim, "if unchastity in a woman . . . be such a scandall and dishonour, then certainly in a man who is both the image and glory of God, it must . . . be much more deflouring and dishonourable" (*CP* 1: 892). As Mary Loeffelholz incisively observes, "Milton wants chastity to find better defenses in *Comus* [than in Ovid], but so long as the chastity defending itself is female the Ovidian metamorphosis will remain a threat, because that chastity is an exchange value whose end is ever to be figured and transfigured" ("Two Masques of Ceres and Proserpine: *Comus* and *The Tempest,*" in *Re-membering Milton,* ed. Nyquist and Ferguson, p. 33).

46. Barbara Kiefer Lewalski, *Protestant Poetics and the Seventeenth-Century Religious Lyric* (Princeton: Princeton University Press, 1979).

47. Quilligan, *Milton's Spenser,* p. 218.

LOST HONOR AND TORN VEILS: A VIRGIN'S RAPE IN MUSIC
(LYDIA HAMESSLEY)

1. "Accenti queruli" is found in *Cantade di Giovanni Felice Sances. A voce sola. Commode da cantarsi sopra Tiorba, Clavicembalo Arpa, o altro simile instrumento. Libro Secondo. Parte Prima* (Venice: 1633), pp. 15–19. I would like to thank Julianne Baird for providing me with information about this piece. Her recording of the piece is available on CD: *Songs of Love and War* (Dorian, DOR 90104, 1990). My thanks also to Martha Mockus and Suzanne G. Cusick for their ideas and guidance on this project.

2. Translation by Julianne Baird and Colin Tilney, *Songs of Love and War*, liner notes, pp. 22–24.

3. E. Jane Burns, *Bodytalk: When Women Speak in Old French Literature* (Philadelphia: University of Pennsylvania Press, 1993), p. 16.

4. For more on the act of ventriloquism, see Elizabeth D. Harvey, "Ventriloquizing Sappho: Ovid, Donne, and the Erotics of the Feminine Voice," *Criticism* 31 (1989): 115–38.

5. Susan McClary, *Feminine Endings: Music, Gender, and Sexuality* (Minneapolis: University of Minnesota Press, 1991), pp. 86–90. One could also argue that the "Lament of the Nymph" consists of two primary levels as Joke Dame does in her "Vertrapte bloemen. Susan McClary's lezing van Monteverdi's Lamento della Ninfa," *Muziek & Wetenschap* 1 (1991). "Lamento della Ninfa" is from his *Madrigali guerrieri et amorosi* (1638), edited in Gian Francesco Malipiero, ed., *Tutte le opere di Claudio Monteverdi*, 8 (Bologna, 1929), 286–94. A recording of this piece, performed by Concentus Musicus Wien, is available on CD: *Claudio Monteverdi, Il Combattimento, Lamento della Ninfa, Madrigali* (Teldec 8.43054, 1984).

6. *Cantade di Giovanni Felice Sances. A voce sola. Commode da cantarsi sopra Tiorba, Clavicembalo Arpa, o altro simile instrumento. Libro Secondo. Parte Prima* (Venice: 1633), pp. 3–9. This piece has also been recorded by Julianne Baird and is available on CD: *Songs of Love and War* (Dorian, DOR 90104, 1990).

7. "Zefiro torna" is from his *Scherzi musicali* (1632), edited in Gian Francesco Malipiero, ed., *Tutte le opere di Claudio Monteverdi*, 9 (Bologna, 1929), 9–20. Two CD recordings of this piece are: *Monteverdi, Lamento d'Arianna* (Harmonia Mundi, HMC 901129, 1984) and *Monteverdi, Il Combattimento di Tancredi e Corinda, Madrigals* (Hungaroton, HCD 12952, 1988).

8. Thomas Walker, "Ciaccona and Passacaglia: Remarks on their Origin and Early History," *Journal of the American Musicological Society* 21 (1968): 318. See also Richard Hudson, "Further Remarks on the Passacaglia and Ciaconna," *Journal of the American Musicological Society* 23 (1970): 302–14.

9. Translation from Sarah Fuller, ed., *European Musical Heritage, 800–1750* (New York: Alfred A. Knopf, 1987), 312. A copy of the Malipiero edition is reproduced in this anthology.

10. The score of "Accenti queruli" included here is my transcription of the original print. Note values have not been reduced, and original spellings have been retained. I thank Robert Whelan for preparing the score.

11. I wish to thank Suzanne G. Cusick for her insights into this reading.

12. Evelyne Barriot-Salvadore, "The Discourse of Medicine and Science," in *A History of Women in the West*, vol. 3, *Renaissance and Enlightenment Paradoxes*, ed. Natalie Zemon Davis and Arlette Farge (Cambridge: Belknap Press of Harvard University Press, 1993), p. 376. Jacqens Duval, *Des hermaphrodits. Accouchemens des femmes et traitement qui est requis pour le relever en santé et bien dever leurs*

enfans (Rouen: David Genffroy, 1612). Evidently, these ideas about virtue, virginity, and rape are still in vogue in some circles. In an article on abortion funding, *The Columbus Dispatch* reported: "There is no need to include rape victims in a state abortion fund because women who are raped don't get pregnant, a state legislator argued yesterday. State Rep. Henry Aldridge, a 71-year-old periodontist, told the House Appropriations Committee, 'The facts show that people who are raped—who are truly raped—the juices don't flow, the body functions don't work and they don't get pregnant.'" Cited in the *Minneapolis Star Tribune*, Friday, 7 July 1995, section E19, col. 1.

13. Ovid, *Metamorphoses*, trans. Mary Innes (London: Penguin, 1955), pp. 146–53 (lines 423–675). For two compelling readings of the Philomela story see Burns, pp. 115–47 and Patricia Klindienst Joplin, "The Voice of the Shuttle is Ours," *Stanford Literature Review* 1 (1984): 25–53.

14. Although one might assume that a man could have sung this cantata in the soprano register, either as falsettist or castrato, the composer Bellerofonte Castaldi wrote in the preface to his collection, *Primo Mazzetto die fiori musicalmente colti dal giardino bellerofonte* (1623), that it is "laughable that a man with the voice of a woman should set about proposing to his mistress and demanding pity of her in the voice of a falsetto." Cited in Nigel Fortune, "Italian Secular Song From 1600 to 1635: The Origins and Development of Accompanied Monody" (Ph.D. diss., Cambridge University, 1953), p. 159. Fortune reports that "castratos and contraltos do not seem to have been very popular" (p. 159). While it is conceivable that "Accenti queruli" might have been sung by a male in the tenor range, I would argue, however, that the text of this cantata would suggest that Sances had a female voice in mind when he set this text.

15. Of course, there is yet another layer to these narratives that I have not discussed—that of the poet. Clearly, the narrator's text, and "his" description of Lidia's rape, is also written by "another," but I am not inclined to discuss this additional complication since I have no information about when, by whom, or for whom the poem was written. I am more concerned with the dual narrative of the poem itself and the way that it operates in the musical setting.

16. Burns, *Bodytalk,* p. 2.

17. I have often wondered if Julianne Baird feels the same apprehension when she sings this cantata. Although her CD recording provides the complete text of the piece, both times that I have heard her perform the piece in person she has not provided texts for the audience. Instead, she summarized the text for the audience before she sang, and each time Lidia's words and the rape itself were not mentioned. The story is changed to one of unrequited love with an ironic joke at the end about being a virgin again. Perhaps there is the fear that the audience cannot enjoy the piece if they know the entire story.

18. Ruth A. Solie, "Whose Life? The Gendered Self in Schumann's *Frauenliebe* Songs," in *Music and Text: Critical Inquiries,* ed. Steven Paul Scher (Cambridge: Cambridge University Press, 1992): 220–22. See also Suzanne G. Cusick, "Gender and the Cultural Work of a Classical Music Performance," *repercussions* 3 (1994): 77–110.

19. Do modern performers and listeners want to participate in this system when impersonation glosses over the rape and effectively silences Lidia once again? Cusick grapples with these same kinds of questions in her study of Jessye Norman's performance of Robert Schumann's *Frauenliebe und -Leben.* What can a woman performer to do with pieces such as these? What do we do with music that is beautiful and yet disturbing? Should one refuse the invitation to perform and to be

swept up in this marvelously seductive music? How? Can there be a resisting reading of works like these? It is not my intention to answer these questions, particularly since I have not heard what I would call a "resisting" performance of "Accenti queruli." Nevertheless, I raise these questions for us to continue to ponder.

EVADING RAPE AND EMBRACING EMPIRE IN MARGARET CAVENDISH'S *ASSAULTED AND PURSUED CHASTITY* (MARINA LESLIE)

1. Margaret Cavendish, *The Blazing World and Other Writings,* ed. Kate Lilley (Harmondsworth: Penguin, 1994), pp. 48–118.

2. Catherine Gallagher offers a fascinating analysis of Cavendish's poetics of absolutism as a means of establishing the female subject; but while Gallagher points to the significance of the "royal martyrdom and exile" in creating "an important imaginative opening for Cavendish" (p. 29), her best textual evidence comes from *Blazing World* and other Restoration-era texts. I concur with Gallagher about the fundamental importance of the experience of exile to her work, but would argue that the work Cavendish produced in exile is far less confident about (if no less attracted to) absolutist resolutions. My essay and its title are indebted to her important study, "Embracing the Absolute: The Politics of the Female Subject in Seventeenth-Century England," *Genders* 1 (Spring 1988): 24–39.

3. Elizabeth I, "Speech to the Troops at Tilbury" (1588). See also Ernst Kantorowicz, *The King's Two Bodies: A Study in Mediaeval Political Theory* (Princeton: Princeton University Press, 1957).

4. See Erica Veevers, *Images of Love and Religion: Queen Henrietta Maria and Court Entertainments* (Cambridge: Cambridge University Press, 1989); and Kevin Sharpe, *Criticism and Compliment: The Politics of Literature in the England of Charles I* (Cambridge: Cambridge University Press, 1987).

5. Christopher Wordsworth, ed., *The Manner of the Coronation of King Charles the First of England at Westminster, 2 February 1626* Henry Bradshaw Liturgical Text Society, (London: Harrison and sons, 1892), vol. 2, v 6.

6. Lois Potter, *Secret Rites and Secret Writing: Royalist Literature, 1641–1660* (Cambridge: Cambridge University Press, 1989), p. 77.

7. D. J. Gordon, "Rubens and the Whitehall Ceiling," in *The Renaissance Imagination: Essays and Lectures by D. J. Gordon,* ed. Stephen Orgel (Berkeley: University of California Press, 1975), p. 50.

8. Stephen Orgel and Roy Strong, *Inigo Jones: The Theatre of the Stuart Court. Including the Complete Designs for Productions at Court ... together with their Texts and Historical Documentation,* 2 vols. (Berkeley: University of California Press, 1973), p. 55.

9. Veevers, *Images of Love and Religion,* p. 43. In this masque the Queen plays the role of Queen Bellesa. Veevers describes the pastoral masque as "a mirror image of the militant England of the 'Virgin' Queen . . . in which the great 'Bel-Liza' becomes the beautiful 'Bellesa, and in which the French-English marriage can at last promote peace, at home and abroad." Ibid., p. 5.

10. *The Poems of Thomas Carew With His Masque Coelum Britannicum,* ed. Rhodes Dunlap (London: Oxford University Press, 1964), p. 160. In *Coelum Britannicum,* the inscription of CARLOMARIA over Jove's door has the power to restrain him from his customary "incests, rapes, adulteries on earthly beauties" (p. 155). For discussions of Caroline masque see Graham Parry, *The Golden Age Restor'd: The Culture of the Stuart Court, 1603–42* (New York: St. Martin's Press, 1981), pp. 184–

229; for texts and commentary see David Lindley, ed., *The Court Masque: Jacobean and Caroline Entertainments, 1605–1640* (Oxford: Oxford University Press, 1995).

11. *The Poems of Thomas Carew,* pp. 90–91. Henrietta Maria also played an Amazonian queen in the masque *Salmacida Spolia* (1640). Orgel and Strong include illustrations of Inigo Jones's costumes for the queen and her ladies, in *Inigo Jones,* pp. 735, 785.

12. William Prynne, *Histrio-Mastix: The Players Scourge* (1633), pp. 201–3.

13. For an extended account of Prynne and the Caroline court entertainments, see Maryann Maguire, *Milton's Puritan Mask* (Athens: University of Georgia Press, 1983).

14. Jane Tibbetts Schulenburg, "The Heroics of Virginity: Brides of Christ and Sacrificial Mutilation," in *Women in the Middle Ages and Renaissance* (Syracuse, NY: Syracuse University Press, 1986), p. 32. See also Jo Ann McNamara, "Sexual Equality and the Cult of Virginity in Early Christian Thought," *Feminist Studies* 3, no. 3/4 (Spring/Summer 1976): 145–58.

15. Schulenberg, "The Heroics of Virginity," p. 32. Not all early authorities, however, felt comfortable attributing to the female virgin an honorary masculinity. Tertullian would vote for a new sexual designation entirely, calling the girl above sexual shame a "sport of nature, a third sex." See Peter Brown, *The Body and Society: Men, Women and Sexual Renunciation in Early Christianity* (New York: Columbia University Press, 1988), p. 81.

16. *Select Letters of St. Jerome,* trans. F. A. Wright. (Cambridge: Harvard University Press, 1954), p. 67.

17. See, for example, Annabel M. Patterson, *Censorship and Interpretation* (Madison: University of Wisconsin Press, 1984); Lois Potter, *Secret Rites and Secret Writing;* Paul Salzman, *English Prose Fiction, 1558–1700: A Critical History* (Oxford: Clarendon Press, 1985); and Kevin Sharpe, *Criticism and Compliment: The Politics of Literature in the England of Charles I* (Cambridge: Cambridge University Press, 1987).

18. Victoria Kahn, "Margaret Cavendish and the Romance of Contract," *Renaissance Quarterly* 2 (Summer 1997): 526–62. Cavendish herself repeatedly disavowed romance as a frivolous form, including in the preface of *Nature's Pictures,* where she declares that "I would not be thought to delight in Romances, having never read a whole one in my life." In the middle of her own romance, Affectionata (as she is called at the time) expresses grave misgivings about the genre, saying: "they extoll virtue so much as begets an envy, in those that have it not, and know, they cannot attain unto that perfection: and they beat infirmities so cruelly, as it begets pity, and by that a kind of love; besides their impossibilities makes them ridiculous to reason; and in youth they beget wanton desires, and amorous affections" (p. 54). This explicit rejection of romance heightens the paradox of a romance of chastity, while it alerts readers to look for more allegorical readings of this tale.

19. Lilley points out the indirect connection of this episode to the foundation of Israel. *The Blazing World and Other Writings,* p. 226, n. 1.

20. The assault upon their sister produces such a violent response from Simeon and Levi that even their father, Jacob, seems troubled: "And the sons of Jacob came upon the slain, and plundered the city, because their sister had been defiled; they took their flocks and their herds, their asses, and whatever was in the city and in the field, all their wealth, all their little ones and their wives, all that was in the houses, they captured and made their prey. Then Jacob said to Simeon and Levi, "You have brought trouble on me by making me odious to the inhabitants of the land. . . . But they said, "Should he treat our sister as a harlot?" (Gen. 34.27–31). Commentators on the passage point out the complex textual history of the literary

sources, which reflect and combine the political history of proto-Israel and the social history of all Israel.

21. This would also represent an appropriation of the more customary radical Protestant identification with Israelites as a chosen and afflicted people.

22. Douglas Grant, Cavendish's biographer, directly connects Cavendish's flight to France with the queen in 1644 to the themes elaborated in *Assaulted and Pursued Chastity*, noting that "the flight of a princess from coast to coast of vague locality, pursued by misfortune in one shape or another, became a favorite theme of her fiction." *Margaret the First: A Biography of Margaret Cavendish, Duchess of Newcastle, 1623–1673* (Toronto: University of Toronto Press, 1957), p. 71.

23. The bawd is a stock figure, often used in female hagiographic tradition as a threat to virginity. A more focused comparison can be made between this scene and Milton's *Mask* (see Shohet's essay in this volume). Unlike Comus, who constructs comparable arguments for the Lady he holds captive, the bawd is not so much *performing* a seduction through rhetoric as representing a client by proxy in a discourse motivated by commercial interest. The bawd offers an anti-type to the Queen of Amity, whose appearance later in the romance marks the possibility of women acting on their own behalf rather than as instruments of corrupted masculinity.

24. For a brilliant analysis of Cavendish's vitalism as well as the "action of virginity" in vitalist theories of the English Revolution, see John Rogers, *The Matter of Revolution: Science, Poetry, and Politics in the Age of Milton* (Ithaca: Cornell University Press, 1996). Although Rogers locates Cavendish's conversion from mechanistic materialism to vitalism in her later Restoration writing, he points out the earlier textual evidence of her struggle against the implications for gender equity in the discourse of mechanism where "the idea of the gendered but complementary forces animating the world was quickly being supplanted by the image of simple dominance of the strong elements of nature over the weak" (p. 186). On Cavendish's use of the skeptical methodology of the new science, see also Lisa T. Sarasohn, "A Science Turned Upside Down: Feminism and the Natural Philosophy of Margaret Cavendish," *Huntington Library Quarterly* 47 (1984): 289–307.

25. This is an allegorical technique Cavendish may have borrowed from Edmund Spenser, although she employs it to construct a very different allegory of identity.

26. Jerome in his *Commentary on Jonah* writes "It is not man's prerogative to lay violent hands upon himself, but rather to freely receive death from others. In persecutions it is not lawful to commit suicide except when one's chastity is jeopardized" (quoted in Schulenberg, "The Heroics of Virginity," p. 24). St. Ambrose, after wrestling with the same problem, seems also to conclude that suicide in defense of chastity is justified in his tract "Concerning Virgins." *De Virginibus* II.VII, in *St. Ambrose: Select Works and Letters*, trans. H. de Romestin, Nicene and Post-Nicene Fathers 10, 2nd ser., (1890; Peabody, MA: Henrickson, rpt. 1994), pp. 386–87.

27. It was not always the woman who was thought to be vulnerable in such situations. The proliferation of antifeminist popular literature more often represented the wars as an opportunity for cuckoldry. Anxiety about the unruly woman was high during a period when familial and political order had been disrupted. See David Underdown, *Revel, Riot and Rebellion: Popular Politics and Culture in England 1603–1660* (Oxford: Oxford University Press, 1985), pp. 211–12, 286–87, and fig. 7.

28. Raymond Anselment, *Loyalist Resolve: Patient Fortitude in the English Civil War* (Newark: University of Delaware Press, 1988).

29. Jean Gagin, "Honor and Fame in the Writings of the Duchess of Newcastle," *Studies in Philology* 56 (1959): 520.

30. Karen R. Lawrence notes the pun on travel and travail in Travellia's name, which she points out "are particularly linked when it is women who wander far from home, attempting to hold up their virtue." *Penelope Voyages: Women and Travel in the British Literary Tradition* (Ithaca: Cornell University Press, 1994), p. 28.

31. I do not mean to diminish the complexity of the effect of Shakespearean or Spenserian cross-dressing. Indeed, I would agree with Marjorie Garber's argument that "[t]ransvestite theater recognizes that *all* of the figures on stage are impersonators. The notion that there has to be a naturalness to the sign is exactly what great theater puts in question." *Vested Interests: Cross-Dressing and Cultural Anxiety* (New York: HarperCollins, 1992), p. 40. Similar arguments might well be made for Spenser that allegory destabilizes any natural sign of gender by making gender itself a sign for institutions, ideas, and other cultural categories. Nevertheless, at the level of narrative, Travellia's motives, behavior, and fate allow her an unusually dual-gendered identity.

32. Linda Woodbridge, *Women and the English Renaissance: Literature and the Nature of Womankind, 1540–1620* (Urbana: University of Illinois Press, 1984), p. 154.

33. In Cavendish, *Sociable Letters* (1664), p. 246.

34. Judith Butler, *Gender Trouble: Feminism and the Subversion of Identity* (New York: Routledge, 1990), p. 141.

35. Judith Butler, *Bodies that Matter: On the Discursive Limits of "Sex"* (New York: Routledge, 1993), p. x.

36. Peter Stallybrass, "Patriarchal Territories: The Body Enclosed," in *Rewriting the Renaissance: The Discourses of Sexual Difference in Early Modern Europe*, ed. Margaret W. Ferguson, Maureen Quilligan, and Nancy J. Vickers (Chicago: University of Chicago Press, 1987), p. 133.

37. Women leading armies is a favorite theme for Cavendish. In her play *The Lady Contemplation*, the eponymous heroine imagines herself married, that her husband is defeated and taken prisoner, and that she dons a "masculine suit" to lead her husband's army. In *Bell in Campo*, the lady Victoria fights alongside her husband with her own army of women.

38. Sarah Heller Mendeson, *Mental World of Stuart Women: Three Studies* (Amherst: University of Massachusetts Press, 1987), p. 22.

39. For an authoritative discussion of the topos of the woman-on-top in early modern European culture see Natalie Zemon Davis, *Society and Culture in Early Modern France* (Stanford, CA: Stanford University Press, 1975), pp. 124–51.

40. This argument was not unique among gentry. Two years after Cavendish published *Nature's Pictures*, Humphrey Moseley published "Phyllon Therapeytikon: An Healing Leaf, Most Humbly Tendred to the Nobility and Gentry of England: As an Essay to Cure the Bleeding Wounds of Themselves and the Nation" (London: D. Maxwell, 1658), in which he argues that by their profanity, drunkenness, fornication, arrogance, and other "heinous sins" gentlemen have brought God's own vengeance upon their own heads. Moseley puts to his reader the rhetorical question: "[I]s this the first time that God hath had a controversie with a land, because of whoredome?" (p. 7).

41. Dorothy Osborne, *Letters from Dorothy Osborne to Sir William Temple*, ed. Kingsley Hart (London: Folio Society, 1968), p. 58.

42. *The Diary of Samuel Pepys*, 11 vols., ed. Robert Latham and William Matthews (Berkeley: University of California Press, 1976), 9.123 and n. 3. Pepys also declares

of Cavendish: "The whole story of this lady is a romance, and all she doth is romantic" (8.186.7). See also entries: 8.163–4, 2.43.

43. Quoted in Douglas Grant, *Margaret the First*, p. 24. See also Samuel I. Mintz, "The Duchess of Newcastle's Visit to the Royal Society," *Journal of English and German Philology* 5 (1952): 168–76.

44. Cavendish, *True Relation of My Birth, Breeding and Life* (1656), p. 374. It was her reputation for extreme modesty as well as her beauty that enabled her to secure a marriage proposal in addition to the attentions of the cavalier William Cavendish, whose amorous exploits were so extensive that his own daughters celebrated them in verse.

45. For an outline of the controversy of female cross-dressing, see Katherine Usher Henderson and Barbara F. McManus, eds., *Half Humankind: Contexts and Texts of the Controversy about Women in England, 1540–1640* (Urbana: University of Illinois Press, 1985); and Woodbridge, *Women and the English Renaissance,* (Urbana: University of Illinois Press, 1986), esp. chapter 6.

46. Nell Gwynne, the most celebrated actress of her day, began her career in the tavern and bawdy house of her father before becoming Charles II's most celebrated mistress. Samuel Pepys would marvel at her performance as the witty beauty, Flori-mell, in Dryden's *Secret Love: or the Maiden Queen* (1667), a role whose onstage antics included passing for both a mad girl and a gallant: "[T]here is a comical part done by Nell . . . that I never can hope ever to see the like done again by man or woman. . . . [M]ost and best of all, when she comes in like a young gallant; and hath the motions and carriage of a spark the most that ever I saw any man have. It makes me, I confess, admire her." This admiration did not, however, prevent him from summing her up as "a bold, merry slut." *The Diary of Samuel Pepys,* 8.91.

47. Joseph Knight, "Margaret Cavendish, Duchess of Newcastle" in *The Dictionary of National Biography,* ed. Sir Leslie Stephen and Sir Sidney Lee (Oxford: Oxford University Press, 1917), p. 1266.

48. Cavendish, *True Relation,* p. 388.

49. Patricia Labalme, *Beyond Their Sex: Learned Women of the European Past,* ed. Patricia Labalme, (New York: New York University Press, 1980), p. 5.

50. Quoted in Douglas Grant, *Margaret the First,* p. 199.

Contributors

CRISTELLE L. BASKINS (Tufts University) has published on Italian Renaissance domestic secular imagery in *Art History, Oxford Art Journal,* and *Studies in Iconography,* as well as in anthologies, including *Gender Rhetorics* and *Sexuality and Gender in Early Modern Europe.* She has recently completed a book, *Cassone Painting, Humanism and Gender in Early Modern Italy.*

MARGARET W. FERGUSON has taught at Yale, Columbia, the University of Colorado at Boulder, and, since 1998, at the University of California at Davis, where she is Professor of English. She is the author of *Trials of Desire: Renaissance Defenses of Poetry* and the co-editor of several books among them *Rewriting the Renaissance: The Discourse of Sexual Difference in Early Modern Europe* and *The Tragedy of Mariam, The Fair Queen of Jewry.* She is currently finishing a study of "Female Literacies and Emergent Empires: France and England, 1400–1688."

LYDIA HAMESSLEY (Hamilton College) has written on manuscript compilation and the reception of the Italian madrigal in Elizabethan England, and she was the program director of "Feminist Theory and Music: Toward a Common Language," a conference held in Minneapolis in 1990. Her recent publications include "Henry Lawes' Setting of Katherine Philips' Friendship Poetry: A Musical Misreading?" in *Queering the Pitch: The New Gay and Lesbian Musicology.* She is currently co-editing, with Elaine Barkin, *Audible Traces: Gender, Identity, and Music.* Her current research is women in old-time and bluegrass music. She is an avid quilter and a clawhammer banjo player.

KATHLEEN COYNE KELLY (Northeastern University) is currently working on a book about virginity and tests of virginity in medieval literary and medical/gynecological texts. She has published in *Allegorica, Arthuriana, Assays,* and *Studies in Philology.*

MARINA LESLIE (Northeastern University) is author of *Renaissance Utopias and the Problem of History.* She has published essays in *College English, Genre, Semiotic Inquiry,* and *Utopian Studies.* Her current work is on early modern representations of female criminality.

KATHRYN LYNCH (Wellesley College) is the author of *The High Medieval Dream Vision: Poetry, Philosophy, and Literary Form* (1988), and of essays published in *Comparative Literature, Review of English Studies, Genre, Studies in the Age of Chaucer, The Chaucer Review,* and *Speculum.*

MAUD BURNETT MCINERNEY (Haverford College) is working on a book about saints' lives. Her most recent publication is *"In the meyden's wombe:* Julian of Norwich and the Poetics of Enclosure," in *Medieval Mothering* (1996).

NANCY WEITZ MILLER (Ohio State University, Mansfield) specializes in 16th- and 17th-century literature. She has published essays on Milton, 17th-century women's persuasive writing, and is at work on a book about rape and the rhetoric of chastity in early modern England. She is also president of the Margaret Cavendish Society.

WENDY CHAPMAN PEEK (Stonehill College) is interested in pilgrimage literature and the representation of Amazons in medieval and Renaissance literature.

WILLIAM SAYERS is an independent scholar and translator who has published on early Irish and Norse languages and literatures. In some recent studies, he has returned to Anglo-Norman narrative, the subject of his doctoral dissertation.

LAUREN SHOHET (Villanova University) is working on a manuscript about the relationship between masque and science in seventeenth-century England.

Index

241